1923

THE MYSTERY OF LOT 212 AND A
TOUR DE FRANCE OBSESSION

NED BOULTING

BLOOMSBURY SPORT
LONDON · OXFORD · NEW YORK · NEW DELHI · SYDNEY

BLOOMSBURY SPORT
Bloomsbury Publishing Plc
50 Bedford Square, London, WC1B 3DP, UK
29 Earlsfort Terrace, Dublin 2, Ireland

BLOOMSBURY, BLOOMSBURY SPORT and the Diana logo are trademarks
of Bloomsbury Publishing Plc

First published in Great Britain 2023

Images © Getty Images; Alamy and author's personal collection, images p.24 (top and bottom)
© BnF - Bibliothèque nationale de France; image p. 66 © Fonds Crolard - Archives de Lorient

A catalogue record for this book is available from the British Library

Library of Congress Cataloguing-in-Publication data has been applied for

ISBN: HB: 978-1-3994-0154-8; eBook: 978-1-3994-0155-5; epdf: 978-1-3994-0153-1

2 4 6 8 10 9 7 5 3 1

Typeset in Adobe Caslon Pro by Deanta Global Publishing Services, Chennai, India
Printed and bound in Great Britain by CPI Group (UK) Ltd, Croydon CR0 4YY

To find out more about our authors and books visit www.bloomsbury.com
and sign up for our newsletters

CONTENTS

'For still, in 1923 it stands not so very far from where it stood in that "giant age before the flood" of nine years since.'

Aldous Huxley, *Vanity Fair*, 1923

1. LOOKING

'If you look at it from very close up . . . you can see all those bridges, hinges, gears, and bolts, and refrains, and all the minor instruments that link distinct, singular and unique events. It is these that form the underpinnings of the world . . . these that launch the phantom trains of thought between things that are naturally strangers.'

Olga Tokarczuk, *The Books of Jacob*,
Fitzcarraldo Editions, London, 2021

After a long and unusually cold June, summer has finally arrived. Now, on the last day of the month, the sun stands high in a milky white sky right overhead the bridge. It casts a strong dark stripe of shadow across the surface of the languid river flowing unhurriedly towards the Atlantic. The bridge's arch, a mighty half-moon of iron, is bisected by the road it carries high above the placid waters of the Vilaine. If you know where to look, you can just about pick out a rider on the bridge. He is nothing more than a tiny dot of white passing rapidly through a picture. You can hardly see him, before he's gone.

FRANCE, AND ITS ABSENCE

This is the story of an obsession. Actually, and more specifically, it's the story of an obsession within a pandemic after which there is a war. These details matter, I think.

It all began in the late summer of 2020, the first year of Covid. I had just returned from spending the best part of a month away from home commentating for British TV on the Tour de France. The 2020 Tour had been an exceptionally dramatic edition of the race, one which had held us in suspense right to the very end when the young Slovene, Tadej Pogačar, turned it on its head, snatching victory in the most ruthless and unforeseeable fashion. His exhilarating win in the final time trial had been orchestrated on the steep slopes of La Planche des Belles Filles, a hilltop I knew well.

This famous wooded climb runs up the side of a hill in the historically disputed Vosges mountains. These humpbacked peaks run along the linguistic and political fault line of western Europe's great schism between France and Germany. The grey villages and mist-shrouded hills of the Vosges, forever caught in a cultural no man's land, had always drawn me in. Their proximity to the German border is what defines them: across that line everything changes so entirely it's like entering a different world. Over many years I had spent long periods of time in both countries, and so the Vosges felt personal to me.

I also knew this particular climb better than almost any other. Over the last decade, the Tour has often battled along the winding road to the top, ribboning up towards a famously steep ramp just before the finish line. Bradley Wiggins took his first yellow jersey on 'La

Planche'. Once, when the race went there, I stayed the night before in an elegant manor house a dozen kilometres from the hill. On my way to work the following day I called into Corbusier's Notre-Dame du Haut chapel.

I sat for a long time on a wooden pew, looking at the tiny block of thickly cut stained glass set deeply into the church's massive, whitewashed walls. Outside, the Vosges mountains were coming to life with summery birdsong. Later that day, as the race approached the final climb, the TV helicopter dwelt for a few seconds over the Notre-Dame, and I was able briefly to recount on air my morning's visit there, before the director cut back to the race beneath. Weaving culture and live action together is the wonderful responsibility of a cycling commentator. No other sporting event balances the world in one hand and the race in another like the Tour de France.

But in the delayed Tour of 2020, our entire production team was forced by Covid travel restrictions to stay in the UK and broadcast remotely. That meant, for the first time in 18 summers, I would not be rolling through France, *département* by *département*, feeling the tilting topography, the changing climate, the differing light. I would not be able to move like a dot on a giant canvas and would be denied that sense of awe to which annually I succumb at discovering new wonders and revisiting old touchstone towns.

Brittany, for example, had always been part of my ritual summers in France. Throughout the long, uncomplicated years when our children were young, we would visit its rocky shores, its hydrangeas, wind-eroded churches and grey cottages straight after the Tour. Creatures of habit, we were drawn back to a certain little village; a sacred-seeming patch of green amid ancient stones. Every year, on a campsite watched over by drifting, thickening white August clouds and fringed by ferns and brambles, I would softly let go the din of the Tour. Here I would unconsciously collect my thoughts and begin to mould them into some sort of shape; the serried impressions of another July spent in France. What I could not have known in the locked-down reality of 2020 was that the mysterious landscape of Brittany was about to come back to me in a most unexpected, entirely different manner.

But before all of that, I had an accident. That pandemic summer I commuted to work at a TV studio in Kent every day by bike. On the final evening of the Tour, after we'd finished off all our commentary duties, I rode back to my hotel room from the studios for the last time. Because the race in Paris had finished late, and because the whole Tour had been delayed until September, I hadn't been prepared for the fact that it would by now be pitch dark as I made my way home. The little bike lights I had with me were wholly inadequate, flashing dimly, instead of illuminating the way. But they were all I had.

It was not surprising that I crashed. Not able to see where I was going, I simply rode headlong into a very deep ditch, where I landed on the damp, stony ground with an outstretched arm and a horrible jolt, knowing straight away I had broken my arm. But I would only gradually realise over the course of the next few hours, days and weeks, quite how badly I had fractured it. I waited nine long days before having a three-hour operation to screw together my shoulder, after which I began slowly to understand how long my recovery period might take.

With my woozy re-emergence from a London hospital post-surgery, there began a period of my life which layered confinement upon rehabilitation, upon self-isolation. I discharged the final few administrative tasks in my working life, but otherwise spent my waking hours brooding, looking at the days getting shorter, and the incidences and deaths from Covid-19 accruing even more threateningly as we headed into our first autumn, then winter, within the strictures of a pandemic. Sitting at my desk, my right arm in a sling, and only able to type slowly with my left index finger, I felt as if the open endless world I thought I knew, already viciously compromised by the virus, was shutting down for good.

It was around then that I got a text message about a reel of film. It came from an ex-paratrooper called John.

THE REVELATION OF JOHN MCDONALD

I should explain how fragile this connection was, how strange and fortunate; and how coincidence and chance have played their spidery part in a web that started to be spun that very moment.

John McDonald is something of a Renaissance man. He's made radio documentaries about boxers, he's been a photographer, a scriptwriter and a soldier, in roughly reverse order. These days his principal occupation is as the Master of Ceremonies for the Professional Darts Corporation. If you've ever watched the darts on TV, you will know him. He's that silver-haired, well-turned-out chap with outstanding teeth and an even better voice whose job it is to call the darts players to the oche for a televised match.

For an irrepressibly verbose man, John's text communication was sparing, to the point of being cryptic. The message he sent me that September morning was simply a link to something he'd spotted online. I wondered briefly whether it was spam, as there were no accompanying words, just the link. In fact, I very nearly didn't open it, for fear it would unleash another unwanted virus into my life. And besides, how many links do we click on every day of our lives? How many of those actually lead somewhere significant? Not many.

That's how the story of the film began, on the most humdrum of terms. But even that probably isn't really the starting point. Tracing back the origins of any sequence of events is a limitless process.

As it is written in the final book of the Bible, in which the end of the world is revealed to another John, the Apostle, *Happy is the man who reads, and happy those who listen to the words . . .* (Revelation 1:3).

JOHN, LANCE AND THE TOUR DE FRANCE

In the late noughties, John and I used to go running along the canal in Wolverhampton when we were both working on a televised darts tournament. Most mornings I would stand there in the half-light of a November dawn in a pair of shorts and some muddy training shoes. I would wait for him by a canal lock, its iron-clad black wooden beam glistening in the morning damp. Then I'd spot him coming towards me through the chill air, breaking into a shuffling jog, upright, a little portly, and wearing a rustling cagoule.

'There he is, all present and correct!' John shouted in that familiar cheerful manner, addressing me from a distance in the third person. 'Well, present, anyway. Let's leave it at that.'

'Morning John,' I replied, and we ran off together.

The canal path was too narrow to accommodate us side by side, so John jogged ahead and I followed behind, stepping carefully either side of the sad little puddles that had collected in the middle of the path. It was better with John in the lead. He was ex-military and leading was a natural state for him. I watched his steps, noting where he placed his feet to avoid the mud. There were twenty-two locks on this stretch of the canal, all the way from the city centre, past the racecourse on the left, dropping under a series of beautiful brick-built bridges to the junction with the Birmingham canal. That's the exact point we'd just reached when John suddenly started, quite unexpectedly, to talk about the Tour de France.

'I just think it's amazing,' he said, lithely dodging another puddle. 'I mean those distances, every day. And those massive mountains.'

John, perhaps innocently, had stumbled upon my favourite subject. 'They used to ride twice as far back in the day, John,' I told him. 'Over 400 kilometres per stage.'

John shook his head in disbelief, as people often do when they hear that for the first time. 'They've got to be the greatest athletes alive, Ned.'

'In some ways,' I suggested, shouting at his back as we ran on. 'But not in every way.'

Even though this conversation happened a long time ago, I had already amassed years of experience at the race. The first three Tours I had covered, from 2003 until 2005, had featured Lance Armstrong at the very height of his powers. Memories drifted back to me as we ran on. The water was lifeless and black. Crows hopped around on bare branches of the trees overlooking the canal, and in the distance yellowish coal smoke rose from the chimney of a houseboat into the still, damp air.

'Take Armstrong, for example,' said John. 'What an absolutely incredible guy. I mean, what a hero. There's just nothing to compare with what he's done. What's he like to meet in person, Ned?'

'Oh, pretty interesting,' I replied. 'Pretty charismatic.' I remembered the dozens of times when I had stood face to face with Armstrong, my words dancing on the head of a difficult question, as he fixed me with his blue-eyed stare. 'Can't trust a word he says, mind.'

'What do you mean?'

'I mean that he doped,' I said lightly, not thinking I was saying anything particularly revelatory. 'We all know he doped all throughout his career.'

'You can't be serious?' John stopped running. 'Armstrong?'

After a short pause, we set off again, but more slowly now. All the way along the canal, to the turning point of the run, and all the way back up the twenty-two locks to our hotel in the city, I furnished John with the details of what I knew, or what I suspected about Armstrong. For a man who liked to talk, I had never known John so quiet. Ever since that day, whenever John and I have met, he has remembered the conversation, almost word for word. 'You remember that morning run, Ned? Down the canal. Lance Armstrong, the biggest cheat there's ever been.'

Time passed. Armstrong came back to race the Tour again, then confessed it all to Oprah Winfrey, a moment I witnessed all alone in a hotel room in Leeds. And all the while my life became more inextricably interwoven with the Tour de France.

By the time the autumn of 2020 came around, I had worked on a total of 18 consecutive editions of the race. It had taken up residence at the centre of my life.

AN AUCTION, A BID AND A JIFFY BAG

A refuse lorry thundered portentously down the road outside, making the windows rattle. So little traffic passed the house during that period of lockdown, that its sudden roar jolted me out of my sullen reverie. I had not left the house, except to dart out to the shops, masked and avoiding any kind of contact, for weeks. My bike stood propped up in the shed, unridden. My arm was broken and my mood was low, every day.

I looked at my phone and John's message. After a momentary pause, I duly opened the link that he had sent me. A page from an online auction house popped up. I squinted at the text that appeared below a small thumbnail image:

'Lot 212. A Rare Film Reel from the Tour de France in the 1930s? Condition unknown.'

From the picture of the reel, it was impossible to know exactly what I was looking at. The metal casing in which the film sat looked a bit battered, and the dark brown film, coiled around its spindle, was impenetrable. It was hard to ascertain from the single photo of the lot what it might actually contain.

Lot 212 was in a category all of its own on the website; an anomalous, overlooked item surrounded by the more mainstream sporting orthodoxy of signed football jerseys, cricket bats and rugby memorabilia, which were clearly attracting the majority of interest in the online auction. Though the date of the sale was some time away, I placed a bid of a maximum £140, feeling both foolish and excited at the same time. I had never even attempted to buy anything at auction before and I wasn't particularly confident I'd win it, having no idea whether my bid was a reasonable one. How do you set a price on such an obscure item? I submitted my bid and then promptly forgot all about it.

A few weeks later, the day of the sale came around. As I had suspected and hoped, Lot 212 had generated very little interest. Though some anonymous online stranger raised me from £100 to £110, a simple extra tenner on top of that bid secured the rather dubious prize. The lot was sold to me for just £120. Just like that. Suddenly thrilled by my achievement, I stood up from my desk and closed the lid of the laptop. Then I quickly re-opened it again to check that I hadn't got the wrong end of the stick, which it seemed I hadn't.

A week later, a jiffy bag landed with a thump in the hallway and nestled up against the radiator pipe. It was only later in the day that I discovered it and took the package upstairs with me to my desk, trying not to break into a run, and closed the door behind me, wanting the moment to myself. My hands, I noticed to my surprise, were shaking just a little.

Inside the jiffy bag, covered casually in a thin layer of bubble wrap, was Lot 212. I walked with it to the window. Very carefully, I unfurled the first half-dozen frames of the film; matchbox-sized images bordered on either side by sprocket holes.

I held them up to the light.

STILL LIFE

A tiny map revealed itself to me. An identical image appeared on each subsequent frame I unfurled. I loosened a dozen frames, then a dozen more. Before long I had dropped a couple of feet from the reel, and all along its fragile length the same map was repeated.

I peered at the miniature lettering. In the top left-hand corner, in capitals: 'BREST'. And diametrically opposite: 'LES SABLES D'OLONNE' with the number 412 alongside. In the centre-left of the frame, the words: '4eme ÉTAPE 412 Km'.

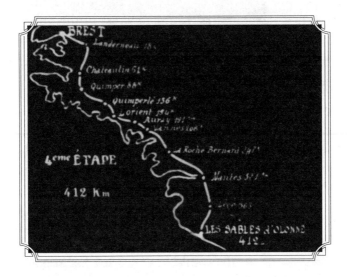

I spooled on, now winding the frames I had seen onto the cardboard tube from the middle of a toilet roll, functioning as a makeshift spindle. The film was dark and felt so brittle to the touch that I was worried it would split. The image of the map replicated itself dozens of times more before there was a sudden cut. The next shot was another caption, again marked out with white lettering against a black background: 'Au contrôle de Lorient.' I rolled the film on.

Finally, I reached a startling black-and-white image. Houses, dark grey against a white-out sky. A string of bunting suspended across a street thronging with people. A man in the foreground, his back turned to the camera, wearing a cap and an elegant long coat. And in the middle of the frame, tiny figures, dozens of them, just about to mount bikes.

The brightly detailed little images were crisp and miniature. With an instant sense of wonder, I realised I might genuinely be looking at a distant and long-forgotten Tour de France.

Metres of film later, over the course of which the figures in the frames moved almost imperceptibly over a series of tiny fractions, I came to another caption. Then, still further, another scene change. Now the riders seemed to be coming towards the camera, racing up a dusty white road, with a wooded horizon behind them. Another longer caption. And suddenly a bridge: a huge structure, almost military in design with a long iron arch, spanning a deep river valley.

At the bridge, I stopped spooling. I estimated that I'd spun through about half of the duration of the film. Carefully, I wound it all back onto the original spindle, for fear that the whole reel would start messily to unravel. I placed it back into the packaging and considered my next move.

The jiffy bag, sitting on my desk now, sat portentously amid the mess of opened utility bills, desiccated biros and half-empty batteries, detritus of twenty-first-century life. Already, if still unconsciously, I had a sense that my reel of film was precious in ways I could only dimly grasp. Again and again I glanced at it, thinking of those tantalising little glimpses my cursory examination of its contents had afforded me. More than anything else, I wanted to see the images move.

I sent John McDonald a message. 'It's absolutely beautiful, John. Thanks so much for flagging it up.'

'Pleasure,' he replied.

'It's made my year!' I followed up.

He didn't reply to that. He could have had not the faintest idea how much meaning I'd stuffed into that simple phrase, since even I didn't yet understand how true it would prove to be.

RESTORATION

A certain, profound sense of ownership settled over me every time I glanced at the reel of film. I was filled with wonder at its dark contents, and would often return, many times a day, to sneak another glimpse at the shards of images from another time. Had they been images of everyday life, just ordinary street scenes, perhaps they might have been of less interest to me. But there was nothing ordinary about them. They were from a distant Tour de France, and therefore they were connected by a direct yet invisible thread to my central obsession.

Over a period of years, the Tour de France had settled at the centre of my life. It had defined not just my professional career, but had shaped my years, giving them contours that nothing else could match. When I counted back through time, trying to bookmark phases of my life, I did so in reference to the Tour de France. The year 1989 – Laurent Fignon and Greg LeMond battling it out on the Champs-Elysées, the same year I was in Germany for the fall of the Berlin Wall. Then

2008 – Carlos Sastre's mournful demeanour even in victory – was the year we moved to this London house. And 1969 – the year of my birth, days before Eddy Merckx won his first Tour, and then the first moon landing. And 2003 – Lance Armstrong's apotheosis, and the birth of my second child. I measured out my life in yellow jerseys, bunch sprints and endless mountain passes. Without my realising it had happened, my sense of the passage of time had fallen into lockstep with the Tour de France.

So to have this reel of film, this fragment of the Tour de France, fall into my hands at this most sensitive time, almost felt like an act of providence. There it lay, guarding its secrets for now, on the dark wooden surface of my desk, beneath the lemon-yellow light of the Anglepoise. My gaze returned to it like a nervous tick, an unconscious impulse.

Getting the film transferred into a digital format was the first and potentially terminal hurdle to overcome. I contacted a few film-restoration companies, anxious about the expense that might be incurred, and afraid that the film might never be viewable: that it might, in fact, be beyond repair.

In the end, a company in Leeds took up the challenge. The extremely helpful film restorer I spoke to over the phone seemed to suggest that it should be a reasonably straightforward process, and that it could be done quickly, too. He also explained over the phone that he used to work in a transmission unit at ITV, for whom I commentate on the Tour de France, and would spend hours of his life watching the Tour, subjected to my commentary while he was at work. He was a devotee of the race and declared himself to be thrilled by the prospect of helping me restore the film. So, I put the reel back in the jiffy bag, sealed it up and sent it in the post to Yorkshire, full of hope.

While I waited for him to get back to me, I read up on the history of those early editions of the race, an era of the Tour de France to which my film clearly belonged, whatever its exact date. The early Tour de France routes did exactly what the title of the race suggested, in that they toured France. The Tour routinely hugged the coastline and the French borders and simply traversed the mountain ranges, rather than dwelt in them. Comprised of stages in excess of 400 kilometres, these races were completely joined up, literally outlining the 'hexagon' of France, in contrast to modern editions, which tend to drop in on certain favoured locations, cross borders for hard tourist-board cash, and ignore entire regions, varying massively from year to year. The early tours were much simpler affairs, albeit almost implausibly vast in scale. Every second day was a rest day, which meant that although there were only 15 stages in total (rather than the modern 21), the race still took a month to complete, starting in the final week of June and filling all of July.

The distances involved were so immense that the race would have to start long before dawn, often at two o'clock in the morning, to allow for sufficient time for the riders to travel over entire regions of France to their distant destination. Every 40 or 50 kilometres they would be obliged to sign their names against the time they passed through at various waypoints, or *contrôles*, to prevent riders from jumping on trains, the earliest form of cheating on the race. That would explain, in the frames of the film that I had unfurled, the checkpoint at the Breton port of Lorient on the Atlantic coast.

In the meantime, I heard nothing from the restorer in Yorkshire, and was beginning to worry. In order to keep myself busy as I waited, I wondered whether the auction house which had sold me the film might be able to cast any light on its provenance. I sent them a long email explaining my fascination with the purchase, trying to instill in them the same sense of wonder that was growing within me. This attempt met with only muted success. 'It came from an auction house in Germany,' was their sparing reply.

That seemed interesting, and rather unexpected. So, I followed it up with another question. 'Could you please tell me which one, so that I could contact them?' I wrote, before for some reason adding, 'I speak German, which might make it easier.'

I got no reply to this suggestion. The thought crossed my mind that they might not want to reveal their suppliers' identities, and a further week passed before I chased them up again. This time they replied more positively.

'We will make some enquiries and let you know.'

I heard nothing more for several days. Then, out of the blue, there was one final exchange of emails.

'The German auction house said they got it from France. That's all they knew.'

Could they be a little more specific? It seemed not.

'People are very protective of their contacts.'

And that was that; a rather threatening-sounding cul-de-sac.

Then the phone rang with a Leeds number. I picked up expecting it not to be good news, and it wasn't. 'The thing is the sprockets are in a terrible condition,' the restorer gloomily told me. 'If we attach the film to our scanner, and get it up to speed, there is a chance that the whole film might tear.'

I agreed with him that this wasn't a risk we could take. He suggested that, with my permission, he would ask around the industry to see if anyone else might be able to help. Inclined to fear the worst, I was already half-resigned to never seeing the images move.

Further weeks passed. I found myself preoccupied by other projects as October drew to a close and turned into the bleak November of 2020 with its renewed regional, then national lockdowns. Somehow the urgency of my interest in the film waned. I forgot about its existence for days at a time, as I wrestled with other deadlines, unconnected in any way with the film. Still, from time to time I'd open the folder on my desktop computer in which I had stored some photos of the frames. I'd look at them, remembering the moment I first saw them and that feeling of releasing something hidden. Then I'd close the folder and refresh my emails, hoping for, rather than expecting, news.

By now the reel had criss-crossed the country. A company that specialised in all sorts of film transfers and restorations was confident it could do something with my film, since they had some sort of clever sprocketless device; a new technology and seemingly the only one in the land. The jiffy bag moved again, from Leeds to London. And then, days later, an email arrived in my inbox.

'I'm happy to tell you that your beautiful film has been successfully transferred. We will send you a link to it shortly, as soon as it has uploaded.'

Not long after that, my film arrived. Over an internet link, I downloaded a 5.68 GB MP4 file. I dragged it onto my desktop, then went downstairs. In the kitchen, I filled the kettle, and stood at the counter watching it come to the boil. I had the house to myself that afternoon, and wanted deliberately to slow down the pace of the day, to extend the moment. The film was about to reveal itself to me. Steam billowed from the kettle, clouding the wall in moisture. It rocked as it came to the boil. Slowly, I walked back upstairs with a cup of tea, and opened the file.

Then I clicked on play.

LIGHT, MOTION AND MYSTERY

My film was a grand total of two minutes and thirty seconds, and not a second longer.

It was, naturally, completely silent. By which I mean that, in a digital age, and viewed as a Quicktime file on a computer, not even the whirring of a projector gave it any kind of acoustic depth. It was a totally mute experience; just light and dark outlines and shaded sepia patterns shifting across the screen.

I watched it through once, my heart racing. I don't think I blinked. It was dramatic in a way I had not imagined it could possibly be. Its huge number of featured characters looked both antique and modern, commonplace and mythical; monochrome genies, escaping their century-long obscurity, released into the unreal light of my computer screen after a hundred years locked away. When it had played out, I scrolled the cursor back and watched it again. This time, I started to concentrate, and made a note of the distinct scenes the film contained:

1 A drawing of a route map.
2 The riders leaving the Lorient control point.
3 The peloton riding along the road to Vannes.
4 A caption, explaining that a rider called 'Beckmann' [sic] has launched an attack over a bridge in 'Laroche-Bernard' [sic].
5 Three scenes of 'Beckmann' at the front, cycling through and past crowds.

Then the film whites out, as if the reel might have melted on a projector bulb and burnt. For whatever reason, it is incomplete. It contains neither the beginning of the stage (which had been in Brest, not Lorient), nor the eventual winner. It was just a fragment, a broken story.

Another email from the film restorers landed, warning me that the film should never have been posted, nor stored in the way it had been. I was told that it was nitrate film, common for its age. As such, it was highly combustible. Nitrate had been known spontaneously to burst into flames and its presence would invalidate home insurance if I kept it in the house. They were shocked that the dangerous package had been posted halfway around the country already, and I certainly didn't admit to them that it had landed next to the radiator in the hallway when it first arrived through my letterbox. They suggested that they hold it in secure refrigerated storage, at least for now. They would look after the reel and keep it safe.

Outside, a watery sunlight fell across the damp roof of the house opposite mine. A gust of wind prised the very last of the damp, dark brown leaves from the spindly tree in front of my window. It was, by now, early December 2020. London had been forced to close down as Christmas approached. But a distant French summer from long ago promised to cast its light.

A GAME OF DATES

I couldn't remember what the old, left-behind, rhythm of my world had been like. Shunted into abnormality by this endless pandemic, I had forgotten how my pre-Covid winters would pass with frosty bike rides along the Thames, a low sun glancing off the water, chilled by London's air that reached in bright stillness towards a morning sky, studded with a daytime moon.

I could scarcely remember how the cold would eventually yield to warmth, how seasons worked, in that misshapen year of 2020 when the Tour de France was in September and the Giro d'Italia had been pushed back from May until October, casting late autumnal shadows over Italian mountain passes. These were profoundly unnatural times. The world was out of whack.

My broken bones shut me down still further. I was months away from being able to ride my bike outside again, and could barely lift my right arm from my side. At some point, I got a home trainer delivered, which I set up reluctantly in our shed. And there I went to ride one-handed, moving through a digital mock-up of the outside world whose passing I had started to mourn. Each day I sat, panting and sweating next to bags of potting compost and garden tools, watching my own virtual progress through a parody of the world.

My family were used to these unsightly rituals. I would come dripping back into the house from the shed, emitting clouds of sweat, hobbling around on cleated shoes. Then, impatient to return to my desk, I would shower, dress and get back to work, with perhaps the most perfunctory of exchanges. 'How's everyone?'

'Good, good.'

'I'm just going back upstairs.'

Upstairs was where the magic happened. It always began in the same way. I opened the video file, and clicked play. The ritual began again.

Which Tour de France was this? What was I looking at?

The first frame of the film was the starting point: The faintly juddering hand-drawn map, charting the outline of the Atlantic coast from Finistère to the Vendée, with way points all marked out, and the principal information clear for all to see: 412 kilometres. From Brest to Les Sables d'Olonne. The first thing I had to establish was the date; the day on which it must have been filmed. Knowing that at least would give me my first point of access into the film's unknown origins, and its uncertain content.

I typed into Google: 'Brest to Les Sables d'Olonne. Tour de France'

I got an instant hit from a reliable and familiar cycling database. I was pleased to see that the rest of the information tallied in every detail with the caption on the screen. It confirmed that stage 4 of the 1923 Tour de France did indeed run from Brest to Les Sables d'Olonne, and it was exactly 412 kilometres long, as the film also detailed. Happy that I had hit upon the correct year in question, I looked no further for a possible date and started instead to read about the 1923 Tour.

1923 was the edition in which a seven-year winning streak of Belgian victories either side of the First World War finally came to an end. At last France would celebrate another winner, when Henri Pélissier would ride in the yellow jersey over the finish line at the Parc des Princes in Paris.

The name Pélissier was hazily familiar to me, as was the case with so many of the pioneers of the Tour in the pre- and post-Great War eras, but I couldn't put my finger on why. Pélissier had been a controversial rider, that much I thought I remembered. Reading a bit further into his history, I was reminded of his part in the most infamous Tour de France story of them all. More notorious than Armstrong, in some ways.

I was reminded about the name Pélissier in a recent edition of the race, as so often happens when the plotting of the race route, the accident of geography forces a connection with a distant past. The first year I commentated, rather than reported, for TV on the Tour de France was in 2016. Stage 2 started at Utah Beach, before the race then passed across the Cherbourg Peninsula. At around 3 p.m., a dead time of day so detested by Jean-Paul Sartre's hero in *La Nausée*, who maintained that it was 'always too late or too early for anything you wanted to do', I glanced at my pre-prepared notes.

COUTANCES

The breakaway had reached Coutances, with its tall Gothic cathedral, too grand really for the modest Norman town beneath it. The 2016 organisation had placed an intermediate sprint there for good reason, as they often do when they want to mark a specific moment in history. Though the town itself was not much more than an unremarkable dot on the map, its name still resonated in the introspective history-addicted world of the Tour, having been immortalised in French cycling folklore for hosting the most celebrated mutiny in the race's long and sometimes inglorious past.

In 1924, Henri Pélissier and his brother Francis, as well as another rider called Maurice Ville, walked away from the race in fury at the draconian regulations imposed on them by the race organisation. What made this truly scandalous was the fact that Pélissier was the returning Tour champion, having won the 1923 edition in great style. That year, in 1924, the race director Henri Desgrange had once more decreed that all riders must start and finish each stage with the same clothing and kit; they would not be allowed to jettison punctured inner tubes or excess clothing. On the early morning start to stage 3, the Pélissiers were both wearing an extra jersey to stave off the chill and intended to discard them later during the heat of the day. Desgrange expressly forbade them, and a row had broken out at the start line.

Not far into the stage, the three mutineers rode off the course and headed for a café where they held an infamous impromptu press briefing. Faced with a clutch of journalists, the brothers poured their hearts out as well as emptying the highly contentious contents of their kit bags. Their pharmaceutical paraphernalia included chloroform and cocaine. 'We ride on dynamite,' Henri Pélissier is reported to have claimed, intent on impressing on his audience the inhumanity of the event and the contempt in which the race organisation held the riders. They were, asserted Pélissier, forced to take all these dangerous substances simply to survive the ordeal.

One of the men listening to their legendary diatribe was the journalist from *Le Petit Parisien*, a certain Albert Londres. He was a well-known foreign correspondent and political journalist, who knew next to nothing about cycling, nor cared greatly for it. Londres had ended up covering the Tour simply so that he could indulge his passion for travelling without leaving the country, as his newly installed lover didn't want to leave Paris. Accidently, he ended up penning a bestseller, in part at least because of the Pélissiers.

Londres' famous account of that meeting is documented in an iconic short book called *Les Forçats de la Route* (The Convicts of the Road). In 2016 I had read this intriguing, and incidentally very funny, collection of reports in preparation for commentating on TV as the riders passed through Coutances.

LES FORÇATS DE LA ROUTE

Now, four years later, I picked the book off the shelf again and looked back through its staccato, explosive prose. It was, after all, written so close in time to the year that my film had seemingly been shot, just one year later. When I got to Londres' famous account of stage 4 in 1924, the next day's racing after the Pélissiers' mutiny, I was drawn up short by the chapter title:

In the Dust – From Brest to Les Sables d'Olonne

It seemed that stage 4 of the 1924 edition of the race featured the same start and finish as in 1923. This revelation threw me into sudden confusion. I read on, and a further detail from Londres' semi-fictionalised account of stage 4 stood out:

At one hour after midnight he knocked on our door:
'It's one o'clock,' he shouted. 'It's time to eat our dust.'
'How many kilometres of it are we going to have today?'
'Four hundred and twelve!'
'Hurray!' shouted the bunch, and sprang out of bed, full of joy.

The race distance that day was 412 kilometres! So, not only did the 1924 route start and finish in the same place as in 1923 but it was the exact same distance too.

I now could no longer be sure that my film was from the year I thought it was. I checked the route of the 1925 Tour. Stage 4 was, thankfully, completely different, having been split into two shorter parts. The race organisation had put in a finish for the first time in Vannes. At least it couldn't be 1925.

But then I looked further back in time. It didn't take long before I established to my growing bewilderment that my film could equally well have been from 1922, 1921 or 1920 as well as the 1923 and 1924 races that I now knew about. All of those years were raced on identical courses. Every year there was a stage 4 from Brest to Les Sables d'Olonne, and every year it was 412 kilometres long. All my certainty about the film's date suddenly evaporated. Five entire editions of the race between 1920 and 1924 were raced on the exact same route, all the way around France.

Which one was it? Answering that simple question became my peculiar mission. Whole days were swallowed up by the internet's irresistible lure, cross-referencing photos and results. I ignored my family, I glazed over during dinner, failed to concentrate during our morbid watching of the evening news with its loathsome Covid statistics. Increasingly now, as the darker evenings drew in, I only had time for rummaging around in the confusion of Lot 212.

I checked the weather reports from the various years in question. In the film it is clearly dry and fairly sunny in every shot. The dust on the unmade roads suggests that it had not rained for some time. There also doesn't appear to be much wind to speak of. It was hard to find detailed, reliable weather reports from the days in question, towards the end of June, on each occasion it was raced. But one website did document that in 1924 after a particularly cold June (it had, a few days earlier, been 4 degrees in Marseille, 7 in Bordeaux, 6 in Lyon, for example), a heatwave rushed in on the 28th of the month. Again, I turned back to the account of that year, *Les Forçats de la Route*, in which Londres writes of 1924's stage 4:

> *There are fanciful people who swallow bricks and there are others who swallow live frogs. I have seen fakirs who gobble down molten lead. These are normal people. The real loonies are these excitable fools who, since 22 June when they left Paris, have been eating dust. I know them well, for I am one of them.*
>
> *We wolfed down 381 kilometres of the stuff from Paris to Le Havre, 354 from Le Havre to Cherbourg, 405 from Cherbourg to Brest. It wasn't enough. When you've tasted it, you can never let it go. . . .*

. . . We were to cross Finistère, Morbihan, the Lower Loire and into the Vendée.

The Morbihan dust isn't as good as Finistère's, and the stuff from the Lower Loire is a bit spicier. As for the Vendée dust; it's a real treat. Just thinking about it makes my mouth water.

Despite the oddity of his turn of phrase and his penchant for slightly surreal humour, this description of endless dust certainly matched the film. But still, something was not quite right. The sense I had gathered about the intensity of the 1924 heatwave is confirmed by this later observation by Londres: *'It is too hot. The Creator is not being reasonable, he's going to kill people.'* I guessed that by 'The Creator', Londres meant both God and Henri Desgrange, the founder of the Tour de France.

I looked at the film again, drawn this time to look closely at the clothing being worn by the people by the side of the road. In Lorient, where it would have been quite early in the morning, they are all in jackets and coats. Perhaps there was still a leftover chill in the air from the night. But even by lunchtime at La Roche-Bernard, they are still for the most part wearing a couple of layers of clothing. Though it's dry and bright, it doesn't look to be *boiling* hot. The riders too have not even chosen to roll up their sleeves, which makes me doubt that these images tally with the description of 1924's intense heat. This annoys me, as I had started to become excited by the possibility that my film dated from that legendary edition of the race. I wanted to believe that it was 1924 but had to confess that the evidence wasn't quite there to back up my hopes.

Then I discovered the French National Library's frankly astonishing online resource. Almost every single edition of almost every surviving French newspaper of note, as well as hundreds of other publications, are available to be viewed online. And with that I disappeared down a sinkhole of scrolling, from which I emerged a few days later triumphantly, if metaphorically, brandishing a small piece of paper that proved conclusively the year in which my film had originated.

After scouring multiple sources for any mention of the attack on the bridge by the rider spelled 'Beckmann' in the caption, I finally got lucky. But in order to get that far in my searches, I had to arrive at the key realisation that the filmmakers had misspelt his name. 'Beeckman' is a not unusual Flemish name, but 'Beckmann' is non-existent. Having established that much, I quickly eliminated 1921, since the rider known as Théophile Beeckman wasn't in that year's race. But he was in 1920, 1922, 1923 and 1924. So without yet being able positively to identify any of the other riders in the clip, nor knowing who went on to win stage 4 since the film stops so abruptly, I would have to look for other clues.

According to the record books, of the four occasions on which Théophile Beeckman raced this stage the best he did was third place. That was in 1924, when stage 4 was won by a French rider called Félix Goethals. When we see Beeckman attacking so vigorously, crossing the bridge alone, he is still 165 kilometres from the finish line. Normally, at least in the modern Tour de France, if a rider expends that much energy that far out, there is no way they'd be able to compete for a podium spot at the finish line. But the race was very different back then, in all sorts of ways. Applying the received wisdom of 2020 race tactics to a Tour from a hundred years ago was unwise. I therefore couldn't rule out the possibility that Beeckman made his attack, was caught by the other cyclists, and then finished strongly in the end. So it could yet be 1924, the day after the Pélissier mutiny, though Beeckman's attack was probably more evidence to the contrary, I conceded.

In the end, it was an incidental detail from a slightly off-piste column on the third page of Henri Desgrange's *L'Auto* newspaper, separate from the main race report, which convinced me that I could accurately date the film. The article in question went to print on 1 July 1923, the day after stage 4 of that year's race. Reading it would be the first of many occasions on which I would exclaim loudly, to no one in particular, as I sat at my desk in the spare room: 'Ha!'

No one in my house responded.

Beeckman Attacks
The front peloton was riding slowly, creeping along the dusty road like a snake joylessly digesting its food. La Roche Bernard was disappearing behind us, vanishing in the clouds of dust created in generous measure by the following cars. Suddenly, like a storm being unleashed, Beeckman attacks and sets off for Les Sables. His back was arched and his pedal stroke was epileptic [sic].

The report described, albeit with certain anomalies, the moment depicted just before the end of the footage. Beeckman is the last thing we see before the abrupt end of the film, the trace of his smile caught on camera and just about visible before the film cuts out. After that we see no more than a freeze frame of white dust with a few discoloured blemishes where the nitrate has degraded over the years.

At last, on reading that report, I could pin a definitive date to the film: The day on which it must have been shot was 30 June 1923.

A NAME AND A FACE

The most advanced facial-recognition software in the world would not have been able to pick Théophile Beeckman out from the available footage. In my film, he is only very partially visible in four different shots. As he crosses the bridge, he is not much more than a bright dot against the dark of the ironwork. In the subsequent three shots, he is much closer to the camera, and occasionally his features come into view, but blurred and obscured by dust clouds which blow across the road.

In that sense, the misspelling of his name seems entirely in keeping with the spirit of the film. Accuracy was something of an optional extra in the 1920s, with multiple variations of facts, locations and names available, and no central and immediate way of correlating them to create any kind of definitive standard. Even the name of the great Henri Desgrange often acquires a rogue 's' on the end (albeit never in any of his own publications, it should be said). Perhaps things such as spelling don't matter as much as we have been trained to believe.

A very few photographs of the Belgian rider are instantly searchable. It's hard to discern much from them save for the fact that he was rather short and very slight. You can plunder Google Images for Beeckman and be finished within a minute or two.

And yet there are, as I later discovered, two quite captivating and detailed portraits of Beeckman stored online in the French national archive. They took a bit of searching for. In both pictures the Belgian has the same disarmingly serious gaze, though in one he appears startled, perhaps from the elation of success. In this image, he holds a victor's bouquet in one hand and his bike in the other, by the side of the track at what appears to be the Parc des Princes velodrome in Paris. The year of this photo is 1925, perhaps in the spring or even late autumn as his bike is fitted with mudguards. It's hard to know.

In the picture above he is married (but only just, as I would discover) and wears a gold band on the ring finger of the hand that clutches the flowers. His legs are filthy, as is his 'Griffon Dunlop' team jersey. His deep-set eyes (I imagine them to be grey/blue, but of course there is no way of being sure) stare intently at the camera's lens. There is not a flicker of a smile. Beeckman was not one for tomfoolery, it seemed.

In the other picture, taken at around the same time by the looks of it, Beeckman appears equally ill at ease, with one arm awkwardly held behind his back. In both photos he stands slightly splay-footed, his stance hinting at out-turned feet. There is an arresting discomfort about Beeckman's demeanour, a certain shyness. Throughout the many months of reading and writing to come, it would be to these two photos that I would return as I paused between discoveries, using his likeness as a touchstone as I passed from the great themes this little broken film was about to throw up.

This unknowing rider somehow became the still point at the centre of the torrent of words, places, people and events that would populate the world I would start to conjure up. Beeckman's stoical silence, staring back at me: the gaze at the heart of the century-old film.

Unlocking his story, I felt, might lead to the unknown answers to a series of silently forming questions which were now only slowly starting to queue up at my door.

BEECKMAN, THE KNOWN KNOWNS

I began to sift through the raw data of Théophile Beeckman's career and it became apparent that he was evidently a very, very good rider; one of the very best of the post-war age.

His results show that he finished fifth, sixth and fourth overall in consecutive years at the Tour de France, just off the podium. He finished fourth in a bunch sprint of six riders who contested the final of the famously gruelling one-day race, Paris-Roubaix, in 1923, in which he had been described by a reporter as 'energetic'. Twice he finished in the top five of the Ronde van Vlaanderen, the already redoubtable Tour of Flanders, close to his home. And he did, in the end, go on to win two stages of the Tour de France, in 1924 and 1925.

Any rider, regardless of the era in which they raced, who can claim to have won multiple stages of the Tour is automatically considered to be elevated into a category above the ordinary. So much for the bare bones of Beeckman's career. That much was easily accessible online and quickly done.

After that, the opacity began. Search as I did, I could initially find precious little else about him other than that. His was a career like countless others which had been suddenly trapped under the ice that formed over the world of recorded facts when the internet came into existence, freezing everything which went before it. For every rocky promontory of an exalted career which still juts visibly above the surface, there are a hundred others buried out of sight beneath. I gathered the very few scraps of facts that most websites agreed upon: Beeckman's birthday, and his place of birth.

He had been born on 1 November 1896 in Meerbeke, a district of Ninove, in East Flanders, half an hour's drive west of Brussels. Eighteen years after Beeckman's death at the age of 59 in 1955, Meerbeke would become synonymous with the great Ronde van Vlaanderen, when it hosted the finish of the race from 1973 until it moved to its present Oudenaarde location in 2012. But Beeckman got there first. He was born, married and died in the very heartland of East Flanders, living his whole life (when he wasn't on the road) in the red-brick terraces of a small Belgian neighbourhood twice invaded by German armies within his single lifetime.

It was to the town archives of Ninove that I turned first during the long, darkening winter of 2020. I sent them an email asking for any information they might be able to provide me regarding a certain Théophile Beeckman, using the most common spelling I had gleaned by aggregating all the available references to him. I got a swift reply from a woman called Sofie who worked there. I don't know whether out of boredom, or a spirit of unmerited helpfulness, or simply because she too was curious to find out more about an almost unknown son of her home town, but Sofie went out of her way to help me in my research.

That December, over the course of a few weeks, emails from Sofie with attachments pinged across the Channel from Flanders to London. I greeted each of their sudden arrivals with the same excitement with which I used to open the doors of a childhood advent calendar. With great exactness, Sofie detailed what she had found out about Beeckman's parents and his many siblings. She also included a copy of his 1925 marriage certificate, on which was typed another spelling of his name: 'Théophile Beeckmans'. The extra 's' on the end of his name is hardly ever replicated anywhere else, not that it matters much. In the certificate that I later managed to obtain, his occupation is listed as '*beroepsrenner*', professional racing cyclist.

Théo, according to the public records, was the eldest child of a civil servant called Camille Beeckmans (sic) and Albertina van den Berghe, both born in the 1870s in Meerbeke. Between them they had seven children, of whom Théo was the first, born in 1896 when Albertina was 21.

1925		11
Maanden Eigennamen	AKTEN VAN HUWELIJK EN ECHTSCHEIDING	

Théophile Beeckman's certificate of marriage to Irène (aka Irena) Wachtelaer

The next two children, Victorina and Maurits, both died as infants. Maurits was only 14 months, and his older sister Victorina died five days short of her third birthday. Théo was almost six already when Maria came along, the first of four sisters who would survive into adulthood, the next being Cesarina, then Malvina and Susanna. All the children were given markedly Latin first names to complement the sturdily Flemish family name of Beeckman. Flanders, especially this part of the region, remains predominantly Catholic. Whichever way you spelt it, there was no mistaking the family's religious inclinations in this most particular corner of Belgium.

In the spring of 1925, twelve days after he'd raced Paris-Roubaix, Théo married Irène Wachtelaer, also of Ninove. The couple had one daughter, Yolande. It proved difficult for some reason to divine her exact date of birth. I doubted very much that Yolande would still be alive, or if she were, she'd probably be into her late nineties. But I continued to wring Google dry of connections, trying to winkle out any semblance of a living descendant of Théophile.

This led me up a succession of false paths, none of which I was able to resist. My mission had become The Mission, and any sense of questioning its purpose had been pushed to one side. Looking back on these hours I passed playing at being a detective, I can only recall the immense pleasure I got from turning over each and every stone as I meandered down those successive paths, taking a new turn at each fork in the road, and drifting further and further from the matter in hand. What had begun as a simple inquiry had started to become a supermarket trolley-dash of matching and mismatching information, a lifting and spreading mushroom cloud of investigation. It scarcely mattered any longer what the purpose of it all was. The process pulled me in, dragged me down and raised me up. I worked alone, lost in it all, and shared only very seldomly any of my discoveries with anyone else. It was all mine.

There are many Beeckmans in Belgium, but when you narrowed it down to certain times and places, not an insurmountable number born at the right time in the same district as Théo (I had begun to shorten his name, as if I were in his inner circle). There was a Pierre Beeckmans, a little older than Théo, but also schooled in the Ninove district of Meerbeke. This made me wonder if he might be a cousin. I found an account of his life: Pierre Beeckmans went on infamously to work with the Nazis under German occupation and to orchestrate the deportation of Jews from Antwerp during the Second World War. I happened upon long accounts of this awful life on a Holocaust memorial site, but happily was unable eventually to make any direct connection between this branch of the Beeckman(s) clan and Théo's wider family.

Another extraordinary but patently false lead pointed to the tragic life cut short of a (nearly identical) namesake for Théo's only child, Yolande. This biography briefly tripped me up, before I realised that the timeline didn't hang together. Nevertheless, a morning passed in which my research into the family of a Tour de France rider led me to the short life of another Yolande Beekman (a fourth possible variation of spelling).

Beekman was a Franco-British spy in the Second World War who, having married a Dutchman (hence Beekman), was sent to Occupied France by the secret Special Operations Executive which parachuted French-speaking agents into enemy territory to support the Resistance in acts of sabotage ahead of D-Day. While their covert operations were occasionally highly successful, many were not, and the agents' chances of returning home to their families were slight. The S.O.E. was also being successfully infiltrated through informers by German counter-intelligence based in Paris, and, just as their activity ramped up ahead of the Normandy landings in 1944, most remaining agents were rounded up across France by the Gestapo, Yolande included. A horrifying journey east began for her and many of her colleagues. For Beekman, this ended with a shot in the back of the head in Dachau concentration camp, as she held the hands of two of her colleagues from the S.O.E. She was far from being the only agent to meet a similar fate.

Yet, as unusual as the name was, this was clearly not the Yolande I was trying to locate, even allowing for misspellings. I began to understand that to dig around in the partially remembered lives of people born into this part of the world at this time in history meant one thing: The two world wars seemed to run like a seam through their biographies. Théo's daughter Yolande in fact survived the war, and, as I discovered with Sofie's help, she started a family of her own, remaining in the same small corner of East Flanders.

When Théo and Irène married, they moved into a house in Brusselstraat in Ninove right next door to Irène's father, her mother having died a few years before the wedding. Then, in the 1940s, the Beeckmans moved house again within Ninove, before returning to live once more in Meerbeke, this time in the prosaically named Tramstratie (there are no longer any trams and the street's name has been changed).

Yolande continued to live in this house after her mother's death in 1951 and her father's in 1955. Yolande then married a certain Frans Vlassenbroek sometime in the later 1950s. In 1959, Yolande and Frans had a child, Thérèse, whose birth is registered to the same address in which Théo was still living at the time of his death some four years previously: Tramstatie 70, Meerbeke. Thérèse therefore seemed to be Théo's only grandchild and might possibly still be alive and contactable. That was my only hope.

I got lucky. There is a genealogy website for Belgian families which is curated and maintained by enthusiastic amateurs, often distant relations with a penchant for family trees and perhaps too much time on their hands. I entered in varying combinations the names of a few of the family members whose identities I had established and was surprised to find an instant result. There was a Thérèse Vlassenbroek listed, who appeared to be still alive and married to a man called Wim de Lendtdecker. I figured out that they had two daughters (by now, if you are losing track, Théo Beeckman's great-grandchildren), Charlotte and Julie de Lentdecker.

These two women were in their thirties and belonged to a generation whose lives automatically came with a substantial digital trace. I remember a friend, who had worked for MI6 under a false identity in China, once telling me that there are huge numbers of operatives who simply sit at their desk all day in London curating fake Facebook and other social-media lives for undercover agents overseas, so that their assumed backgrounds check out under the scrutiny of a Google search. Charlotte and Julie's names both yielded a surprising number of plausible and possible hits.

Fortunately, I had a pandemic in which to try and pick a way through. The almost silent tapping away at my laptop keyboard would become the soundtrack of the 2020/21 winter. From time to time, I'd leave the desk to pace around. These were the moments when self-doubt crept in. I'd leave the room, sometimes I'd leave the house altogether, dragging some family member reluctantly with me on a dutiful walk. We'd encounter other households in the park, keeping exaggerated distances between us as we passed.

'Can I tell you about the film?' I'd shyly request of my family member, quite overcome by the sudden urge to say out loud the things I had been thinking.

'Sure.' My family were nothing if not polite.

'The thing is, I don't know if I'm getting very far.' We'd walk on in silence watching dog walkers looping tennis balls for the animals to chase. 'I don't really know what it is I'm looking for.'

Once, I remember being told, 'Just keep looking. You'll find it.'

And so I would return to take my seat to re-watch the short film, paying particular attention to the thin figure of Théo Beeckman, stamping on the pedals and accelerating away from the town of La Roche-Bernard.

At other times I'd issue another muted shout of vindication or success when I stumbled across some little fact that added to the picture. I would scrape the chair back across the wooden floorboards, pushing back from my desk. Standing up abruptly, with just a hint of accompanying dizziness after hours spent hunched over, I would take the one and a half steps to the window to the left of my desk, whose curtain I had drawn in order to keep the morning sunlight from intruding on the dull sobriety of the scene. Now, reflecting on each tiny successive discovery, I could look with sudden and renewed interest at the real world outside. The opera singer who lives across the road was once again standing at his piano on the first floor. Though he had the window shut today, I could just about make out the other-worldly drift of the aria he was rehearsing. The guy next door to him, who would occasionally drop by to pick up the post from an otherwise empty house, was scurrying to his car. And overhead, a rare Airbus was turning slowly in the sky and looping towards its final approach on Heathrow, the roar of its engines suddenly dropping in pitch as it descended. That sound would drift from the spare room down through a mostly silent house, to be heard by no one in particular. On the couch, one of our cats might have momentarily pricked up an ear.

I was helplessly lost in the story of Théo Beeckman now. I had no desire to leave it alone. Real life could wait. These little desk-bound discoveries were all I had to mark out the passing of my days. But in the tiny withdrawn world I had slipped into, they were fireworks.

One day I spotted the two names of Charlotte and Julie de Lentdecker appearing together on the programme of a contemporary dance company's performance from 2011. The production was called *Terra* and was, it seemed, a choreographic exploration for 18 dancers of the 'bond between man and earth'. It had been performed for two nights only in March 2011 in a venue in Aalst, East Flanders, scarcely 12 kilometres from Ninove, where Théo Beeckman had been buried some 56 years earlier. I was convinced that these two sisters were descended from the same Beeckman family.

Though 10 years had passed since the performance, the website of the dance company still seemed to be active, and so I contacted the chief choreographer, a certain Francine de Veylder. I wrote a garbled and confusing email to her in which I tried to explain that I was attempting to contact two of her former dancers about something I had found relating to their great-grandfather and a piece of discarded film. When I wrote it down like that, it didn't seem a promising approach. But the path I had chosen left me little option other than to hit 'Send' and wait for a reply. So that's what I did. Then I had to wait, which was the hard bit.

As I waited, I returned to study the film again, but this time frame by frame, face by face, shot by shot. And when I had done that, I started to look outside of the framing entirely. I wanted to look just around every corner, behind every spectator and into every house.

A MAP

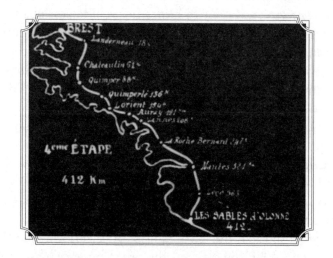

The first six seconds

The outline of the Breton coast, white against black. Riddled with inlets and coves, bays and estuaries, it twists, switches back upon itself, and winds ever further south-east. At the far top left of the map, BREST is marked with a round white point, and is capitalised in what looks like neat handwriting, the careful work of the Pathé lettering artist. At the far point of the map, in the bottom right-hand corner, the destination: LES SABLES d'OLONNE. Between the two points, along the line which traces the route of the race on the map, are all its checkpoints along the way:

> *Landerneau 18k*
> *Chateaulin 61k*
> *Quimper 88k*
> *Quimperlé 136k*
> *Lorient 154k*
> *Auray 191k*

Vannes 208k
La Roche Bernard [sic] *247k*
Nantes 321k
Légé 363k

On the left of the frame, filling the ink-black space where, in reality, the dark waters of the Gulf of Morbihan seethe with their Atlantic energy, the stark distance of the race:
4ᵐᵉ ÉTAPE
   412 Km

The whole map drifts back and forth minutely in its frame, the white outline of the coast and the inland race route moving like a tiny organism caught in the light and gaze of a microscope. Like shooting stars on a time lapse, flashes of white, slashes of white light flicker across the screen; there for a fraction of a second, a frame or two. And then gone.

BREST, AFTER THE GREAT WAR

Brest was another beginning to the story, to the events of that day in 1923. This was a place I had often visited while covering the Tour de France. I remembered having flown there once in 2008, travelling on a small propeller plane in the company of Mark Cavendish, just days before the great sprinter won the first of his flood of stages at the Tour de France. We had only ever met a handful of times prior to that encounter, and I wasn't to know what future awaited him, though I suspect he did. As we'd disembarked from the plane and walked across the tarmac at the tiny provincial airport, I remember asking him for his mobile phone number, and his polite but unambiguous refusal. It would be over a decade before he finally obliged, and I could add him to my contacts. A decade and 34 Tour de France stages later.

I remember Brest as being grey, windy. Unremarkable, actually, as so many places of mythical importance to the Tour de France reveal themselves to be. The race graces them with temporary significance, but moves on, leaving behind it only a dissipating echo of itself. What remains is simply a road, a corner, a field, a town. How strange that this film's insertion into my mental wanderings would bring the city back into the foreground, changed vastly by time and war. Brest is an iconic stop-off point in the history of the Tour de France, and now it was a mythical citadel in my imagination of a distant past.

The Breton port was almost ever-present on the early Tours, representing the furthest possible point to the north-west of the 'hexagon'. Referred to by Henri Desgrange as 'le grand port du guerre Breton', Brest sits on the finger of coast known as Finistère; the end of the land in Europe pointing across the expanse of the Atlantic towards America. This was about as far from the metropolitan sophistication of Paris as it was possible to get in France. Stage 4 had started in the middle of the night. I imagined Brest's interwar streets, ink blue and coming to life with clatter from side-alleys and firing motors. I prowled along them in my mind, seeking out the Café du Commerce, looking for the start of the Tour, and the deeper I went, the further I found myself from my starting point.

From my distant perch, across the water in London, I looked over towards Brittany and it drew me in. Spending time and money on the French booksellers' websites, I bought and read books on Brittany, the Morbihan, the growth of Lorient as a port, the Resistance in 1944, and the impact of the Great War and the Spanish flu on the region. They arrived from second-hand booksellers in France and piled up on my desk.

A red notebook that I had been given by a Tour de France team sponsor before the 2011 Tour and which I had never used, now filled with ever tinier scrawlings as I tried to get a sense of what the world was like on the night when Théo Beeckman and the other riders of the 1923 peloton set off from Brest. This was a liminal city, edged on the one side by the vast nothingness of the Atlantic, and inland, the rolling immensity of an endless continent whose war engine was still ticking as it cooled.

In 1923 the port was only just returning to a semblance of the normality that it had known before the turmoil which 1914 brought with it. Though geographically far from the front lines of the First World War, the city had nevertheless been thrown into a state of chaos by the distant calamities of Verdun and Flanders. And when, on 6 April 1917, President Woodrow Wilson of the United States of America declared war on Germany, Brest's immediate future was altered at a stroke.

I read for days at a time, and transposed my new-found scraps of understanding onto the threadbare fabric of my film. I learned how boundless the American war effort was in its industrial ambition, as the new superpower considered what could be done in Europe. The numbers! The US Army had the declared intention to land one million troops in the following six months, two million by 1918, and over five million a year later should the need arise. While ports as far down the western coast of France as Bordeaux and up along the Channel to Le Havre were designated to receive the bulk of the heavy artillery, machinery and supplies, Brest was earmarked as the most suitable point of disembarkation for the millions of American soldiers about to head over the Atlantic to join the fighting.

The huge steamer SS *Leviathan* played a central role in moving the troops across the ocean. Originally named *Vaterland*, it had been constructed in Hamburg and was one of the three huge commercial ocean liners built to make the Atlantic crossing. The ship had only been working the route for a year when war broke out and it found itself stranded in New York's harbour. When the Americans entered the war, they confiscated the liner and converted it to carry troops: 12,000 of them at a time, packed into bunks and heading for Europe's fields of slaughter.

Alongside other vessels, the *Leviathan* was responsible for landing hundreds of thousands of soldiers in Brittany, where, before continuing their journeys east, they might spend a week or two in one of the myriad makeshift camps that had sprung up to accommodate this vast new temporary population. Wooden barracks were built in record time. Some 1,200 were erected on one site just inland from Brest, with a huge refectory that could serve up to 5,000 meals at a sitting, and even a theatre with a massive capacity of 3,000 to give the troops something to keep them entertained while they waited for whatever fate had in store for them in Flanders. Such a welter of temporary construction required sudden and huge amounts of raw materials, most notably timber to construct the acres of duckboards and thousands of accommodation blocks to replace the tents which had been used at the beginning of the landings.

Of the many beneficiaries of this unexpected boon in trade with Brittany's new tenants were two men whose names were unknown beyond the immediate locality. But they were names that would be destined to become known by everyone in the country some six years later, when they both gained a macabre notoriety that would fascinate the public for generations in France, throughout the summer of 1923 and even until the present day: Pierre Quéméneur and Guillaume Seznec.

Quéméneur had been a local politician of some standing in the *département* of Finistère. He was a successful timber merchant from Landerneau, through which the 1923 race would pass shortly after leaving Brest, 'illuminated by a round moon whose image rippled on the surface of the river like a Japanese lantern', according to *Le Matin*. Seznec owned a sawmill in Morlaix, the picturesque port on the north coast of the Côtes-d'Armor, the closest town to the campsite I used to visit when my children were young.

Both these men, vague business associates, would profit from the trade with the Americans. Likewise, for both men the US 'invasion' would ultimately be their undoing. A pivotal event in their unhappy collaboration would fall fatally into place on the very morning, some years later, that the Tour de France left Brest in the darkness of the early hours on 30 June 1923.

One of them would be murdered, and there would be a warrant for the other's arrest.

A CASE OF MISTAKEN IDENTITY

I was losing myself in the urge to discover. Each successive detail I unearthed drew me further in, the allure of a mysterious name, the wonder of a hitherto unknown story, the gathering complexity of the landscape I was constructing around the bare bones of the film's simple narrative: a town, a road, people and riders. These incidental discoveries of a parallel world locked within the film's imagery simply drove a desire for me, fed a growing addiction for more. In this manner, whole days were swallowed up. Before I knew it, the light outside had faded into the early evening's gloom, and it was time to flick on my desk lamp. The yellow pool of light that now fell across my notebook was as wonderful to me as any sunset.

I sent another speculative email, this time to a cycling club based in Landerneau.

Landerneau was the first checkpoint on the route after the *départ* from Brest. The peloton would have reached there after about three-quarters of an hour of riding, and it would have been pitch-black still.

I was trying to make contact with a rider I vaguely remembered from my many years of covering the Tour de France. Though he had been retired for a few years, I still recollected bits and pieces of his career, in particular his presence on the podium after the opening stage of the 2011 Tour de France; a race that began in the Vendée before heading for Brittany, as if retracing the length of stage 4 from 1923 in reverse.

That day in 2011, a rider from Landerneau had won the *Prix de la Combativité*, a discretionary award for the most aggressive rider of the day. It went on that occasion to Perrig Quéméneur. I'd interviewed him in broken French that afternoon, as he was paraded past the waiting media beside the podium. Landerneau, I discovered, was also the home town of Pierre Quéméneur.

The cycling club kindly forwarded my email on to Perrig, who responded a few weeks later, curious as to why I'd contacted him out of the blue. I replied, apologising for the strangeness of the question, but asking whether or not he was related in any way at all to the infamously disappeared Pierre Quéméneur.

It took a couple of days before he got back to me.

'Hello Ned. Well, it's been a long time since I've been asked that question! The "Seznec Affair", named after the presumed assassin of Pierre Quéméneur! I've gone back to my parents to check with them again. But I regret to inform you that it seems I have no familial ties with said Pierre Quéméneur,' he wrote. Before enthusiastically adding, 'However, it does remain one of the greatest mysteries of our region.'

We exchanged a few more messages, and I expressed the wish that I could at least buy him a coffee in Brest, assuming he'd be in the city when the Tour de France started from there in July 2021. We arranged, in principle, to meet at the exact same location where stage 4 of the 1923 Tour had rolled away in the night, a few hours before an arrest warrant for Guillaume Seznec was issued.

'See you soon, perhaps, on the terrace of the Café du Commerce, watching the Tour de France, Perrig,' I'd written.

'That would be really good! See you in Brest in July next year!'

Two things meant that this meeting would never happen, sparing us a confusing conversation about a distant murdered relative from his home town who wasn't a distant murdered relative at all. In the summer of 2021 the Covid-19 pandemic prevented us once more from travelling to cover the Tour de France. To a limited extent, Brest was once more cut off from the wider world by infection, a century after the Spanish flu had ravaged it. And, more pertinently, the location of the stage start in 1923, the Café du Commerce, no longer exists. In fact, nothing prior to the Second World War remains of the square on which it stood. The Allied air forces would flatten Brest from above where the First World War had merely shaken it up.

As a British newsreel from 1945 intones in its clipped narration, filmed from the air, Brest was nothing but 'acres and acres of devastation. As you look down, you'll see that almost every building has been burnt or blasted into a hollow shell.'

A PLAGUE AND A BLACK MARKET

Quéméneur and Seznec were not alone in finding their lives radically altered by the friendly invasion of 1917 and the consequences that followed.

The influx of Americans had brought with it the Spanish flu, an infection that had truly taken hold in the United States but was yet to reach Europe in such great numbers. That was about to change. From early 1918 through to the summer of 1919, given Brest's importance as the main port of arrival, the city remained an epicentre of the infection throughout the period during which the disease was racing unchecked through Europe. Heartbreaking stories are recorded of rural communities using barns and other farm outbuildings effectively as pest houses, with large families forced to separate across the generations, the healthy elderly watching the infected young dying, sometimes literally within hours of infection. From my own partial Covid isolation, I read how schools were shut to those who could not produce a doctor's certificate, and cinemas and places of public gathering indoors were closed.

France lost an estimated 400,000 people, many young citizens, in just over a year. Most of these fatalities occurred during the deadly second wave of the pandemic in the autumn of 1918 when mortality rates were running close to 25 per cent. The appalling death toll only abated when the majority of the vulnerable had either succumbed or survived, and a herd immunity was achieved at devastating cost to human life and without any vaccine.

Even without the fresh horror of the virus, when the war ended, Brittany was destined to descend into a brief but wild state of disorder. France was indebted to the United States for the quite unimaginable sum of 63 billion francs. It was a debt so vast that it was not repaid in full until 1963 and goes a long way to explaining the very particular politics which saw France explore ever more punitive foreign policies aimed at preventing Germany from reneging on its own repayment schedule under the terms of the Treaty of Versailles.

In order to recoup some of the funds it owed, the French state was put in charge of liquidating the American stock of war assets left on French soil as they withdrew during the course of 1919. This meant the fire sale of thousands of military vehicles, cars, motorbikes, and huge amounts of various other commodities, from typewriters to cigarettes.

The American withdrawal was not an orderly process. Profiteering turned to racketeering, then theft and widespread looting, as during the spring of 1919 more than 120,000 troops left Brest for their distant home every month, leaving behind them a whirlwind of quick money and sharp practice.

In one incident 200 cars were stolen from Nantes, while another amazed eyewitness report describes an abandoned American depot which had been ransacked and vandalised. Massive piles of rice were sinking into the mud, surrounded by broken machinery and supplies of all descriptions. Orders were handed down to the local authorities that looters would be shot on sight if caught in flagrante. The German black market was being illegally supplied from sources within Brittany, trading in stolen American goods while the French authorities looked on largely powerlessly or looked the other way. Though by 1923 the real anarchy had subsided, high net-worth items were still being traded, criss-crossing the country and indeed the continent, en route to ever more obscure destinations.

THE MYSTERIOUS DEATH OF PIERRE QUÉMÉNEUR

It was in this context that the two associates from the pre-war years, Quéméneur and Seznec, made a fateful trip together from Brittany to Paris in May 1923 to discuss some opaque business involving the sale of American cars that the pair had invested in. It was a trip from which Pierre Quéméneur would never reappear.

Few facts from this murky case emerge as incontestable, the most pertinent being that the popular *conseilleur général* of Finistère was never seen alive again. His body was never found, nor was it definitely proven that he had been murdered. But as the police started to investigate the case, interest in it spread like wildfire across the histrionic, wildly unbalanced and florid French written media of the age. And, fanned on by the more lurid commentaries in some of the papers, suspicion grew day by day that Guillaume Seznec, Quéméneur's companion on the business trip, had murdered him and disposed of his remains in a crematorium in Morlaix.

Assuming Seznec was the guilty party, dozens of theories started to circulate as to what his motivation might have been, according to Bernard Roux's account of the scandal, *L'Affaire Quéméneur-Seznec*. Quéméneur's politics were largely pragmatic and centrist. He was a Republican Democrat, openly suing for reconciliation with Germany. That meant he often came into conflict with the various nationalist and socialist groupings that had a powerful voice in post-war France. So was Quéméneur's a state-sanctioned execution carried out by Seznec working as an agent of the state? Or was Seznec about to be framed in order to protect corrupt politicians involved somehow in the illegal sale of American vehicles to Bolshevik Russia? There was more conjecture than evidence.

Day after day, even as the 1923 race had got underway with stage
1 to Le Havre (coincidentally a waypoint on the Quéméneur-Seznec
business trip too), the Tour de France competed for column-inch
space alongside the growing obsession with the supposed murder of
Quéméneur, and an increasingly tense situation in Germany.

On the morning of 30 June 1923, just a few hours after the race
had left Brest on stage 4 of the Tour, the peloton reached Lorient, 154
kilometres away. This is where it was light enough to start filming and
my fractured newsreel began. The sun had now risen and it was broad
daylight. Having been held for two minutes at the Lorient checkpoint
so that the paperwork could be satisfactorily completed, the peloton
continued.

At exactly the same time as this was happening, the examining
magistrate to the Quéméneur inquest in Brest, where stage 4 had started,
issued his own paperwork: a warrant for the arrest of Guillaume Seznec.

Thus did two stories, one sporting, the other criminal, cross physical
paths with one another, as copy was filed down the same telephone lines
in a frenzied network of correspondence for the next day's morning
papers.

The Seznec trial, held in the Breton town of Quimper the following
year, did little to clear up the confusion over what might really have
happened. But it ended with Seznec's conviction and sentencing to
hard labour in perpetuity, only avoiding the death penalty because
premeditation could not satisfactorily be proven. It was a sensational
case. According to most historians, the Seznec Affair riled up public
opinion in an echo of the Dreyfus Affair which had reached its
conclusion in nearby Rennes some 25 years previously.

DREYFUS AND SEZNEC

Dreyfus: One of those dimly lit corners of my memory.

Though I knew its two syllables were somehow of central importance
to the development of French nationhood, my understanding was fuzzy
at best. Feeling that it was central to the story, I refreshed the negligible
nub of what I knew.

In 1894, Captain Alfred Dreyfus of the French Army was convicted
of treason. His alleged crime had been passing military secrets to the
German Embassy in Paris. He was sentenced to exile on Devil's Island

in French Guiana. Dreyfus was, however, two things: Jewish, and innocent.

The military establishment had framed him, and his innocence became a *cause célèbre* when no less a figure than the towering literary giant (and, incidentally, massive cycling enthusiast) Émile Zola wrote a public letter titled *J'Accuse* in which he condemned Dreyfus's persecution. Public opinion polarised, became dangerously binary. Though Zola was roundly reviled in much of the popular debate, many from France's literary and scientific community sprang to his defence. The actress Sarah Bernhardt was one, as well as the future Prime Minister Raymond Poincaré's cousin Henri, a leading theoretical physicist who would lay the foundation for Albert Einstein's later work. Certain other figures, like the socialist Jean Jaurès, even changed their minds and came to defend him. Dreyfus was eventually exonerated and released from exile, but only after a period of incarceration which had lasted over a decade.

Now, in 1923, in the same manner that the French commentariat had been either 'pro-' or 'anti-dreyfusard' in a defining moment in the nation's evolving politics, so most French newspaper readers were either convinced by the defendant's guilt or considered themselves to be 'Seznecophile'. It was, it goes without saying, not on the same scale as the Dreyfus Affair, but it was a curious after-echo.

Seznec himself was, just as Dreyfus had been, deported to a penal colony in French Guiana, from which both men were eventually returned to France, and then released. Seznec was granted some clemency and released in 1947. In 1953 he was hit by a van in Paris, and sustained injuries from which he would never recover.

Over many decades, Seznec's family and descendants continued and still continue with their attempts to clear his name. As recently as 2018 a cellar was excavated and unidentifiable bones were discovered in the mansion that was once owned by the Seznec family, as the hunt for Quéméneur's body goes on. The mystery endures, past the point at which it can ever be resolved. Not everything has an answer.

The warrant for Seznec's arrest was issued on that morning in Brest, 30 June 1923, when stage 4 of the Tour de France got underway. His detention began with his arrest on the day of stage 6 into Luchon, and during the 1923 Tour's rest day in Perpignan he was charged with murder. He spent the next 24 years in exile, before eventually being released.

ONE DAY, MANY STORIES

The real world was on pause. Try as I might, I could summon no enthusiasm for the ghastly parodies of life that lockdown imposed. Face masks had started to appal me. The rituals of social distancing were starting to erase the point of everything. There was no joy in going for a walk with a friend and staying two metres apart, or shivering over a coffee at a table outside. Even the comings and goings of the cycling world, which normally kept the journalist in me busy throughout the year, came and went but I scarcely noticed. The fragility of everything confounded my natural optimism. I reluctantly dragged myself to and from the garden shed and the virtual world of my turbo-trainer. But that was it, as far as I was concerned, for the twenty-first century. I had little patience for it. Instead I spent my days like some sort of flatfish, wafting along the almost bottomless depths of the French national archives. Drifting through 1923.

Sometimes the race made the title page of the day's papers, but more often than not most of its reporting was buried within. I scoured each and every publication from the following day, 1 July 1923, looking for Beeckman, looking for the Tour de France, looking for the written testimony which would lend a context to the images I had discovered: something that felt like a faraway rumble of things past and a portent of much more to come.

Regardless of the political leanings of a given newspaper, one story dominated the agenda. It was an event which had happened just as the riders of stage 4 of the Tour were assembling for the start of their 412-kilometre race from Brest to Les Sables d'Olonne. Like the arrest warrant for Guillaume Seznec, it also took place on the exact same day that my film was shot: 30 June 1923.

Report by report, piece by piece, I started to cross-reference the timings, and I realised that two simultaneous events had occurred on either side of France; to the very western Atlantic coast and as far east as it was possible to go and still claim to be under French authority. The definition of France's borders stretched unusually far in 1923.

DAWN IN BREST, A DISTANT BRIDGE AND A TRAIN

There are whole hours of the race which were never filmed at all. The cameras of the age would have had no chance of capturing the action, since the race began in the middle of the night. No amount of starlight would have been enough to light up the road sufficiently for a 35mm film camera of the age. Therefore, these imagined kilometres, ridden under moonlight, these nocturnal gatherings of riders breakfasting at midnight, will always remain the preserve of our imaginations; false images we can conjure up, night dreams.

The Belgian cycling press on the race felt the strangeness of Brittany too; its introverted population and particular privations. The Tour de France correspondent for *La Dernière Heure* viewed the region as being a 'tragic and tormented land in which the menhirs and dolmens invoke the druidic ceremonies of antiquity, where even the sea is more hostile and sombre than on other coasts of France's beautiful land'. Brittany has a quality that is hard to define, but it has a distinct edge of menace to it, among other characteristics.

But whether filmed or not, it was a matter of fact that at 2 o'clock in the morning of 30 June 1923 the riders of the Tour de France were assembling for the start of stage 4 in front of the Café du Commerce in Brest.

The darkened street scene would have at least been partially illuminated by the glow from the ornate lamps inside the café. The proprietors of the establishment on the Rue d'Aiguillon were well versed in hosting the Tour. They would have known what to expect from the demanding race director, Henri Desgrange, and his dozens of acolytes, and how to look after them. A little hospitality on their part, in return for column inches in all the newspapers the following day. That was how the Tour worked back then; a mutuality of concerns that still does business to this day on the race.

The great French race favourite, Henri Pélissier, was there, small, compact, moustachioed, flanked by his lanky smooth-shaven brother Francis. These two riders were the star attraction for the crowds across the land. René Lehmann would write in the August edition of *La Revue de France* that they were both 'stubborn, intelligent, nervous and proud' but they would 'animate the race in a manner of which only they were capable'.

The Pélissier brothers would have been able to reflect with pleasure on the race that had finished some 36 hours previously, when Henri had won stage 3 from Cherbourg to Brest. But it was Pélissier's young Automoto teammate, Ottavio Bottecchia, who would start stage 4 in the yellow jersey. The Italian now led the race for the first time, at his very first attempt. And there he was standing outside the café wearing the distinctive *maillot jaune.*

No film then nor photos have survived from this frigid, misty night. The few reports that dwell on the scene at all pay homage to the large crowds that had made their way to the café, as the order to start was given. Perhaps stage 4 had a perfunctory feel about it; something of a routine event for Brest – and the fifth year in succession that people had watched the peloton depart from the café since the end of the war. And for the fifth successive year the route to Les Sables d'Olonne was identical.

Buried somewhere in the middle of the pack was Théo Beeckman. He, along with his compatriots, the Walloon Alfred De Busschere from Brabant and the moustachioed Achille De Pauw from Loppem near Bruges, was among the very first to sign on that morning for the race. Beeckman was almost certainly speaking to no one. In truth, it seemed, he seldom did, preferring to keep his thoughts to himself. Away they went, waved off in the gloom with a cheer as behind them the horns of the convoy sounded their departure from Brest, just as so many thousands of ships had done before. The race cast off on an inland voyage down the Breton coast.

At the exact same time, across the breadth of France, and into the occupied Rhineland of the Weimar Republic, a military troop train was approaching the Duisburg-Hochfeld bridge across the river. It was the darkest hour of the summer night, and a detail of Belgian soldiers might have been dozing as the carriage in which they travelled went bumping and grinding across a series of points that led onto the grand old river crossing. There were a few dozen soldiers on board, looking forward no doubt to the journey home to Belgium, where they could spend a few days on leave with their loved ones. Their work in the Belgian occupied zone, where they were deeply unwelcome, was dangerous, and the atmosphere in occupied Germany was getting bleaker by the day.

Some of them would have been gazing out of the window, perhaps looking down at the steady flow of the Rhine heading north, its ripples catching in the moonlight. The moon was almost full, the night was mild so far inland. And all across the continent, summer was finally rolling in.

THE OCCUPATION OF THE RUHR

I began to understand how a stage of the Tour de France could intersect with the seething politics of post-war Europe, how the two events coexisted on the now yellowed pages of the French press.

After the war, bicycle races had played their part in a national introspection and moral outrage which often found its expression in acts of bitter memorialisation, particularly in France. In May 1919 the infamous and ghastly *Circuit des Champs de Bataille* was raced through heavy rain across terrain still marked by ruin and unexploded ordnance. The race itself was designed to be an act of defiance, as was the running of the 1919 Tour de France, expressly routed at the behest of race director Henri Desgrange through war-shattered Picardy and along the new German and Belgian borders. And in November 1919 the *Grand Prix de l'Armistice* was raced on the 10th and 11th. Symbolically it started in recaptured Strasbourg and finished in Paris, reuniting the capital with the eastern territory it had surrendered to the Prussians 50 years previously.

I knew something of the rancorous aftermath of the Great War for Germany, the descent into turmoil in the Weimar Republic, and the rise of the Nazis. But I didn't know how, why, and what role the French and Belgians might have played in all this. I didn't know the detail.

I didn't know, for example, that France had simply marched into Germany and confiscated their resources, accusing their former enemy of breaking the terms of the Versailles peace treaty. The 'Occupation of the Ruhr' was a new phrase to me. In the spring and early summer of 1923, French and Belgian troops had pushed ever deeper into German territory, annexing still more of the Weimar Republic's industrial and mineral output, and transporting its steel and coal away from Germany. They moved into the Ruhr Valley, the main tributary to the Rhine.

It had begun with the occupation of the Rhineland. This had been the prescribed consequence of the Treaty of Versailles, signed four years previously, under whose strictures defeated Germany had to meet the most swingeing of repayment terms to France and Belgium, who had seen vast tracts of land laid to waste by the fighting. France considered the destruction of so many of its towns and villages to be a moral abomination, perpetuated by a pitiless enemy who must, once and for all, be brought to heel. The French press, broadly speaking, fell enthusiastically into line with the rhetoric of the republic's political classes. The French daily, the *Petit Journal*, for instance, went as far as to drive a radio car painted red, white and blue up and down the streets of occupied Recklinghausen playing patriotic French songs. Such actions found no shortage of cheerleaders.

Belgium, having suffered the partial or complete destruction of nearly 300,000 houses during the war, was already four years into rebuilding the territories laid to waste (a process that would not be formally completed until 1967) as well as making safe the hundreds of square kilometres of battlefield. It was inclined to fall into line with Paris. For the first time in their short history, Belgian troops crossed the border into Germany as occupiers.

Germany, for its part, was still reeling from its own powerlessness in the face of a rapid and unforeseen defeat and was being torn asunder by internal revolutionary factions. Many Germans considered the war to have been a fully justifiable act of self-defence in the face of sabre-rattling from the powers which had surrounded it in 1914.

The occupation measures and confiscation of assets were bitterly contested. Germany, unable and unwilling to accept the national guilt being urged on it for having started the war, and itself riven with violent political unrest, was united in a feeling of resistance against the occupying armies. But France had ended the war having lost 1.5 million lives; more per capita than Germany and twice as many as Great Britain. And it didn't end with her dead either. As Jonathan Fenby writes in *A History of Modern France*, 'of the 6m survivors, half were wounded, mutilated, shell-shocked or confined to a wheelchair'. It was an arms race of grievance.

France's allies were alarmed at the stream of ever more strident pronouncements coming from Prime Minister Raymond Poincaré, a statesman who had been the country's president throughout the war. Poincaré seemed intent on bringing Germany to its knees. He and Georges Clemenceau had jointly campaigned from 1919 onwards as the father figures of the right-wing coalition *Bloc National*, whose slogan simply read, 'Germany will pay!' Unhappy with the extent and success of the occupation of the Rhineland, Poincaré made it known that he wanted more. He declared on 22 December 1922 that 'whatever happens, I shall advance into the Ruhr on 15 January'. Poincaré was as good as his word. In early 1923 he duly marched French troops into the valley, the essential tributary to the Rhine, along whose banks Germany' great industrial cities were built, the true economic beating heart of the land.

The subsequent confiscation of 70 per cent of all goods and materials, including 85 per cent of Germany's coal and 80 per cent of its steel and pig iron, sent the German Reichsmark into a tailspin and set in train the call for passive resistance, the widespread strikes and then the hyperinflation which led to the complete bottoming out of the Weimar Republic's economic, social and political life. Fear spread across Germany, as some sections of the population faced the real prospect of starvation, that the French army was gearing up to march on Berlin.

For days in late June 1923, the French press had anxiously been carrying the latest from London and from Rome, as France continued to turn the screw on its old enemy across the Rhine. In London, the newly installed prime minister, Stanley Baldwin, demanded in writing that France and Belgium explain their policies in the newly occupied Ruhr. And from the Vatican, in the heart of Mussolini's Rome, a warning shot was fired in the form of a letter from Pope Pius XI to his Secretary of State Cardinal Gasparri, in which the leader of the Catholic Church spoke of the risk that France's policies towards Germany might provoke 'an extreme misfortune for the whole of Europe' and lead to 'resentments which would remain a continuous threat of new and more ruinous conflagrations'.

AN EXPLOSION AND A CHECKPOINT

Against this backdrop, perhaps wholly innocent of the larger political machinations at play, a train driver was moving his rolling stock westwards across the Rhine. The Belgian soldiers might have been roused from their slumbers by the train passing over junctions in the track. Having pulled out of Duisburg main station at exactly 1:04 a.m., they had just passed under the twin towers of the Duisburg-Hochfeld bridge, with its huge, mock-medieval crenelations on the eastern riverbank.

George Rigaud, a Belgian guard posted at the tower, watched it pass and must have seen how the train was approaching the middle of the first of three elegant spans. Little would have been heard above the steel-on-steel grinding of the train as it slowed to cross the river. As the last carriage passed under Rigaud's watch tower and onto the bridge, an enormous blast tore into the night. A ball of light and a deep crack of splitting metal and wood as the sides of the train blew out, scattering human debris and torn materials far and wide. All across Duisburg, windows either rattled or shattered. A large piece of shrapnel from the blast caught Rigaud on the head and hurled his corpse 40 metres through the air. The last two carriages of the train had been pulverised by the explosion. Then silence descended.

When rescuers eventually got inside the remains of the train they would find personal belongings from the soldiers' suitcases strewn all around, and the dismembered corpses of nine men, four of whom had been decapitated by the force of the explosion.

The bomb was not heard far away on the western coast of France. But the riders of the Tour de France were now on their tortuous way, lit by the same moon. Wordlessly for now, the peloton went about its bleak task, pushing through the chill of a sea breeze drifting inland on the night air, following the lights from the convoy of cars, their jerseys already moist with sweat, if they had dried overnight at all. The longed-for first light would finally begin to appear somewhere just after Quimper, almost 100 kilometres into the stage, at first bluish, then ever whiter as the rising sun started to get to work on the morning mist that had rolled in towards dawn. The sun would eventually come, and with it, good spirits.

By Lorient, at the checkpoint, it was already high in the sky. The usual big crowd had assembled. They had strung bunting out across the Rue de Brest, by the Café Gloux, as they always did. The press had arrived too, bringing their cameras, and the filming could begin.

No one yet knew what had just happened in Germany.

LORIENT

Seven to eight seconds
Another caption replaces the map and holds our attention for a few seconds. It announces the checkpoint at Lorient.

Au contrôle de Lorient.

Then, in an instant, as if the lights are suddenly switched on, the first scene is revealed. The film now seethes with life – after the long black seconds of the titles, such a richness of detail is almost too much to take in. Everywhere there are people, hundreds of them, spilling out of houses, riddled with movement and life. The camera points down a tram-lined street, above whose houses on either side are suspended a series of flags. The strings of bunting recede into the dusty distance. A dozen riders are lined up in the middle of the picture. On either pavement crowds of onlookers are packed together, straining for a glimpse of the riders, and held back by police officers. The boys all wear shorts and caps, the men variously in long coats and trilbies or even straw boaters. Officials stamp twitchily around in front of the peloton, clutching sheaves of paper. There is a tension in the air. The tableau vibrates with small gestures. It is straining to break loose.

HENRI DESGRANGE

In the midst of all this flux, I spotted him. Or, at least, I thought I did: Henri Desgrange.

Desgrange was to all intents and purposes the founding father of the Tour de France. The great race came about in 1903 when Desgrange took up the suggestion of Géo Lefèvre, one of his journalists at his newspaper *L'Auto*, that there should be a Tour of the whole country.

Until that point, all the races had been one-day races, or out-and-back kind of affairs. A *Tour de France Cycliste* would serve both as a handy, and extremely successful marketing tool, as well as a statement of national celebration and unity, at the beginning of an era in which patriotism would be tested and proven time and again. It would bring, Desgrange announced in *L'Auto*, the 'most beautiful manifestation of the sport of cycling' to 'entire populations who had never witnessed it'. It would also teach the French about France. There was that, too.

Géo Lefèvre, not Henri Desgrange, was initially tasked with the job of accompanying the riders around France as race director. He jumped on trains with his heavy bike to try and reach the finish line before the winning rider, a task which he failed to manage on the very first stage in 1903 in Lyon. But it wasn't too long before his boss Desgrange decided that he himself should be on the race, rather than directing affairs from his distant Paris office. And from 1910 until his death in 1940, Desgrange did not miss a single stage. His core values ran through the race like a stick of French rock. His beliefs shaped the race.

From my distant perspective across the Channel and a couple of centuries removed, I had always lazily thought of France as a finished product, something eternal and unchanging. But now I began to understand the unfinished, turbulent nature of the project, from Robespierre through to Napoleon and beyond. At the birth of the Tour, more than a hundred years after the Revolution, France was still in the process of convincing its constituent parts – various peoples, dialects, classes, professions, political ideologies and languages – that it was indeed a whole and coherent entity; one worth devoting one's life to, or even dying for.

It's true that the 1870 Prussian (German) invasion of France through Alsace-Lorraine and the siege of Paris by the Germans had done much to foster a sense of national purpose and grievance. But, with the subsequent Dreyfus Affair splitting the political classes asunder, and the steady rise of anti-Semitism, nationalism, socialism and communism, which found its physical manifestation in the Paris Commune of 1871, there was also plenty of dissent. Distant regions, with their own animosities and sense of injustice at the hands of overbearing Parisian coercion, still resisted or refused to accept the primacy of the capital and the untrammelled authority of the nation state, governed by distant Paris. This was another reason for the Tour, symbolically, to begin and end at the centre, to bind it to the capital. Desgrange did this by design.

Born in 1865, Desgrange had been too young to fight the Prussians in 1870, and when eventually the conflagration of the Great War came about, he was far too old to fight. Nonetheless, he signed up. He was 50 when he joined the war effort, serving as an ordinary *poilu* ('hairy one', or squaddie). All the while, writing under the wartime pseudonym of Desgrenier, he exhorted his readership to enlist, support the war effort, and strive to defeat the Germans in a war which he persistently described as being a kind of giant game; the ultimate sport between the youthful manhood of competing nations. No amount of Flandrian mud along the Ypres Salient, or blood spilled in the siege of Verdun seemed to dispossess him of that ideal.

These were values which were pursued with great ardour by the unambiguous Desgrange. A former champion cyclist from wealthy Parisian stock, he had gone on to become the director of a brace of velodromes in Paris alongside his journalism; positions that yielded great wealth and considerable political clout and status.

For almost 40 years, Desgrange dictated terms at the Tour de France; the route it would follow, the riders and teams who would compete, the structure of the competition, even the winners on any given day, as I would later discover. His position at the heart and head of the race was undisputed, and though he made many enemies over the years of his tenure, his primacy was never once seriously challenged; this despite the rivalry of men like Victor Breyer (I would discover), a former colleague who, by 1923, was the editor of a rival sports newspaper, as well as holding directorships at other velodromes and organising his own cycle races. Desgrange was one of the most important men in the land.

But was he there, in my little film?

The clues had been there from a long way out that a particular figure might indeed be Henri Desgrange himself. There was something about this mysterious man that seemed almost to remove himself from the scene in which he was placed. And though he was standing with his back almost completely to the camera, and off to the side of the shot, it was almost as if he stood centre stage despite himself. Smartly dressed, immobile, upright, and seemingly in complete command of all that he surveyed.

He seems to be holding something in his right hand, perhaps a sheet of paper, though it's very difficult to see. He glances down quickly, and resettles his weight upon either foot, resuming his powerful stance. A huge figure in a long, somewhat shabby-looking coat stands at his side, looming over him. The two men converse for a few seconds, after which the tall man strides with a lolloping gait over to where the riders are lined up. In the middle of all this competing detail, it is clear that this is the man who actually gives the order to the riders to get going. He pauses for a second with his back to the camera, facing the peloton whose undivided attention he now enjoys. Then, with an expansive gesture, he points down the road and retreats rapidly towards the crowded pavement with half a dozen backward steps.

Cross-referencing the few detailed reports of this moment, I hit upon a name which was as unfamiliar to me as that of Théo Beeckman before the arrival of this broken reel of film in my life. I find myself reading a scan of a faded regional newspaper from nearly a hundred years ago. It's a paragraph in the report carried by *L'Ouest Éclair*, buried deep inside the body of the paper, so hardly front-page news. It describes the moment I had paused on my laptop screen. I shrink the window with my film down to fit alongside that of the scanned report, so that the two could almost be followed together – word and image:

Lorient – 08.40 – A few minutes ahead of schedule – The sun is already high.
    Desmarets steps out onto the road and orders them all to stop (2 min neutralisation) so that they can all sign. 31 riders line up under the multi-coloured bunting strung up by the Comité des Fêtes de Kerentrech – Everyone is in good shape and still very fresh. Finally, Desgrange gives the signal to depart – riders and official cars pull away at great speed.

This report definitely places Desgrange at the control in Lorient that morning. It is the race director himself who gives the order for the restart. But it is also clear that he is being assisted by a Monsieur Desmarets, whose role in actually giving the signal to start the race in Brest is corroborated by a report in *L'Auto* from the same day.

Robert Desmarets (pictured here), known as '*Le Grand Bob*', was, it seems, an instantly recognisable figure. He was physically perfectly suited to his role, as he stood a head above everyone else. He was an important ally of Desgrange's, with a brain that understood the commercial side of the race. Indeed, some accounts suggest that it was he who started to develop the notion that brands should pay the Tour to be part of the spectacle; a concept that ultimately gave birth to the publicity caravan which is an important part of the post-war and twenty-first-century Tour de France experience.

Even in 1923, Desmarets has an eye for turning a few sponsorship francs. The pages of *L'Auto* proudly announce that *'Le Grand Bob'* is driving the route of the Tour de France in a *'15 hp De Bazelaire'* luxury automobile. The car had been supplied to Desmarets by the eponymous French car manufacturer Ferdinand de Bazelaire, who in 1912 had even raced one of his own De Bazelaire vehicles in the Tour de France Automobile, a motor-sport race around France which pre-dated the Tour de France Cycliste by four years.

That it is Henri Desgrange to whom *'Le Grand Bob'* is talking at the beginning of the clip is equally beyond doubt, despite the fact that we never see the man's face. It is enough to see the interaction between the two men to know what is being imparted; who is giving the orders, and who is carrying them out. The punctilious, immaculately dressed Desgrange is wearing the kind of fine tailoring in which he is pictured in all the other existing images of him; the same coat, the same hat. It is Desgrange from whom everything flows, not just in the stream of action which follows, but in the history of the Tour itself.

I could, and can, find no other existing movie-camera footage of the founder of the Tour de France.

I made my notes and paused. I closed the film down and shut the laptop for another day. I gazed from the window, which was my habit when slowly re-emerging from 1923 and re-entering the locked-down reality of the latest Covid wave. A muted London sky gazed blankly back at me, offering no encouragement, no sign of better times to come. Yet, I was curiously content. The jigsaw of my film had moved in to take the place of my anxieties. Bit by bit, piece by piece, the picture in my head, the faces in the film, were becoming more and more detailed. Here were Desmarets and Desgrange; along with Beeckman, they were labelled, identified, digitised. Captured.

Many months later, en route from Germany back to London, I would find myself standing on a Parisian street, the same laptop open, trying to explain to a complete stranger through both a face mask and my inadequate French, quite how important it was that I had in my possession the only film I had ever seen of the man who started the Tour de France. But that encounter was still some way off.

OUTSIDE THE CAFÉ GLOUX

Nine seconds
To the extreme left of the frame stands Henri Desgrange with his back to the camera. The leather on the heels of his shoes is highly polished and it catches the morning light. He wears an elegant, long, light-coloured coat, well-tailored trousers, and a snugly fitting white cap. He is in conversation with 'Le Grand Bob' Desmarets, who stands a good six inches taller than anyone else in the febrile atmosphere of this tableau. Desgrange's chauffeur stands behind him, in a long leather coat, goggles and a driving cap, his hands on his hips. He is waiting for his boss to get going. The two men, Desgrange and Desmarets, are exchanging words.

In eight brisk strides, Desmarets crosses the No. 69 tram lines of the Rue de Brest, throws his right arm out and steps rapidly backwards. As soon as he starts to walk across to the front of the line, every moving part in the scene starts to jostle and break up with sudden urgency. Some riders have already mounted their bikes or are trying to. In the front row, the furthest rider to the right pulls one of his spare tyres completely over his right shoulder then throws his right leg over the frame of his bike, as he sees Desmarets moving towards the peloton. The rider almost loses balance, rocks back towards the thick crowd behind him on the pavement, and then tries again. He is one of the first to roll forwards when the signal is given.

The Tour de France moves off, as the crowd surges forward and the officers push them back. Only Desgrange stands planted and immobile, watching on, until he too is forced to take one step back as the riders accelerate away and fill the road, seeking out the space to ride. A moustachioed man in a long white coat and cap briefly, partially, blocks the camera's view of Desgrange. The man pirouettes smartly on his heels, turns through 360 degrees and carries on his busy way. In his gloved left hand he holds another glove. He must be a driver. The cars will follow on after the riders are on their way.

Twenty-one seconds
The riders stream past the entrance to the Café Gloux on whose stone façade the warm morning light is now spilling. The sun is high enough to have rounded the corner and is starting to cast its rays along the Rue de Brest. The wrought-iron gas lamp on the corner of the building trails a strong shadow across the stonework. And on the other side of the entrance, on the corner, newly installed brackets hold telephone lines in suspension above the street below; the rows of white ceramic insulators catch the sun. The rider in a light coloured jersey, perhaps the 'maillot jaune', seeks the inside line as they slowly file left past the café and drop down onto the Rue du Pont.

From his position on the balcony above the Café Gloux, a gentleman in a dark suit and straw boater with a dark ribbon stands and gazes down on the scene below. A lady in a robe, as if stretching off the night's sleep in the morning light, walks out from the entrance to the café, her outstretched arms reaching languidly out for either side of the door frame. Just as the riders pass, she takes five hurried steps down onto the pavement and disappears behind a sea of heads in the crowd. Behind her comes a waitress from the café, dressed in black and with a white apron and traditional Breton white lace coiffe upon her head. She stops on the top step and places a hand contemplatively on her left cheek. A colleague of hers, identically dressed, rushes from the dark interior of the café into the brightness, shielding her eyes against the glare.

The riders, all labouring on their bikes in their single gear designed for much higher speeds, continue to stream past the front of the café. The camera now follows them, panning right to reveal the perpendicular Rue du Pont. They begin to descend past the little bar on the right with its two light awnings drawn down to shade the clientele from the morning glare. As far as the eye can see, as the road sweeps down to the river Scorff, the pavements are lined with onlookers, standing patiently five or ten deep.

Thirty-seven seconds
Walking with purpose, a photographer arrives on the scene from the right in a short black coat with a light cap on whose brim a pair of driving goggles are perched. He wears a tie, and moves with a bouncy stride, his trousers just an inch too short perhaps. He's a man who knows exactly what he's doing. Perhaps he too has been there and done this every year since the race resumed after the war. He heads into the middle of the junction, walking uphill and against the flow of the bunch. Just as the lead riders start to pick up speed and disappear from view, the smartly attired photographer approaches ever closer to where the film camera is shooting, until he becomes the biggest figure on the screen.

Behind him, a man in the throng of onlookers in the shade of a tree has spotted one of the stars of the Tour as he turns the corner, points him out to his neighbour, *then folds his arms in satisfaction. Above him the branches of the tree are gently waving in the morning breeze, which catches too at the flags suspended above.*

At the same time, before the photographer has even come to a halt, he lifts his camera to his right eye and slows to a standstill to take the picture. He is framing up the scene which the film has just left behind as it pans round: the café, the crowd, the bunting, the riders still passing. The man in the boater all alone on the balcony has watched them go. The scene cuts before we see the photographer press the shutter and take his shot.

A PANDEMIC AND A RETREAT

Idle days came and went. They became weeks, then months. Of course, I was not completely cut off. I talked to the family, saw how they were all progressing through the long weeks of our shuttered-off life, tried to allay their fears as best I could, keeping spirits up. But I was lacking in method or belief, and my words rang hollow. The kettle boiled with relentless regularity, as liquid days disappeared to its bubbling rhythm.

I wish I had known how to react in the face of something so entirely outside of my control. Wars, pandemics; these things were completely beyond all our experience. I believed them to have been declared impossible. Our lifetimes had suggested as much, and the evidence of our eyes had only reinforced that understanding. None of the living generations, including mine, could grapple with the reality of this altered world with new, seemingly awful and unfamiliar rules.

I stirred another cup of tea, made my excuses, and trudged slowly up the single flight of stairs towards my desk once more. I had been doing this for months. There was even a time, at the beginning of the pandemic, when I didn't feel it was right to go outside for exercise and would instead run up and down these stairs a hundred times at four o'clock every single day, listening to the press briefings from Downing Street. My 'covid steps' had driven everyone to distraction. Now I just walked the stairs, which at least was quieter.

And all the while, though I was not always aware of it, my heart was hatching an escape plan. Somewhere at the core of this hundred-year-old world I had been building around the film, I had started to place myself. I longed to walk the roads I knew only from these old shadows that flickered in the quiet darkness at my desk. I would go there, one day.

MAPPING THE FILM

Scrolling forwards, using the cursor, I found I could agitate the peloton, making them pedal with a sped-up slapstick cadence. When I noticed something of interest, I dragged them backwards, holding them in an unnaturally suspended action, in slow motion.

I began comparing the buildings by the side of the dusty roads in my film with screenshots from Google Street View. Occasionally I got a match, where the house in the film still stood.

The Rue de Nantes, 1923   The Rue de Nantes, present day

This information I squirrelled away, dreaming of a time when I could explore the countryside for myself. I imagined how I might visit, perhaps by bike, perhaps in the summer. I thought about how I might catch a train to Brest and spend a few open, solitary peaceful days retracing the route of the race, all the way to Les Sables d'Olonne. I would ride the same roads if I could find them, though that was no simple matter.

In order to map the route exactly, I contacted one niche organisation after another, trying to winkle out the tiniest bit of information of significance any way I could imagine. The Association for the Preservation of the Windmills of Morbihan never responded to my email. They weren't alone in meeting my uniquely obscure questions, penned in shaky and probably comical French, with the blankest lack of interest. Some Facebook group of local historians declined to respond to my questions about the bridge over the Vilaine. Undeterred, I downloaded from their page an MP3 of some Morbihan folk-singers whose accordion-based album included one song that had a quite unrevealing reference to the old bridge of La Roche-Bernard. I listened to it a couple of times, then no more.

Thinking that no one knows roads better than a professional bike rider, I attempted to forge contacts with local cycling clubs and personalities from Morbihan. This led me, eventually, to the considerable figure of Guy Tréhin, a rugged Breton rider who had raced alongside the great Antonin Magne and the even greater Raymond Poulidor. For 50 years, Tréhin had also been president of VCP Lorient, the local cycling club, and was a much-venerated organiser of local amateur races; in effect, he *was* the heart and soul of Lorient's cycling scene. I was certain that he might be interested in the film and might potentially help me identify the stretch of road between Lorient and Vannes over which the peloton is seen to pass.

On the road to Vannes

Guy Tréhin's contact details proved to be stubbornly elusive to get hold of. But, during my searches, I quickly found out that his son Roger was now a *Directeur Sportif* on a French team. I managed in turn to elicit Roger Tréhin's details from a British pro on the same team, Connor Swift, with whom Tréhin worked closely. Connor, who himself expressed a heartening interest in my reasons for wanting to talk to his sports director, was only too glad to pass on his number.

Roger Tréhin, before moving into sports directing, had been a well-respected semi-professional from Lorient, and was now an important part of the backroom staff at Arkéa Samsic, a team that invariably competed at the Tour de France. I copied a link to the film onto a message for him to see. He seemed, initially, to be greatly interested by the film. *'C'est vraiment excellent Ned!!'* he replied to me. This felt like validation of the highest order, and I began to believe that what I had embarked on could have a more general appeal than just my own increasingly strange compulsions might suggest.

But thereafter, Roger too drew a blank. *'Je reconnais juste le départ à Lorient.'* He was only able to recognise Lorient. And even that was only a polite half-truth, I suspected. Lorient, I reckoned, was identifiable *only* because of the graphic announcing it as the location. The street corner on which the scene is staged had been altered beyond recognition 20 whole years before Tréhin had been born.

Over and over again I looked at the junction between the Rue de Brest and the Rue du Port, where the riders drop down to the left and away from the town, comparing it with what now stands in its place. I discovered that neither road exists any longer, in name or matter. The raw geometry of the town layout mostly persists, but Lorient was so heavily bombed by the Allies between 1943 and 1944 that almost nothing of its stoical bourgeois character remains to allow a sense of how things were in the film, nor in the half-dozen contemporaneous black-and-white postcards I unearthed in the online municipal archives. Lorient before the Second World War was a place of wide avenues, boulevards and trams. It was a city for pedestrians in long coats and hats, taking a stroll along the ample pavements.

Nothing of that feeling remains as I prowl Lorient's bland twenty-first-century austerity on Google Street View, looking for a single surviving reminder of the film. The two roads at the junction on which the Café Gloux once stood have both been subsequently renamed. They are now called the Rue Paul Guieysse, named after a notable engineer and socialist from Lorient, and the Rue de Verdun after the great French victory and longest battle of the First World War. The name changes came about a long time later. Perhaps, in 1923, the memory of the many lives lost was still too close for Verdun to be commemorated in such a manner.

44 LORIENT — Rue de Brest   Artaud et Nozais Nantes

But topography's tracery persists. A hill is still a hill, a river a river; harder to eradicate than a street name. The drop down the sloping road is still apparent, the way the Rue de Verdun falls away towards the water. Even though there are none of the original buildings to recognise it by, this is still the same patch of now-asphalted rather than cobbled earth over which the photographer strides to frame up his newspaper shot of the peloton departing in front of the Café Gloux.

GLOUX

This time I'm in the online Lorient archives. I want to see what I can establish about the café and its owners. I wonder if the lady in the doorway, whose relaxed, almost entitled gesture seems so suggestive of ownership, might have been the proprietor.

And I wonder about the older gentleman on the balcony above. Her father? Her husband? Did the apartment on the first floor belong to the café owners? Was he the café's owner?

But there are scant mentions of the Café Gloux anywhere to be found. It appears that the conflagration of the Allied bombing had erased the café's existence almost entirely, save perhaps in the memories of a dwindling number of very elderly survivors. There are a few photos of the old Rue de Brest which feature its imposing façade, but very little else besides.

I do, however, happen upon a pair of purchase receipts which for some reason have been preserved in the Lorient town archives. At some point, recently, someone must have taken the time to scan, upload and label these incidental fragments, not imagining for a second that they would ever be searched for, found and scrutinised. But here I am, staring at them from my house in the capital city of a foreign country.

They date from the early 1930s and are signed by a Madame Quentel of the Café Gloux and detail the purchase of alcohol, medications and groceries from the Epicerie J. Pasco and the Société Audiau et Cie. It's possible, I imagine, that it was the same Madame Quentel who was filmed in the doorway of the café on 30 June 1923. And it is possible, I suppose, that it was her father, or her husband, who gazed down from the balcony. On the other hand, Quentel might have been an employee of the establishment, and not the owner or a member of the owner's family. But it was pleasing to bestow a name on her, however erroneously. At least I could be confident that no one was going to contradict me. It occurred to me that this is how certain histories are falsely written, and pass into fact. I get to decide.

The name Gloux is heavily Breton, but fairly unusual. That makes it both easier and harder to mine any connections. From 1952 I discover a memorandum from a secret meeting of the municipal council during which a support package is granted in a case of hardship on the part of a M. Gloux, an electrician in the Lorient Arsenal, in respect of his children's education. M. Gloux's address is given as 4, Rue de Kerguélen, just a stone's throw from where the old café had stood on the corner. Had the family perhaps been re-housed nearby after the Second World War? Had they fallen on hard times? Is the electrician the grandson of the man on the balcony, perhaps the child of the woman in the doorway? Was she indeed a Gloux and not a Quentel?

This is guesswork, just a stab in the dark. Each turn in the film offers me up a further invitation to discover. But each find can also lead me further away from knowing, piling instead incoherent scraps of information upon one another, until the truth is buried. But already, in my addled mind, they have joined up to create an illusory narrative; a story which exists that may be complete fiction. It starts with a bike race, and a café caught on film, and I cannot imagine where it might end.

A PHOTOGRAPH

Then I happen upon a photograph in the municipal archives which seems at first glance to replicate the scene from my film exactly: an image of the riders setting off in front of the café; the same light, same crowds, same proliferation of straw boaters and cloth caps, the same hunched figures on the same bikes. Moreover, it seems to have been taken from precisely the spot on which the photographer in the film stopped to take his photo. The shadows fall across the doorway and balcony of the hotel at exactly the same angle, and with the same strength. Its likeness is arresting.

I look at the two scenes more closely, pausing my film on the frame which best matches the still photo. I set them side by side, and, with a lurch of disappointment, I realise that the two images could not have been created at the same time.

The two images were close, astoundingly so. Both scenes actually took place at least a year apart. Nonetheless they testify to the familiarity of the ritual to which Lorient had become accustomed. Save for tiny fluctuations in the human landscape, they might as well have been recording the same events.

In the film still, 'Madame Gloux/Quentel' is standing in the doorway. In the photo she is not there. The door is open, but there is only shadow, broken by the tiny detail of a couple of men emerging from the gloom, just their faces visible as they step into the morning sunlight of the street corner. And 'Monsieur Gloux/Quentel', standing alone to the far left of the balcony in my film, has company in the photo. He is dressed identically in both images and occupies the exact same spot on the balcony. But in the photo from the archives, he is not alone. A boy of perhaps twelve or thirteen is with him. Perhaps, I think to myself, this is his grandson. Perhaps he was the boy who would go on to become an electrician in the Arsenal, in need of financial support. Or most likely he was no relation. In the absence of a definitive version of the story, others rush in to fill the void.

The images were non-identical twins, separated by a slice of time; something almost replicated, one of which had happened either before or after the moment I was trying to anchor it to. The compression effect of a hundred years of history had made the differences negligible, to the extent that the two events appeared to be simultaneous; chronologically almost indistinguishable from one another. Looking at these years from a distance was like fluttering the pages of a flip book. Time had been crushed.

BEECKMAN, DELAYED

I had reasonably expected to find Théo Beeckman in either, or indeed both, of the shots of Lorient, perhaps at the very front of the peloton. He was after all an established 'ace', even if he wasn't yet a rider of the very highest calibre. He'd been at the Tour already in 1920 and 1922, the latter a race in which he had impressed. I continued to hunt for him in the still shot, poring over it, shuttling the film back and forth in the hope that his quartered cap would somehow appear in the mass of riders, but to no avail.

Then, sifting through the Belgian press, I realised that I was looking for a man who wasn't there in the film. Théo Beeckman couldn't have been in the scene from 1923, for good reasons.

A surprisingly detailed report suggests that he was riding hard to get to Lorient on time, but would in fact arrive too late to be included in the footage of the mass restart. The first 60 riders of a peloton which now totalled just 97 (meaning that 41 riders of the original 138 had already abandoned the Tour since it had left Paris) arrived en masse into Lorient at 8.04 in the morning. According to the French-language Belgian daily, *La Dernière Heure*, there had been 'huge crowds' there to greet them. But Beeckman wasn't among the first to arrive.

The 18-kilometre passage from the previous checkpoint in Quimperlé had not been without the odd incident. Léon Scieur, for example, the rugged champion and Walloon winner of the 1921 Tour de France, took a blow to the head when his front wheel simply buckled. To add to his misfortune, a following car failed to hit the brakes in time and ran over his rear wheel as his bike lay in the road. Scieur, known by the press as 'The Locomotive', was seen hitching his bike onto his shoulder and running off into the nearest village in search of a workshop where he could fix it (these were still the days when any form of mechanical assistance was sanctionable). Astonishingly, he finished the stage and only lost around a quarter of an hour. He must have raced like a beast for the rest of the day.

At some point thereafter, Beeckman suffered a puncture. It was not the first time on that Tour. On stage 2, he'd been riding in the final selection of the day, in the same group as the Pélissier brothers and the eventual stage winner Ottavio Bottecchia. The elite riders were close to the approach to the finish line in Cherbourg when Beeckman punctured, and his chance of victory evaporated in the late afternoon dust.

Bad luck had continued to dog him into stage 4, and this time almost from the very start. In fact, at a feed zone in Rosporden, just outside Quimper, Beeckman reported that he had already punctured six times (though riders were routinely prone to exaggeration, and often made quite unverifiable claims). Nevertheless, as a result of having to change his tyre by the side of the road, he reached the checkpoint outside the Café Gloux in Lorient four minutes down on the field, two minutes after Desgrange had halted the peloton to allow all 60 riders to sign in.

When Desmarets gave the signal to restart, the peloton rode away at such a moderate pace, enjoying the early morning sun after the hours in the dark, that Beeckman, along with one or two other stragglers, was able to get back on. But even that came at some cost for the chasers: they had been off the back for a further 22 kilometres, only finally rejoining the front of the race at Landervaut.

As with the precise origins of the photographs, the truth sometimes remains invisible to the naked eye. Perhaps, I had to concede, I would never be able to find out what was going through Beeckman's mind that day; and why he attacked when he reached that big bridge.

THE ROAD TO VANNES

Sur la route de Vannes.

Forty-one seconds. Sur la route de Vannes
For three seconds, the caption sways gently from left to right, before recentring itself. Then the film cuts to the second scene, filling the frame with a chalky

whiteness, far brighter than the previous scene in Lorient. We are in the open countryside now. The sky is a monochrome haze, filling the top half of the frame. It is met in the distance by a low range of hills. Hardly hills, in fact. More like a gently rising ridge of farmland, dotted with the odd copse. Closer to the foreground there are two windmills, whitewashed and rounded. The nearer of the two is perhaps a kilometre away from the point on the unmade road that the riders have reached. There is no wind, and the windmill's wooden blades are immobile in the sultry morning air, facing away from the race and into the greyed-out distance.

On either side of the road there are crumbling dry-stone walls, partially overgrown by what looks like gorse. And on the left-hand side of the road, more newly installed telegraph poles carry 10 lines alongside the race. The riders are coming towards the camera but are still perhaps 50 or 60 metres away, gaining on the camera. They pass a tiny, narrow car, almost comically small; big enough only for the driver. It is parked on the verge and the figure of a man is just visible standing next to the bonnet, watching the bunch pass him by.

The road is pure white; the brightness of the misty sky is amplified by the surface. Dust is being kicked up in little clouds from all the movement.

LES GÉANTS DE LA ROUTE

Were any of the other riders in my film identifiable? I welcomed the extreme difficulty of the challenge, which would certainly involve hour after hour of tapping away on my computer and studiously avoiding the real world. Fiddling around in Google Images, staring at the angle of the pedal stroke, the pattern of socks, the positioning of water bottles and handlebars seemed a far better use of my time than becoming an amateur epidemiologist. Outside in the world, anxieties continued rearing up like snakes in the form of horrifying bell-curve graphs. But inside the world of my film, inhabited by its ghosts on bikes and its amorphous hatted and suited onlookers, endless sunny contours filled the landscape as far as the eye could see; stacks of words and thoughts and faces telling tales of another time, distant and yet familiar enough almost to reach out and touch. The story of the 1923 Tour de France, and how its looping course brushed up against all these great themes straining at the leash across the continent of Europe and beyond. This was the story I shored up against the reality of the Covid pandemic. It was simpler to close the door and return again to 1923.

At first glance all the riders seemed interchangeable, floating cyphers of their age, each one equipped with the same set of age-appropriate features: light-coloured *casquettes*, pilot's goggles, inner tubes strapped around their torsos, two aluminium bottles attached to the handlebars. To differentiate them from one another was going to take a forensic mind, something I had never believed myself to possess. I considered this difficulty with a rising sense of panic. If I couldn't identify them at all, if it were to prove impossible, it would bring to a shuddering close the sense of purpose that my enquiry had brought to my life. I lived in dread of that finality. I couldn't return to the reality of the pandemic, so I persisted, even when it seemed futile. By pursuing this questionable obsession, I discovered a doggedness I did not know I had.

I searched for the basic information available on each of the key names from the 1923 peloton but was left perplexed by the lack of detail which each search threw up. Often, even when returning results on the biggest stars of the era, the links revealed not much more than a few endlessly recycled photographs accompanying the same sparse biographical details, which themselves relied to a great extent on a mutual rehashing of stories or supposed facts. There really wasn't much to go on.

It was almost by chance that I figured out with a sudden and absurd cry of excitement the presence on film of the race leader on stage 4, Ottavio Bottecchia.

I was looking at him now, perhaps the first person in almost a hundred years to see him move. The Italian star is riding on the dusty road to Vannes in the yellow jersey, which is distinctive in tone even in black and white. Bottecchia's much-lampooned and caricatured sharp nose catches in the light from time to time, peeking out from beneath the shadow cast across his dark features by the peak of his cap. Knowing that I had unearthed footage of the *maillot jaune*, and that quite clearly it was him on camera, lent the scene a further gravitas. The Italian's presence, along with that of Desgrange, gave these images genuine weight.

Squat, unusually broad-shouldered and very upright on the bike, few riders were as distinctive a figure as Bottecchia. But he was as unfamiliar to me as he would have been even to the well-informed cycling public by the side of the road. Though he was well on his way to stardom, he was making his debut at the race that year, so they were seeing him for the first time. Reading the reports of the day, Bottecchia's name is written large in all the narratives. Having started the day in first place overall, he finished by relinquishing the lead, though he would regain it a few days later.

Ottavio Bottecchia in the maillot jaune, 1923

Spotting Bottecchia was a big breakthrough. But it was followed a day or two later by the startling realisation that the two Pélissier brothers were also in the film; the biggest names in the French peloton. In the case of Henri Pélissier, I had discovered footage of the man who would go on to win the overall race in Paris. But for now, here were the brothers in the same shot as Bottecchia, holding the edge of the road, riding to the right of the Italian.

With the benefit of hindsight, Francis Pélissier was easy to spot. He is huge, the tallest man in the peloton by far, and sits bolt upright on his bike, from which perch he briefly adjusts his goggles, as the dust is blown in their faces by the camera car. His older brother Henri was less simple to figure out, until I realised that Francis was accustomed to taking a position just to the rear of Henri on the road, acting effectively as his back guard.

Henri Pélissier on the road to Vannes

The Pélissier brothers pictured later in the 1923 Tour

There is a photo of Francis from 1923 in *Le Miroir des Sports* riding behind his brother jokily wielding a stick, accompanied by a caption which warns against upsetting him or trying to get to Henri. The similarities in both men's postures on the bike leave little room for doubt. The rider in front on the film matches the rider in the photo with unexpected precision. Henri is the protected leader, and he sits on the bike with the same unfussy intensity with which a skilled artisan might take his seat at a workbench.

ANOTHER HENRI

Later on in the day, and in just the same way that he had the previous year, Henri would puncture and Francis would be ordered to ride on without him. That outwardly selfless-seeming decision was typical of Henri's flaky relationship with the Tour, though: the most stubborn and unreliable of race favourites who blew hot and cold and sometimes didn't seem to give a toss; the same champion elect who drove Henri Desgrange to distraction. How those two Henris sparred, Desgrange and Pélissier.

The year 1923 would be Henri Pélissier's race, however. I look at him pedalling in my film. While the riders around him are distracted by the novel presence of the camera to break the monotony, Pélissier remains unmoved, noticeably ignoring the outbreak of frivolity around him, to which even his hard-nosed brother Francis eventually succumbs.

Henri Pélissier's story is no less incredible than many of the lives which found themselves bound up in the history of the early Tours. In that regard, it is not so unusual for a man whose life trajectory spanned the First World War, and who specialised so brilliantly in an activity as patently grand and cruel as the Tour de France. Pélissier, who excelled in so many of the other great races in the calendar, was already well into his thirties when the war was over.

And yet evidence of Pélissier's unreliability was considerable. He failed to finish either of the identical 1919 or 1920 editions of the Tour, twice ending his race just after stage 4 had been completed. The 1919 Tour had started so well for Henri, the gruff, moustachioed rider. The first Tour de France after the Great War was famously brutal, passing as it did through battlefields only recently cleared of the most glaring residues of conflict. Perhaps this grim landscape brought out the best in the largely cheerless Henri Pélissier. He'd won stage 2 to Cherbourg, and his younger brother Francis won stage 3 to Brest the following day, keeping it in their somewhat intimidating family ranks. Henri then completed stage 4 to Les Sables d'Olonne, but unexpectedly didn't start stage 5. He just climbed off and left the race. He was Henri Pélissier, and he did as he pleased.

This pattern of unpredictability persisted into the following year. In 1920, having almost abandoned the Tour in Morlaix with bronchitis on stage 3 before going on to win the race in Brest, he then took the following stage 4 to Les Sables, claiming back-to-back wins. Pélissier suddenly looked unstoppable. This time he started stage 5, but in the pouring rain, and without a word of explanation, he stopped riding somewhere near Rochefort. It was just before four in the morning. He was a long, long way from the finish of the monstrous 482-kilometre stage. Only retrospectively did he let it be known that he had by now succumbed to a heavy cold. Or so he said. You never quite knew what to believe with Henri Pélissier.

This explanation came too late for the newspapers, first among them *L'Auto*, which was filled instead with snarky insinuations about his temperament. Desgrange himself, whilst refraining from pointing the finger directly at Pélissier, nonetheless wrote that he wished 'our star riders, apart from their muscular valour, possessed a moral fortitude at least on a par with children from Year 2'. Thus there continued a toxic public as well as private relationship between the biggest star of French cycling and the man who ran the show.

But in 1923 Henri Pélissier made it through the psychological barrier of stage 5 and Bayonne. And this despite the fact that on the ill-fated stage 4 to Les Sables d'Olonne, which had twice spelled the end of the race for him in previous editions, he'd punctured towards the end and lost a huge amount of time, finishing almost half an hour down on the stage winner. He remained confident that the overall race was not gone, however. And he was as good as his word. He would regain an amount of time in the Pyrenees, and with the Alps rearing ahead of them, he would finally fulfil his promise by taking the yellow jersey and holding it all the way to Paris.

In their 1981 biography of the Pélissier family, *La Légende des Pélissiers*, Roger Bastide and André Leducq wrote an imagined response which Henri Pélissier might have made to Desgrange's not-so-veiled accusation of a lack of moral fibre:

You saw me on the road to Les Sables d'Olonne all on my own, my eyes glazed, twenty minutes down, zigzagging across the width of the road. Perhaps you thought I'd quit, as was my custom. I told Francis not to wait for me, which could have been interpreted as a bad sign. Somewhere in the fog of my brain a little mechanism was still working and did not stop repeating 'No, not this time . . . this time you go all the way to the end and you win.' I did not give up hope. Not for a second. There was still a long way to go.

For Henri Desgrange, the ambivalence he felt towards the obstreperous Pélissier and his lanky brother was tempered by the champion elect's undeniable physical prowess, as well as his undeniable Frenchness. A compact, powerful rider, at home more than anywhere else in the high mountains, Henri Pélissier also exhibited tremendous tactical awareness. Despite the annoyances (and the worst of these was still to come the following year, in 1924), Desgrange knew a great champion when he saw one. And after all, his race was about valour and honour, as much as it was about France itself and the vaunted currency of *Patrie*.

Desgrange's considerable heart was sustained by such lofty ideals. They were his bread and water, but also his inspiration. He strove all his life for a perfected unity of purpose in both mind and body, a theme he had explored in his early cycling training manual, *La Tête et les Jambes*, first published in 1895. As Henri Pélissier closed in on victory in the 1923 Tour, Desgrange would describe his value to cycling as being as important as Debussy's to music, Manet's to painting and Zola's to literature. Body and soul.

BLOOD

In 1923 this fusion of the physiological and the metaphysical was nowhere more complete, nor more literal, than in the meting out of justice.

The literal principle of an eye for an eye was still in many quarters an unquestionably just equation, as assorted nations picked at the wounds of their victimhood. Whether it was France exerting retribution on

Germany, or the state taking its pound of flesh from criminals, there was little room for empathy when great ideals like justice were at stake.

In Germany on the morning of 30 June 1923, the newspapers were full of vengeance for injustice. Even before news broke of the attack on the Duisburg-Hochfeld bridge, there were unsettling, violent reports coming out of the occupied Rhine. The French military court in Mainz had just handed down seven death sentences to alleged saboteurs. The oldest of them was 26-year-old Max Hahne, a locksmith from Berlin. The youngest was Alfred Schneider, a servant. He was just 18. They were all to be shot by firing squad.

The *Deutsche Allgemeine Zeitung* was not alone in declaring that seven new French 'blood sentences' amounted to the 'latest, monstrous outrage perpetrated by the creature Poincaré . . .'

That was the morning the bomb went off in occupied Germany.

PLAYING TO THE CAMERA

Fifty seconds
The bunch are little more than 10 or 15 metres away now from the camera, which has slowed to allow them to approach. A rider to the right of the group sits back in the saddle, and waves vigorously towards the camera. As he gets ever closer it becomes

apparent that, far from greeting the camera, he is waving away the vehicle which is carrying it. Too much dust is getting thrown up by the wheels. You can see the filth on the faces of the riders, as the chalk dust has mixed with their sweat.

Behind him, another rider makes the same gesture. They pass a group of five young men on the path to their right. Two of them hold the bikes they have ridden down to see the race. The rider who passes immediately in front of them, bobbing stolidly on his way, is none other than Henri Pélissier.

But it's not Pélissier who the boys recognise. As they watch the riders push past them (the road is slightly uphill, enough of a gradient for their progress to look laboured), one of the boys spots the yellow jersey of Ottavio Bottecchia. The Italian is minding his own business on the other side of the road, not getting involved in the gesturing or the chat which is breaking out in the riders around him. Square-shouldered, Bottecchia pedals elegantly and sits effortlessly still on the bike, his gaze impassively forward-facing.

Next to Bottecchia rides Jean Alavoine. Now that he is closer to the camera, we can see his expansive features, his wide cheekbones. It was he who was doing the waving. Though he doesn't know it, he is just a couple of days away from winning back-to-back stages in the Pyrenees. But for now, he's horsing around in front of the camera, enjoying himself. He pulls his goggles up onto his cap and smiles broadly, taking his right hand from the bars and letting it fall loosely at his side.

Perhaps unconsciously wary of Alavoine's ragged position on the bike, or maybe to avoid the very worst of the dust, Botteccia moves into the middle of the road, away from the Frenchman. Now Henri Pélissier becomes agitated, urging the camera vehicle to speed up and leave them alone. Behind him Romain Bellinger raises his right hand, and with pointed fingers draws a circle in the air, three times. Bellinger will finish the day unexpectedly in the yellow jersey, to only muted celebration in the French press which knows that he is not a real contender. For now he tucks back into the pack, taking the wheel of Robert Jacquinot, the muscular, square-jawed winner of the first two stages. The riders are over the top of the slight rise now, and the tempo is picking up.

Finally, the camera speeds away from the bunch, passing a rider on the right who had somehow ridden off the front by a few bike lengths. He gestures impatiently, as he is engulfed in dust. As he recedes from view, another rider comes alongside Alavoine, puts out his right arm and places his hand on the back of another man to his right. There seems to be an amount of animated talking among the riders.

Pushing her bike through the weeds and grasses at the side of the road, a lady in a skirt and long cardigan walks in the opposite direction to the race, and barely affords the riders a glance as they pass by. And then the film cuts again, just as the disappearing bunch is erased entirely by a gathering cloud of fine dust.

1923, A VIRUS

The year 1923 is under my skin. It may be a virus, I think. But then, that's a poor metaphor. The virus is real, this isn't. But sometimes I feel as if I can no longer separate my waking hours from the process, whatever it is.

That was a year of intense contradictory impulses, simultaneously brimming with ambition and yet deeply insecure. This strikes me as a better description of my state of mind, as I descend again into the ironed-out folds of the newspapers, the little alleyways, the blunt dead ends and unexplored fire escapes of a certain midsummer day, in a particular year, in a country I love and miss. Perhaps this is simply an account of where the mind can go during a few years spent in the wintry thrall of a pandemic. How it can tumble.

2. FALLING

'It's such a shame we can't go in and devastate Germany and cut off a few . . . kids' hands and feet and scalp a few of their old men but I guess it will be better to make them work for France and Belgium for fifty years.'

Harry S. Truman, Letter to Bess Truman
from the front line, 1918

THINKING, KILLING AND RACING

France was a febrile nation in 1923, in which the arts in all their extraordinary and sudden modernity were running off in all manner of uncontrolled and opposite directions. The latest activities of the various Parisian avant-gardists jostled jarringly for the public's attention alongside the grave political news of the day as well as the universal interest in sports like horse racing, car racing, aviation, boxing and cycling. Newspaper reports of art exhibitions were often accompanied by advertisements for ointments to cure piles or keep rodents at bay, which only added to the dissonance: such products paid the wages of the thousands of journalists, opinion-mongers, authors and sketch-writers whose work appeared in ever more florid form above their adventurous *noms de plume*. The mundane gave rise to the aspirational.

The very fact that Henri Desgrange, the editor of *L'Auto* and founding director of the Tour de France, also chose to launch a sister newspaper, *Comoedia*, dedicated to the arts, tells you much about the cultural landscape of this battered yet flourishing country. The hunger for knowledge and for culture in all its forms was omnivorous, and the lines were often blurred between what was good for the body and what was beneficial to the soul.

France still entertained a tradition of celebrating, and even fetishising, the act of thinking, dating back to Descartes and beyond. They still do. And in 1923, even by French standards, there was a great deal of thinking going on. The idea, the *Pensée*, was proudly celebrated, even if each disparate thought was hotly, even bitterly, contested by myriad opposing positions. It was a land which espoused a moral high ground but was populated by contradictory factions, buffeted by belief systems that had been weaponised by often fatal hardship, existential threat and the technological revolutions of cinema and telephony. Looking down from my hundred-year perch, I began to form a vision of the France of 1923 as a landscape of great hope, perpetual despair, joie de vivre and daily violence.

One tiny example of such quotidian violence springs off the page, but it is one of so many: on the same day as the film was shot, 30 June 1923, Séraphin Sleuraul, a resident of Hervafaing in the Vosges mountains, was murdered by his wife, Célestine. Her motive was not recorded. She confessed immediately to having struck him six times with a billhook, a sharp hand-held scythe she had been using for pruning.

You read of murder in the newspaper, and your eyes move on without the slightest hesitation. Yes, but what's happened in the Tour? Is Bottecchia still in the lead? Where's Pélissier now?

PÉLISSIER, LIFE AND DEATH

Henri Pélissier was stern, taciturn; hard to approach. I assemble the constituent parts of his biography, which offer explanations, but no excuses: because, actually, he was a terrible man. Born in 1889, he had grown up in a violent world and he left the world in violence, murdered by his lover in 1935.

His father was a self-made man from the Auvergne who had left home for Paris as a penniless teenager. Pélissier senior had somehow gone on to acquire a little land in Levallois, a small town just to the west of central Paris, hemmed in by the Seine and the Bois de Boulogne. Levallois is now a fully urbanised central suburb of Paris, but in the late nineteenth century there was still just enough pasture there to graze a small dairy herd and eke out a subsistence living. Along with their older sister Augustine, the young Pélissier boys (four in total, of whom the youngest, Charles, would eventually win 16 stages of the Tour, including a record 8 in a single edition) were often sent out to the nearby Place Victor Hugo to rip out grass from the lawn inside the square to supplement the animals' feed. That stark detail speaks to the liminal nature of the Pélissier family's existence.

Life was as hard as you might imagine it to be on a small dairy farm on what might now be considered 'brown belt' land. Four o'clock morning starts, the work relentless, and the diet terribly poor. Henri, the oldest of the brothers, often fell seriously ill. Once when he was 12 he acquired anaemia, from which it took him months to recover. Another time when he was 19 a bout of pneumonia left him in a coma for 10 days. And illness struck yet again when he was dismissed from the army in 1910 on medical grounds: Already underweight, he had started to waste away in the barracks at Verdun. But far worse than that was the pain inflicted on him at home. His father resorted to regular beatings to make his point. Henri left home as soon as he could get away, and balancing a job as an apprentice electrician with his ambitions as a racer, began to build a name for himself.

The war acted, as it did for an entire generation, as a potentially lethal hiatus in his career. It did indeed cost the life of Jean, the second oldest of the brothers, when he was blown apart by shrapnel on the Western Front. Jean's death, as well as that of his brother-in-law Eugène, a year later at Verdun in 1916, prompted Henri to try and enlist again in the army that had initially rejected him. This time, with the war machine running at full throttle, they took him on though kept him away from the front line. He survived the rest of the war serving at first as a cycling courier in Paris, then as a telegraph operator for the air force, exploiting his ability with electrics.

He may have lived through the hostilities but he did not escape injury. With cruel timing, on the day of the Armistice, 11 November 1918, he was hit by a truck and sustained a serious blow to the head. There is no knowing how this injury might have affected Pélissier's behaviour thereafter, but it's interesting to note.

In 1919 the world of racing resumed. For Henri Pélissier it represented a chance to continue his slow rise to the top, which in 1923 resulted in the apotheosis of his career: his singular overall victory at the Tour de France.

The older Pélissier brothers, Henri and Francis, were a formidable double act. Young Charles's career had not yet begun. And besides, he would prove to be a wholly different character to Henri and Francis: charming, urbane, open-minded, and hugely interested in the Parisian arts scene. How different were his older brothers. They seemed to behave as a hermetically sealed unit, not in need of any outside help, operating according to their own interpretation of the regulations as well as the law, and not without a certain sense of entitlement.

The two-minute time penalty that Henri sustained for throwing away a tyre on stage 5 in 1923, against the rules and in blatant and full view of the *commissaires*, is quite a revealing detail. Especially when you consider that it was an exact copy of the two-minute penalty he'd been handed for an identical offence three years previously, in 1920, a punishment which many believe had led directly to him abandoning the Tour that year for the second successive time. By 1923, when he was handed a penalty again, he had attracted the almost open disdain of Desgrange. It was almost as if Pélissier didn't care; which judging by the way he shrugged the time penalty off ('I can take the time back easily in the mountains'), perhaps he didn't. He was, after all, a brilliant rider; and he had won almost everything there was to win, except for the Tour. And in 1923 he would even put that right.

His 1924 defence of his Tour title ended the following year with the famous mutiny on stage 3. This stage would also represent the remarkable apotheosis of young Théo Beeckman's racing career, as I subsequently discovered, but almost nobody remembers that detail in their retelling of the Pélissiers' wanton abandon, remembered as the most significant rebellion in Tour history. Their protest claims a greater place in the collective memory of the race than even the riders' strike in 1998 when the race was being consumed by a doping scandal. At least on that occasion the eventual winner, Marco Pantani, didn't simply pack up and go home.

Henri and Francis, having made their point by quitting in 1924, nonetheless completed the journey to the finish line in Brest by train in order to collect their various personal belongings, which had already arrived ahead of the race during the previous rest day. The brothers proceeded to hold court in one of the local cafés until late into the night. The following day, Henri was observed having a loud altercation with a ticket inspector on board the Brest–Paris express train. It seemed he had a second-class ticket but was sitting in first-class, and was volubly refusing to leave. In the end, and after impassioned protestations, it was only the threat of being removed by the gendarmes from the train altogether that persuaded Pélissier to relent.

By rail and by road, the Pélissiers were trouble. Accounts of their petulance and boorishness abound in the reports of the era. The previous year, a local businessman near Épernay was driving back home one afternoon only to find himself stuck behind a slow-moving car on the Route de Paris. Driving a more powerful vehicle, 'Monsieur D' (as he is referred to in an account of the incident) tried repeatedly to overtake. But the car in front continually blocked his passage by zigzagging across the road to prevent the manoeuvre. After he'd eventually managed to get past, 'Monsieur 'D' was so incensed by what had just happened that he stopped in the road and waited for the offending car, presumably to give whoever was driving it a piece of his mind. When the car behind reached the roadblock and came to a halt, the door opened and the Pélissier brothers both climbed out armed with a gas canister and a wrench. An unequal fight ensued, in which 'Monsieur D' came off the worst.

In 1925, Henri Pélissier rode (and abandoned) his final Tour de France but raced on elsewhere until his late thirties. In 1927 he packed it in for good, aged 38. But Henri's retirement was not long and it was not happy; neither for him nor for the people closest to him. Unable to find a satisfactory role in life, he drifted half-heartedly around the fringes of the cycling scene, variously managing as *directeur sportif* the Peugeot cycling team as well as working on the track as a moto-pilot in 'stayers' races, pacing the cyclists on a curiously adapted motorbike made for drafting. But nothing replaced the feeling that racing and winning had given him, and its accompanying raison d'être.

According to many who knew him, it was often noted that Henri Pélissier was seemingly incapable of happiness. His marriage was falling apart. He was violent and unfaithful. Living through a personal hell, his wife Léonie, known to her friends as Nini, fell into a state of jealous despair and towards the end of 1933 died by shooting herself with a pistol Pélissier kept in the house.

Not long afterwards, Camille Tharault, Pélissier's lover, an ex-painter's model and over twenty years his junior, moved into the grand marital house at Feucherolles which the champion cyclist had bought from the proceeds of his racing career. Camille's younger sister Jeanne moved in as well. And 17-year-old Jeannine, Pélissier's daughter from his marriage to Léonie, was also a resident in this deeply unhappy home.

Pélissier drank heavily and beat both the teenage Jeanne and his own daughter Jeannine. But the worst abuse he reserved for his lover Camille, known as Miette. She in turn often had to intervene to spare the younger women.

On 1 May 1935, with two dinner guests waiting in the dining room at his home in Feucherolles, a violent dispute broke out. The cause of the anger had seemingly been an intervention from 19-year-old Jeanne which had sparked off Henri Pélissier's incandescent rage. He had been drinking heavily all day since lunch. Taking the argument into the kitchen, Henri hit Jeanne hard in the face, then turned his attention to Camille. He forced her up the stairs to their bedroom. There he brandished a revolver, hit her across the head with a kitchen ladle he had brought with him, punched her and kicked her in the stomach until she passed out. That done, he rushed downstairs again and attacked Jeanne once more in a fury, this time with a knife, cutting her face and scarring her for life. Jeanne managed to cry for help, 'He's going to kill me!' Camille, woken from her unconscious state by the screams, rushed from the bedroom to come to her sister's defence, having grabbed the pistol that Henri had left there.

She shot five bullets, one of which tore his carotid artery and killed him instantly. In a remarkably dark twist of fate, Pélissier had been killed by his lover using the same firearm that his ex-wife had used to end her own life.

Camille Tharault was eventually handed a one-year suspended sentence for his murder. Summing up the case, Judge Peyre, President of the Versailles Court of Assizes, said of Henri Pélissier, 'He was one of the great glories of French cycling. But he had a character which was irascible, violent and perverse.'

You might say the very same thing about the years in which he raced.

BEECKMAN, ALONE

Brusquement, Beckmann s'échappe et passe seul au viaduc de Laroche-Bernard.

One minute and twenty-two seconds
The massive bridge, with its humped iron back, appears to sway gently as the camera moves from left to right. The eye moves with it, loosely.

There is a rider on the bridge. You can just about make out his cap and his shoulders behind the wall. The rest, his legs, his bicycle, are obscured by the parapet of the bridge. He will be riding close to it, though, in the gutter. This is something riders of the Tour do every year, knowing that the road is smoothest there.

He outpaces the camera, leaving the frame, and riding off the bridge and onto the riverbank. His speed temporarily disrupts the camerawork. As he disappears completely from view, we catch a fleeting glimpse of half a dozen men who have gathered on the bridge to watch him pass. The rider, Théo Beeckman, is pursued by another man on a bike. But he is no racer. You can see that he is wearing a normal work jacket; its tailcoats flap in the wind. He's just trying to keep up, for the sheer joy of the experience, but he can't hold the pace for long and drops back.

Beeckman has vanished entirely now behind a cloud of dust kicked up by the car. They have turned now 90 degrees to the right, to the south-west, and are heading along the river valley.

Out of nowhere two horses appear on the road, close to the camera. They are in harness, pulling a covered wagon in whose dark interior no driver is visible. The larger of the two animals appears to be dark, and the other white, or at least light grey. They are agitated, their big nostrils tipped up and flared. The wagon is veering erratically across the road. Perhaps the horses have been spooked by the passing car. Their trot is barely restrained, verging on uncontrolled. And behind it the lone rider is nowhere to be seen.

BEECKMAN, FORGOTTEN

A week after stage 4, on 6 July, the film was shown for the very first time at the spanking new Montrouge Palace cinema in Paris, just two years old in 1923. Pathé's report from the Tour de France was merely the support feature, with Beeckman briefly taking the spotlight. Three stages were documented in each of the Pathé despatches from the Tour, making a total of five newsreels throughout the duration of the 15-stage race. This fragment, therefore, was the beginning of the second reel from the 1923 race.

The newsreel was projected ahead of the main presentation of the evening, *Heurle à la Mort* ('The Silent Call', 1921), which was a heart-warming adventure about a dog called Flash who is falsely accused of sheepicide by local farmers and has to go into hiding in the mountains. The film starred a famous German Alsatian called Strongheart, a dog that would eventually meet a grizzly end, dying of severe burns and a tumor suffered during the filming of a scene in Hollywood in 1929. *Heurle à la Mort* was the main attraction, and Strongheart was the star turn of the evening. The Tour de France was the hors d'oeuvre.

I imagine the dimming of the cinema lights, the heat inside the theatre, and the fug of tobacco all around, before the whirl of the projector and the sudden sweep of the curtain. In all that velvet darkness, the contrast of the strong Breton sun on the light-coloured stone of the houses with the deep shadows in doorways and windows. A related sense of wonder was common to both my experience and that of the seated masses in the Paris cinema. There had been a certain magic at play then, and there still was for me, reading the juddering caption with its revealing misspelling. Some of the audience too might have been asking themselves, 'Who is this "Beckmann" [sic]?' At the heart of the spell lay the unknowability of the film's central protagonist.

His real name was Théophile Beeckman. Attacking, alone, on stage 4 of the 1923 Tour de France and staying off the front for a good few kilometres was not the biggest thing he had achieved to date in his chosen career, nor does it compare to what he went on to achieve over the next couple of years. But strangely this is going to be the thing for which he will in fact be best remembered. And stranger still, I have a part to play in that memorialisation, as do all future readers of these words as I write them. As do you.

Maybe if there hadn't been a pandemic which had shut down the world, I might have let the moment go, allowed it to drift away like the dust kicked up by the horses and the car. But instead the little figure of Théophile Beeckman assumed a bloated significance in my mind. The more I learned about him, the less I knew. And the less information I gathered from the dwindling resources I had plundered, the more I wanted to know.

I was not alone in my ignorance. The lack of any trace of Beeckman's career in Belgium, Flanders or indeed the wider Dutch-speaking world was extraordinary for a rider of his considerable ability. It was only when I chanced upon a Dutch blog which briefly profiled his career that I realised quite how vanishingly small a mark he had left on the sport. On a nostalgic historical website called *Muizennest* (Mouse Nest) there was a page all about him, which didn't really tell me much I didn't know except to confirm my suspicions; namely, that no one knew anything about him.

'He has been completely forgotten as a cyclist,' bemoans the Dutch author of the blog, 'except in Meerbeke and perhaps by a few very fanatical cycling fans outside of town. I fear that any kind of monument to him in Meerbeke is missing.'

I briefly exchanged a few messages by email with the blog's author, who could offer no further information. In fact, he seemed surprised and faintly suspicious of my particular obsession with Beeckman. 'May I ask,' he wrote, 'why you are so interested in Beeckman? You even have his photo as your avatar on social media.' Unable to think of a cogent explanation, I simply stopped corresponding with him, feeling faintly embarrassed, as if I had been unmasked.

I began instead to daydream about visiting Ninove. Though the pandemic would keep me at arm's length for some time to come, Meerbeke, the humble district on the south side of the river Dender in

Ninove, had become as totemic in my imagination as the bridge over the river Vilaine, where my film first affords a glimpse of Beeckman. I knew, after all, the addresses in Ninove and Meerbeke at which Beeckman had spent most of his adult life. I knew where he had grown up. I had digitally walked along these streets on the internet, turning the compass cursor of Google Street View to spin through 360 degrees, following the arrows on the named roads, looking, often in vain, for a sense of history. It was a trick that had only partially worked for me. Deep down, I knew that *being there*, feeling the bite of a Flandrian wind, hearing the actual traffic on the road and real Flemish voices talking into their mobile phones around me; there could be no substitute for that. But it was impossible to travel. The world was still closed and any plans I might have hatched seemed a long way off. I would have to be patient.

Besides, who would I visit? Who could I talk to, face to face? I refreshed my inbox daily, hoping for news from Belgium. I had heard nothing yet from the dance company, nor therefore from Beeckman's great-granddaughters who I hoped might be reachable. A mild panic started to creep in, that if I got no response that way, there might literally be no other avenue to explore. Drawing a total blank would be a forlorn end to a journey I did not want to end. So, I returned to the film. I looked again at the moment that Beeckman gets up to speed and almost draws level with the camera.

What was he thinking? Was there the trace of a smile on his lips, in those fleeting fractions of a second when he was close enough to the camera to see his features? Or was it a grimace?

This became the central question of my enquiry: Why did Beeckman attack that far from the finish line? He still had 258 kilometres to go, which was a greater distance than is ever raced on a single day in the modern Tour de France. It made no sense. A solo rider could not possibly hope to hold off an organised chase by the peloton on such flat roads, even allowing for the differences between the way the race worked back then and how the tactics are coordinated now. Beeckman was not particularly noted for his flamboyance, rather for his tenacity, modesty and resilience. This move seemed out of character. Or at least that's what I thought until I started to aggregate the different voices in the press which had severally told the story of the day.

In most of the accounts of stage 4, Beeckman's aggressive move barely gets a mention, is merely noted in a few sparing words, or simply doesn't exist. After all, it was soon snuffed out and was of little consequence beyond its own short time span. It's quite possible that Beeckman himself went on to forget about it entirely; just a forgotten detail, like so many other insignificant moments in a race.

Except, that is, for the quirk of fate which has meant that Beeckman's attack, rather than anything else, is what has survived a hundred years of history and ended up on my desk. In essence, what made this attack different to an almost infinite number of other, unrecorded moments, is that somehow, it had dodged oblivion. It still existed to be witnessed.

ARE YOU CRYING, MR. BEECKMAN?

Perhaps the key to understanding his attack lay in the previous hours of racing. By the time they had reached Vannes, Beeckman was seemingly close to an emotional breaking point, according to some reports. Whatever was affecting the quiet Belgian, his frustration had begun to bubble to the surface long before the waters of the Vilaine appeared ahead of him, the houses of La Roche-Bernard cluttering up the steep slopes of the riverbank on the other side of the bridge. Something happened to him that day, shaking him out of the lethargy of the day's interminable grind southwards following the high sun's rise in the sky.

Having already punctured on several occasions in the pre-dawn darkness before Lorient and having chased back on, he reportedly reached Vannes, the last checkpoint before La Roche-Bernard, in yet another group of four riders off the back. As in Lorient it seems, Beeckman had signed in two minutes after the front of the race had done so. But this time in Vannes he had also incurred a penalty from the race commissaires. They issued him with a 50-franc fine for 'tenue incorrecte', which is intriguingly vague, but means 'improper dress'. His crime may have been something greatly trivial, even if the amount of the fine was not inconsiderable.

That morning local schools had reportedly broken off their lessons, though they had scarcely begun. Out in the Morbihan countryside schoolchildren in remote villages had already set off and were walking for kilometres with their teachers to get to the side of the road and see the race. Their chorus of joyful, inarticulate support would greet the riders as they shot past. The passage of a bike race meant an enforced interruption to the normal routine, then as now: roads, schools, offices closed for an hour or two, only the railway timetable did not bow to the exigences of the Tour.

The correspondent from *Le Matin* had gone ahead to Vannes to wait for the riders to come through the checkpoint. The author described some of the individual spectators by the side of the road waiting to see the riders cool down by plunging their heads into buckets of water placed for that purpose by the side of the road. A hazy heat had descended on the town. He stood next to a few locals who always turned out to watch the race come through, their annual pilgrimage. There was a Monsieur Asse, the local notary who always ensured he took a day off work to celebrate the passage of the Tour. Standing next to Asse there was a 'charming old lady holding a parasol and a bag of sweets'. She seemed to know all the riders by name and called out to them one by one.

'Are you crying, M. Beeckman?' she asks.

But Beeckman, drying his eyes with the back of his arms, leaves without a word in reply.

'*After all,*' writes the reporter, '*he really can't explain to the lady why he has been handed a 50-franc fine.*'

This is a scene I could picture especially vividly. In my role as reporter at the Tour de France, I had often posed an innocent question to a rider only to find them unwilling or perhaps unable to respond, whether through exhaustion, frustration or anger. It was strange to stand dumbly in their presence awaiting their non-response, while they gazed into a distance you couldn't possibly know. Or perhaps Beeckman didn't dare say a word for fear he'd explode with rage at the injustice of it all. I'd seen that from riders, too.

The approach to La Roche-Bernard was hugely congested, that much was well documented by numerous sources. People had flocked there, on foot, by bike, and most notably, by car. The roads were so busy with vehicles and spectators that the riders were briefly impeded by the chaos and the race almost ground to a halt. Perhaps Beeckman, having left Vannes a couple of minutes down, had already rejoined the peloton again. Or maybe he was still off the back and the delay on the road had allowed him to make contact again with the bunch. But by common consent that was the moment at which the Flandrian chose to attack, taking advantage of the mêlée and the resultant lack of organisation from his opponents. The Flemish reporter from *Sportwereld* witnessed the congestion of cars on the approach to La Roche-Bernard, and saw how Beeckman seized his opportunity, as the rest of the race was brought to a standstill:

Suddenly Beeckman jumps through a hole left in the middle of the following riders, and he hits the front on his own. In the group, there doesn't seem to be much desire to chase him, so he reaches the checkpoint with a 500m lead.

With the rest of the bunch having crossed the bridge and begun already to labour up the steep approach to the centre of the little town, Beeckman had already dropped his bike, signed on and remounted, holding onto his slender advantage:

Will he keep it? It seemed possible!

The reporter for *L'Auto* misrepresented the facts. In his account, Beeckman attacked as they *left* La Roche-Bernard, which was clearly not the case, as my film shows. Somewhat awkwardly for the writer in question, this misreading of the race was flatly contradicted by his boss, no less a figure than the paper's editor, Henri Desgrange. In his column Desgrange wrote a different account of the events, but one which tallies correctly with the video evidence. '*Let's get to the facts*,' Desgrange wrote:

A few kilometres before La Roche Bernard, Beeckman, probably overheating in the sun, threw a tantrum, attacked, took 500 metres and the peloton chased. Believe it or not, the peloton wasn't able to swallow him back up until Pontchateau. That's 25 kilometres!

The original report, despite misplacing the moment of the attack, described Beeckman's attitude faithfully, painting a picture of a '*storm being unleashed*' and how his '*back was curved and his pedal stroke frenzied*'. The film did indeed suggest that Beeckman was in full flight, making an unsustainable effort to break free and stay away.

Despite scouring acres of newsprint, I did not find a single quote from Beeckman. It was almost as if he had taken a vow of silence. And yet, the strongest evidence I could find of Beeckman's more emotional side was bound up with the moment, caught on film, of his attack into La Roche-Bernard. The slightly wayward report from *L'Auto* also described how his attack, for all its costly vigour, had been almost entirely anonymous. Had it not been for the film's existence (and subsequent rediscovery), as well as these few words, the whole moment might have been eradicated entirely from history:

Unfortunately it was midday, time for aperitifs and for lunch and no one was there to see Beeckman's attack except those who, like certain others, were eating the contents of one of Machurey's lunch bags [Machurey had been the race *commissaire* at the checkpoint in Vannes, I later discover]. *And Beeckman, after a pursuit which lasted an hour, was caught. Only two or three following cars, a few villages, and a thousand Bretons in clogs witnessed the attack and the Belgian and how he was subsequently caught.*

LA ROCHE-BERNARD

Two minutes and two seconds
For the first time we see Beeckman clearly. He has deftly mounted his bike, almost cyclo-cross style, in motion. And now he is pushing the single gear he has at his disposal, a gear designed for rolling along at pace in the bunch, not starting off. It is hard work, each revolution pushes his front wheel from side to side, as his slight frame bobs with the effort. He is wearing a light-coloured jersey, which looks heavy in the heat. He has two inner tubes around his torso and has a casquette that is quartered, like a jockey's cap.

Suddenly the bike rights itself as Beeckman, up to racing speed, accelerates vigorously through a puff of dust towards the camera. He pushes past the half-open first-floor shutters of the café/tabac. Its striped awnings are lowered below, to keep off the midday sun. In front of the café the crowd pulls back to let him past, whilst craning to get a view of the lone rider at the front of the race. Two finely attired gentlemen, one with a folded parasol. A lady to his right is drawn to the sight of the camera, and briefly looks away from the approaching Beeckman just before he passes her. A tall young man with slicked-back hair stands half a head above the others, hatless in the lunchtime heat.

On the other side of the road where there is no shade, the youngsters have gathered. Most are straining to catch a glimpse of the rider, but one boy breaks rank. In his excitement, he sets off just after the camera has passed, sprinting for a few steps. The boy then abruptly stops and turns just in time to see the Belgian. On the other side of the road, tall ladders are propped against a house which is being renovated. Three workmen have climbed a few rungs of ladders to get a better view.

Beeckman races on, passing the Docks de l'Ouest grocery shop, in front of which there is a racing bicycle propped up with a pedal against the kerb. Either side of the bike are three parked cars, their round headlights and polished chrome grills glinting. A man walks towards the cars, against the direction of travel. In his right hand he carries two bags of shopping, and with his left he holds the hand of a young child. They barely look up to see Beeckman, his goggles lifted onto the peak of his cap, find his rhythm. As the camera car slows to negotiate a sharp left-hand turn in the road, Beeckman dives out of shot on the right, undertaking the car and disappearing from view. The shot becomes unstable.

Before the cut, there is an ephemeral glimpse of two women, one younger than the other, dressed in long white dresses and white stockings, with another younger girl, in black. Above them is a woman peering from a first-floor window. The camera jerks off to the left as the car takes the bend in the road. It reveals the dark stone, small rose window and austere façade of Saint Michel church. A flash of a black road sign with white script pointing back down the road Beeckman has attacked on. It reads, 'Vannes. 40k'.

THE GIRL CHEWING GUM

It's London. A dull, grey evening.

I have assembled downstairs a projector (we long since abandoned television, though we can stream videos). Though our living room is not large, we have a white wall, big enough for an image to be displayed to fill the space. It feels like a tiny cinema, and its luminance and scale gets us through troubling times. Tonight is a good example.

I watch a short film from 1976 that has been recommended to me by a filmmaker friend. *The Girl Chewing Gum* is a benchmark in avant-garde cinema, and was filmed during 1976, in London, the year of the drought, which I just about remember. On a street corner in Dalston, people come and go. The camera observes them moving, ignorant of its presence. An omniscient-seeming narrator seems to be directing them, ushering them into position as if he had prior knowledge. One by one, he calls them onto stage, anticipating their movements, which he knows with infinite detail. He seems God-like.

But, and here's the twist, the narrator turns out to be a fraud. He is in fact nowhere near the scene on which he is commentating, and is making it all up. The lives he tried to own knew nothing of his presence, as he knew nothing of their realities.

BEECKMAN IN A CROWD

What stories surround him as he finds a way through the throng and heads for the open road again? What are those kids thinking, in the foreground, whose attention is caught halfway between the film camera itself and the rider who's about to come past them. One of the smaller boys, agitated into instinctive excitement, darts out from the pack and starts to run alongside Beeckman, simply for the joy of it.

It is impossible to imagine what the lives were like for the people, young and old, in the town that day. Some lives cut short, perhaps. As if war wasn't enough, the particular cruelty of the Spanish flu was that, especially in the second and most lethal wave, it predominantly claimed the lives of young adults. And even without war and pestilence, childhood mortality rates were still unimaginably high at the beginning of the century. Very few families came through the rigours of the age intact and unscathed. Perhaps none.

The Beeckman family was not unusual, though even now it is shocking to learn of their ordinary family tree, riddled through with infant mortality like so many millions of others. I wondered how often Théo remembered from his childhood his younger siblings who had died one after another in little over a year. What did he recall of baby Maurits, who was dead at the age of just one? Or, a year later, little Victorina, who died just days short of her third birthday? There is no doubt that the same genealogical scarring would have been present in the lives of those prosperous townsfolk of La Roche-Bernard who thronged the dusty road to see the great race pass. Beeckman was a total stranger to them, but his life was not so unfamiliar.

BEECKMAN, COMMITTED

Two minutes and twelve seconds
A jump cut of a handful of seconds. Beeckman is riding much closer to the camera now, almost looking at it. To his left extends a tall, rough-hewn stone wall along the roadside. In the background of the shot, you can just about make out the church, which is rapidly fading into the dusty white. Beeckman's muscled upper arms are tensed against the handlebars, and his slender legs work a steady cadence. He is picking a jerky route through the potholes and ruts of the road. He passes a stationary delivery lorry with a big canvas covering. The camera is accelerating clear again, and Beeckman's figure gets smaller. He rides by a house on his left with two advertisements on its side wall. One is for beer, the other for stock cubes. There is no one by the side of the road, save for an indistinct shadowy figure standing in the partially opened doorway entrance to what seems to be a barn.

BEECKMAN, A QUESTION

Now he pushes furiously to keep his advantage, swinging left-handed past the church and heading out of town into the open countryside, leaving behind him, suspended in the hot air, the last lingering shouts of encouragement from the Breton supporters at the side of the road. He settles into a sustainable rhythm, a half-smile appearing to play across his features, as he determines to enjoy the ride, roll the dice, and see what becomes of his audacious move. *'But Beeckman's attack appears to be a straw fire,'* continues the correspondent from *Sportwereld*, *'and after a few kilometres, through the work of the Pélissiers, the man from the Denderstreek is done for . . . which isn't to say that the guy doesn't deserve praise for his cheeky attack. At least it brought some life into the game.'*

Accounts vary as to how long he held on for. It was perhaps something between a handful of kilometres and over twenty-five; a total distance as unknowable as his motivation. The film cuts out long before we see him caught, leaving his fate dangling off the front, forever unresolved.

This is maybe the lesson to be learned as I move backwards, arms outstretched through the fog of partially recorded time, misted up like the soft lens of a silent film camera. We will never know the inner lives of others, whether they really come past us at speed, so fast we catch a breath of wind as they pass, or whether they only exist many years later as a ghostly moving image, recorded and preserved semi-incidentally.

If Einstein's theory of time travel holds, I know exactly how I would take advantage of his proposition. I would go back to 30 June 1923, and I would check into a *pension* in the seaside resort of Les Sables d'Olonne, where I would have lunch, looking out over the Bay of Biscay.

Then, as evening started to settle, I would make my way down to the finish line, amid the crowds of women in their startling local costumes, complete with their headdresses. I would watch the stocky Albert Dejonghe raise his arm in victory, but I would scarcely register him. Instead, I would gaze down the dusty finishing straight. There, I'd see Ottavio Bottecchia in the yellow jersey he was about to concede, pushing hard to finish in 10th place, supported by Francis Pélissier. I'd wait for a further five minutes to see Théo Beeckman come to the line in 14th place.

I'd walk over to him as he came to a halt in the late afternoon sun. I'd introduce myself. Tell him I'm writing a book about him.

Then I'd ask my question: 'Why did you attack in La Roche-Bernard?' But somehow, when I imagine this encounter, he never speaks.

DIE DEUTSCHLAND TOUR

The next summer, much to my surprise, since the pandemic was still barely being contained, I travelled to Germany to commentate for TV on their national Tour. The *Deutschland Tour* was a paltry-seeming four days long, compared to the 21 stages of a Grand Tour like the Tour de France.

It was a thrill to be on the road again. I'd lived in Germany when I was in my early twenties, about the same age that Beeckman was when he was racing the Tour de France. It was an unsettling country in the early 1990s, undergoing the prolonged birth pangs of reunification, and still grappling with all the seismic upheavals of a century of brutality and defeat. But it was *my* foreign land, one into which I willingly disappeared until, after many years, I had an ear and voice for the language and a strong feeling for the country; one I found hard to explain, perhaps.

It was strange therefore that France and French, whose quicksilver vowels and soft consonants made up the other half of my linguistic universe, had more recently come to occupy an equal and sometimes opposite place in my heart, and brightness in my imagination. My work at the Tour de France had bent the beam of my affinities back again towards the west, crossing the Rhine in reverse. Now my affections straddled both cultures, differently and equally.

What made the week's race across Germany even more heavy with meaning was the fact that I was working for a French race organisation team, all of whom had boarded a chartered flight from Charles de Gaulle airport to Hamburg, where I met up with them. The Deutschland Tour is owned and operated by the Amaury Sports Organisation, ASO, the proprietors of the Tour de France, and the natural and legal inheritors of Henri Desgrange's original Grand Tour.

With the local TV production crew all being German, there were frequent times when I was called upon to interpret between sets of colleagues from either side of the linguistic divide who found themselves mutually incomprehensible. On one occasion on a long motorway transfer, I had to explain in French, under the specific instruction of our East German coach driver, that we would stop at the toilets for no longer than eight minutes. If the passengers weren't back at the coach by then, he'd drive on without them. He had expressed a concern to me that, being French, they'd all want a smoke, and delay our journey. He wasn't wrong, I noted, as I gazed out of the stationary coach window at a row of leather jackets and ponytails from which plumes of cigarette smoke were emanating.

That year the route of the Deutschland Tour followed a trajectory southward through the former East Germany, passing through Weimar, the birthplace of the fragile interwar German state. It ended up at one point in the city of Erlangen in what had been the West. Along the route of the race, there were echoes of at least three different iterations of the German state, and plenty more duchies, kingdoms and principalities besides, depending on how far you wished to go back. The morning before the race arrived there, I walked through the elegant grounds of the famous Erlangen University which had given birth to the Siemens industrial empire and I ended up in an academic bookshop. It was only when I walked in that it occurred to me how one-eyed my understanding had been of the Franco-German rift which defined politics in 1923.

Erlangen University

Moving freely for the first time in months in the real world, and wonderfully released from simply scanning for material online, I took time to browse the shelves. I ended up carrying a handful of books published only in the German language to the till, hoping that they might shed some light on this other side of Europe, on the Weimar Republic, its nerves, its people and their fears in 1923.

The Deutschland Tour came to a close in the pouring rain in Nuremberg, and a day later I flew back with my French colleagues to Paris, my books in a little cabin bag by my side. Not long after we had taken off on the short flight, we crossed the Rhine itself, a broad silvery width, fringed with green cliffs and dotted with barges. I nodded off, and only woke when we landed with a bump on French soil, in Paris.

PARIS, PATHÉ AND A HOMECOMING

My plan was to connect with a Eurostar home to London later that evening. This meant that now, rather happily, I had the best part of a day to spend in Paris. It was the first time I had been there since the final stage of the 2019 Tour de France, ignorant then of how changed the world would be by the time I finally made it back again.

It occurred to me that this accidental afternoon in the French capital might be usefully spent on my quest to make contact with Pathé Cinema France, the originators of my film. Founded exactly three days before Théo Beeckman's birth, in 1896, Pathé rapidly became the biggest film-production company in the world. In 1908 they invented the newsreel, short sequences to be shown in cinemas before the feature film.

The newsreel changed the world, and in the case of the Tour de France, catapulted it into ever greater heights in the public consciousness. To this day, Pathé retains its Parisian headquarters, and is still a major film and TV concern with interests across the continent. It is a cultural monolith, a giant symbol of French pride. And then there was me, with my little box of film, and my increasingly obsessive story to tell.

I needed to talk to someone at Pathé for a number of reasons. Firstly, there was the issue of intellectual rights to the film, which was unclear, but seemed to suggest that they were the owners. But that in itself was a curiosity, since I was convinced that they not only had no idea of the film's existence, but that I had the only copy in the world of something which they might feel they would want to include in their archives. I hoped that they might show good faith and share the rights with me in exchange for the return of their lost property. It was a complicated affair, incredibly important to me, but possibly of negligible significance to them. I had already sent them a couple of emails in hesitant written French which had remained unanswered. So, I thought I might as well just go and knock on their door, since I happened to be in town.

Until this point I had shared my discovery with very few people, but that was about to change. Once I had actually landed in Paris, I started to become unsettled by the risk I sensed, of the dangers of exposure I now felt. Waiting at the stubbornly immobile baggage carousel, I contemplated my onward journey to the film company's archives on the Avenue des Gobelins at the Jérome Seydoux-Pathé Foundation. And I imagined with trepidation how I might begin to introduce myself and my precious film written in binary code onto the hard drive of my laptop.

'*Qu'est-ce que tu fais maintenant, Ned?*' asked one of the editors I'd been working with in Germany, wanting out of friendly curiosity to know how I was going to get home to London.

I told him that I had a late train out of town and I was going to Pathé's archives because I had a film belonging to them. Straight away

I knew that this rather gnomic pronouncement would need explaining, and suddenly I was committed to telling the whole story. Before long, as I unfolded the laptop and started to play the film, half a dozen of ASO's staff had surrounded me, and were staring with genuine interest at the black-and-white images that flickered across the little screen. I pressed pause.

'*Et lui?*' I said, enjoying their fascination. '*Lui, c'est Henri Desgrange.*' I pointed at the figure of the father of the Tour de France, proud of my ownership of his pixels.

'*Non, c'est pas vrai…*' Their astonishment was now audible; a succession of soft whistles and admiring gasps. The meaning of this moment in Terminal Two's baggage reclaim at Charles de Gaulle airport suddenly filled the space around our spontaneous little huddle: I was showing them their founding father. The reason we were all standing there around a laptop almost a hundred years after the event was because of the neatly dressed old man in the long coat, with his back turned to the camera. Our presence at that spot and at that time was traceable back to this moment, as Desgrange gives Desmarets the order to set them off again, and the riders remount their bikes as the morning sun starts to warm their backs in Lorient on 30 June 1923.

Arriving at the Gare du Nord from the airport, I dropped off my heavy suitcase at left luggage and, with my laptop and notebook in a leather shoulder bag, jumped on a Vélib hire bike and started to head south. Passing Oberkampf, I crossed the Seine at the Pont d'Austerlitz, retracing in place names Europe's warring past.

The leaves on the plane trees were still full, green, and gently drifting in a soft breeze from downstream, lifting the morning clouds and allowing the sun to break through. I was overwhelmingly happy to be there, in that city to which I had been used to making an annual pilgrimage on the Tour de France. And here I was, back again in unexpected circumstances, my little briefcase in the basket on the front of the bike, bumping around on the cobbles. I put my hand out to steady it against rattling around.

Docking my bike near the Place d'Italie, I soon found the Pathé Foundation's impressively sized, modern headquarters. But, as I had anticipated, like so much of France, they were closed on Mondays. The doors were locked, and as I peered through their tinted glass, there was no sign of life behind them. There was, however, a separate entrance for authorised researchers; film students who had access to the archives even when the rest of the exhibition space was closed to the public. Not being even remotely authorised, invited or expected, I lacked the necessary code to open the door and swan in. But there was a bell and video entry system whose confusing menu I navigated and rang. I had come this far, after all.

'*Allo?*'

I launched into my semi-coherent spiel, sprinkled with what I hoped were endearing apologies and as politely as I could muster, like some kind of low-rent French-speaking Hugh Grant. I had, I assured the lady on the other end of the line, just a '*toute petite question*'. The question was actually as big as a Zeppelin in my mind, but she needn't know that. After that, there was a slight hesitation, in which I figured I could almost hear her mixture of curiosity and infuriation in the intercom's crackle. And then, '*Attendez. Je descends.*'

So it was that, a minute or two later, I was standing on the street in Paris discussing the 1923 Tour de France with a total stranger I had met just seconds previously. Or rather, I was discussing it, and she was looking at me discussing it. As the buses roared up and down the avenue, I tried to summarise my convoluted obsession with a fragment of newsreel through the several disadvantages of patchy French, a face mask made to German standards which rendered my speech almost totally inaudible, and the fact that I was talking to a woman who was simultaneously suspicious, confused and seemingly completely uninterested in cycling. I told her the film contained rare, if not unique, footage of Henri Desgrange. Behind her mask there was scarcely a flicker of discernible excitement. This prompted me to leave out my noteworthy identification of Ottavio Bottecchia and skip lightly over what I knew about the Café Gloux's possible owners.

She asked me what I wanted to do with the film. I explained I wanted to clear the rights with Pathé so that I could make use of it in a forthcoming book, to reproduce some of the images. Her brow furrowed. She mumbled something about it being really rather old, though I thought I could tell she was actually thinking that it was really rather boring. I told her that, in return, I would like to present the Pathé Foundation with a copy for their collection. Again, not a single flicker of interest. She asked me to send her an email. I told her I had. She seemed to suggest I hadn't. At this point, I confess, I sighed.

I opened my laptop and showed her the email I'd sent her. She thought that was strange and asked me to send her the email again. Just as our discussion was meandering its way to the unsatisfactory if inevitable conclusion that communicating with one another 300 miles apart over the internet was her preferred means of dealing with me, a colleague of hers approached along the street, perhaps returning from her lunch break. She radiated alarm.

'*Tout va bien?*' she asked her friend in urgently concerned tones and shot me a look which made me feel like the predator I suddenly inwardly and outwardly resembled. I tried to offer my reassurances that this was a perfectly normal transaction, as I stood on the street with an open laptop, beaded with sweat after my cycle ride, in front of two wary women. I sensed that I had gone as far as it was prudent to go on this particular journey and that any further insistence on my part might firmly label me as a person of concern, and lead to copies of my likeness being circulated for the attention of all Pathé staff. I thanked them, bade them farewell and strolled off, imagining the scandalised conversation inevitably ensuing behind the closed doors of the Jérome Seydoux-Pathé Foundation.

But by the time I had reached the Rue Mouffetard, 10 minutes down the road, she had already emailed me. It seemed that they had indeed received my original correspondence and that they would deal with the issue and respond '*rapidement*'.

I went for lunch, after which I sat down at the Cave La Bourgogne on the corner of Rue Pascal to think things through over a perfect, crisp glass of Sancerre. I watched a kid on a bench play something intently on their iPhone, while her mother chatted to a friend. Two students flashed by on hired scooters, and a steady trickle of people came and went from the steam baths opposite the bistro.

Perhaps Pathé already had multiple copies of the newsreel in their archives, I suddenly thought. That would knock the wind out of me if it were the case. I had so much invested in the notion that I was the sole custodian of the story. Or what, still worse, what if it became obvious that I was the only person in the world who cared about this broken fragment of film from an unremarkable day during a forgotten race?

A rather perverse part of me now almost wanted that to be the case. I think a bit of me wanted to be alone and to keep it to myself. I drained the glass and ordered another. How I'd missed Paris.

BAD NEWS, MAD NEWS AND A VOLCANO; THE WEIMAR REPUBLIC, 1923

Eventually I headed for the Gare du Nord, where I often used to find myself on the Sunday evening at the end of another Tour de France. Like so many times before, I took the escalator to the mezzanine level and joined the various queues for the Eurostar, watching despondently as a young French man from London was taken to task by British passport officers who were insisting he had the wrong paperwork to enter the country. A border I had crossed without noticing for almost all of my life was being partially raised once more.

I fell asleep on the train, masked and unsettled by odd half-dreams, waking only as an artificial darkness fell suddenly outside. We were entering the Channel Tunnel, leaving the continent behind. I picked up one of the books I had bought in Erlangen and started to look at the tumult of 1923 from a new angle. All through Kent's rolling fields, I read about Germany's fevered state of mind during that year which started with an invasion and ended with a putsch. Eventually the train slowed as we ground our way over the junctions of track which led eventually to St Pancras station. And when I got home, I tested myself for Covid, and spent a day or two nervously awaiting the results.

Though we had lived for years already in an era of saturated bad news across all the panoply of twenty-first-century media we couldn't resist consuming, still the anxieties of our age bore scant comparison to the absolute tone of the Germans' state of despair after the end of the Great War. Whether apolitical, communist, fascist, or any number of shades in between, those times were close to unliveable for many people. And life for Germans in the occupied Rhineland of 1923 was dictated by the whim and grace of the French authorities.

Sometimes personal appeals were a matter of life and death, as is revealed when I started to look through the surviving dossiers of the Haute Commission Interalliée des Territoires Rhénais. Dossier 12628, for instance, documents the request of the Social Democrat Franz Michel Witsch of Neunenahr that he might be permitted to carry a firearm for self-defence. He had recently been attacked because of the work he did with the occupying regime. In another dossier, the widow and children of Graf Ulrich von Schack were demanding compensation after the count had been run over and killed by the driver of a French military vehicle in March 1923. I could not find out whether compensation was granted, but I did discover that one of the children, Adolf von Schack, would later be executed in January 1945 by the Nazis for his part in Operation Valkyrie, the failed assassination attempt on Hitler. As ever, the future cast its long, dark, reverse shadow over the year.

The HCITR held sway not just over the exceptional, but the more everyday too. And that included the humble desire to race bikes. In 1923 the Deutsche Radfahrer-Union (the national cycling federation of Germany) requested permission to organise a race from Berlin to Cologne via Hanover, all trace of which has been eradicated now from the history books, but which must have existed at some time. And simultaneously, Germany's oldest one-day race, the famous Rund um Köln (which is still being raced to this day), requested permission from the French authorities to be allowed to be organised. The race had been paused for the war and now found itself needing to be authorised by the occupying French. In 1923 a certain Fritz Fischer won. Fischer had been the best amateur rider in the 1914 edition of the race, the last edition to have been run before the war had temporarily prevented it from happening.

The Rhineland occupiers were kept busy with all this mundane, yet extraordinary bureaucracy, as tensions were running high on both sides of the border. The French and the Belgians might have been the target in the occupied territory, providing a common enemy, but in the rest of Germany, politics was splintering into violent factions. According to the press reports, in just one single 24-hour period, the day before the

Duisburg-Hochfeld bomb, on 29 June 1923, Germany counted a startling number of violent scenes the length and breadth of the country. A fight between communists and *Stahlheme* ('Steel Helmets') war veterans in Eisleben in Saxony left 22 men with stab wounds. Five more were injured in Munich, where young workers and a band of swastika-carriers clashed. An illegal Steel Helmet flag consecration ceremony was broken up by the police in Hamburg and there were pitch battles with republicans. And there were several wounded after a fight broke out between socialists and the Hitler Youth in Dramburg (now Drawsko Pomorskie in Poland).

To pour petrol onto the flames, an untethered German economy hurtled toward the very peak of hyperinflation in November 1923. At that point, at the very crest, the Reichsmark peaked out at an exchange rate of 1:4,200,000,000,000.

Yet, amid the gathering cluster of crises, the fevered state of the country's politics, and a rapidly dissolving fiscal floor, there was nevertheless still time in the German public consciousness for diversions, some of them outlandish, perhaps the result of a sudden loosening of the ties that bind, as if defeat had somehow engendered a form of liberation. The reality of the capsising Weimar Republic was fertile ground for a wave of creativity that expressed itself in countless different ways. Theatres flourished, Walter Gropius and the Bauhaus movement in Weimar were setting about remodelling their physical and spiritual universe and creating a better template for humanity. Their grand schemes were announced at a seminal exhibition in the Republic's capital city throughout the summer of 1923.

While in Berlin, the artist Käthe Kollwitz, a grieving mother to a fallen soldier in the war, was forging bleak beauty from the desperation she so keenly observed; her stark renderings of pain, dignity and anger still have the power to move us a century later.

Art was splintering into a million creative and noisy factions and hyperinflating in its own proliferation. Musical experimentation accelerated in particular across the German-speaking world, much of it delighting in challenging the norm. It was in 1923, for example, that Arnold Schoenberg published his revolutionary twelve-tone system, *Zwölftontechnik*, which broke all the accepted rules that had defined musical composition in Europe since as long as anyone knew. Ten years later, the Jewish Schoenberg, while on holiday in Paris and following Hitler's rise to power, would be forced to flee to the United States.

By 1923, Dada too had taken root in Berlin, where it found its own often angry expression. For a few Reichsmarks you could buy a ticket to one of George Grosz's shows, for example, in which his actors spent the duration of the performance simply screaming abuse at the audience. 'We were complete, pure nihilism, and our symbol was nothing, a vacuum, a hole,' wrote Grosz. 'We scorned absolutely everything, nothing was sacred to us, we spat at everything, and that was Dada.' It was the parody of a revolutionary movement, the ultimate expression of individual freedom after years in which those freedoms had been repressed by the institutions of war.

But the desire to look away from the abyss was perhaps just as strong as the urge to gaze into it. Evidence of that unspoken longing to be diverted from the present danger is to be seen in certain popular enduring vestiges of the age such as the slightly yellowed and delicate pages of *Zeitbilder* ('Pictures of the Times'). This photographic supplement was published alongside the weekend edition of the Berlin daily, *Vossische Zeitung*, and its pages tell a story of how the people of Germany, like so many across the continent, sought out diversion from the commonality of troubles which afflicted their daily lives. Normal life clings on with tenacity even through chaos, holding surprisingly firmly to the hull of sinking events until the very last second before it crashes through the waterline when it must let go. Only at the bitter end does total anarchy descend.

Flicking through its 1923 editions, you might be forgiven for thinking that Germany wasn't in crisis at all. The photographs in *Zeitbilder* pay scant attention to the gathering storm clouds in the occupied zone. Inside the magazine there is only a fascination with exotica and athleticism, two forms of contemporary escapism. There's a striking photograph of the stretched limbs of two mighty racehorses, Augias and Canelon, battling out the victory in the German Derby in front of tens of thousands of spectators in Hamburg. It's hard to believe that such massive communal celebration could exist in the midst of the worries of the age. I read up on the race and discover that the tote that day would pay out over 1,000,000,000 Reichsmarks, a colossal-sounding prize which probably didn't amount to much and would anyway have devalued dramatically overnight.

I continue turning the pages. There is a portrait of the elegantly suited Alexander von Bismarck posing in the cockpit of his ungainly glider in which he had just completed a noteworthy 9-kilometre flight in just 42 minutes. There's a lovingly reproduced selection of bronze sculptural work from Benin. Expressionist dancer Mary Wigman is photographed with her troupe of experimental dancers, posed in a field, dressed in tunics and bowed against one another, arms clasped or raised aloft in various gestures of despair and imploring. And alongside this there's an advertisement for a perfume called *Mystikum*, the 'heavy, substantial scent of the imagination'. Though its pages drip with yearning for any form of mental, spiritual or even physical escape, not everything in *Zeitbilder* could ignore the unseen forces shaping the world in all manner of obscure ways.

Life would get better in the Weimar Republic (though in 1923, of course, no one was to know that). In fact, once inflation was capped with the abolition of the Reichsmark and the introduction of the 'Rentenmark', pegged to the dollar, stability returned, and for half a decade, especially in Berlin, a kind of carefree, reckless optimism took hold, personified by the cabaret scene, and accompanied by a flourishing of the arts and sciences (the Nobel prizes of the 1920s were almost a German monopoly). By the end of the decade, though, the boom was bust. Those years of decadence were short-lived. They had only ever papered over the cracks; fissures which ran deep.

ETNA

On its front cover on 1 July 1923, the day after Beeckman's attack on the bridge and the real explosion on the train track over the Rhine, a national newspaper carried an image of the 'first pictures from the most recent eruption of Mount Etna'. It shows the figure of a Sicilian woman wearing a headscarf and dressed from head to toe in black, carrying what might be a painting or a tapestry across the stony surface of a rough bridge over a stream. Two men leaning against the parapet watch idly on, while another man seems to be rolling a barrel towards the bridge, kicking it along. Behind this scene stretches a narrow road flanked on either side by stone cottages, one of which has been entirely collapsed by a seething wall of black, smoking lava that is moving down the hillside towards the town of Fiumefreddo. I find myself poring over the fuzzy black-and-white picture, with its moving caption that declares how 'the last inhabitants were leaving the locality'. It's a scene of desolation and powerlessness, an echo of a ruined Flanders village at the other end of Europe.

In June 1923 the reality of Etna's sudden and prolonged convulsions was shockingly violent. The volcano made headlines even as far away as the distant United States. The *New York Times* reported on it in fascinated detail and horror on 18 June 1923, a week before the Tour got underway. The paper's Catania correspondent wired the following report: 'The eruption of Mount Etna, which has been going on for the last fortnight, suddenly assumed alarming proportions last night, when, after a series of loud explosions accompanied by violent shocks, a large number of new fissures appeared on the north-eastern side of the volcano, flooding the vineyards and a whole forest with molten lava . . . the inhabitants have fled in terror to the countryside.'

For 10 years, the volcano had been completely dormant. For the duration of the Great War, while fissures in the earth were being torn instead by the billions of artillery shells launched through Flandrian skies, Etna had remained unmoved. Only now, during this tense, troubled peace that had fallen like a shroud over Europe, did Etna choose to remind the populations of Europe that the ground beneath their feet could never be trusted. In 1923 the earth's crust was indeed thin. The German economy was in the process of blowing apart. While events in Sicily attracted the attention of the *Zeitbilder*, another publication, the *Berliner Börsen Zeitung*, printed a story that was much closer to home.

On 30 June 1923, the day of my film, the newspaper listed on its back page the latest figures released by the treasury. As of 20 June, the pending debt of the Weimar Republic ran to 2.5 trillion Reichsmarks. The debt had increased by over 1,000,000,000,000 Reichsmarks in the 10 days since it had last been reported. In that time period alone, Germany had paid 245,000,000,000 marks to France and spent 150,000,000,000 marks on gold to send to Belgium. That was reported on the same day that a train bound for Belgium exploded as it crossed the river Rhine. Instead of gold, it was carrying soldiers.

And yet, at the same time, offstage, out of sight, Germany's war-machine was still firing off tiny signals that it was neither cold nor entirely disabled; its cells were still capable of quiet reproduction, invisibly readying themselves for what might be to come.

Banned under the terms of the Versailles Treaty from the manufacture of aircraft in Germany, Fokker, Junckers and Zeppelin had simply relocated overseas, sneaking out of the country almost unnoticed. In Sweden, Russia, Denmark, the Netherlands, Romania, Spain and Italy, airships and aeroplanes were being designed and constructed by German engineers; even then, in 1923. France and Germany were not finished with one another, not by a long way. And Belgians still had good reason to be alarmed.

FIN

Two minutes and sixteen seconds
The only part of Théophile Beeckman that can be seen is his quartered cap, and even that only occasionally. The rest is dust. Behind the rider, a grand-looking car has appeared, just about visible. It could be that Desgrange has managed to get to the front of the race, perhaps having been held up by the congestion in the town. The race is now passing through a hamlet in which a good few dozen people have gathered. A brace of young men to the right hold newspapers. A stout man, also on the right, swivels as the race passes. He is dressed in an open white shirt and vest with a tall hat. Other men wear flat caps and a clutch of young girls have gathered on the opposite side of the road, set back a few steps towards the houses. A boy of about 10 runs in step with the passage of the race.

Beeckman is now through the dust, moving ever closer to the camera, and almost appears to be smiling. As the road levels off, he's picked up some speed, now shooting past an imposing restaurant or hotel, outside which a horse-drawn carriage and a large car are parked. A chicken darts jerkily away from all the movement and makes for the shelter of a low, scrubby thorn tree.

Still Beeckman passes isolated groups of people by the side of the road, agitated and compelled by the excitement to lean forward and try and look the lone rider in the eye. A man with a conical straw hat, a portly lady in a long black dress.
Now white and burnt-golden holes and splotches appear on the film. Beeckman turns his pedals once more, slumps minutely lower on his drops. And then the holes suddenly expand like sped-up bacterial colonies on a petri dish, the film explodes into pure white, and there's nothing more.

RUBBLE, DREAMS, UTOPIAS

The year 1923 was a watershed moment in the European story, as suggested by the German historian Daniel Schönpflug in his book *Kometenjahre*. Schönpflug describes 1923 as '*eine echte Zäsur*', a real caesura. That is to say, it is one of the moments in the twentieth century when things start to fall apart in a different way, the point of interruption or the moment of pause between two distinct movements, like a boundary between tectonic plates. Like the Vosges mountains, raised up as the Rhine *graben* sank.

On the one hand, the immediate aftermath of the Armistice was finally coming to a close, with a slow and now almost complete laying down of arms from the multiple conflicts that endured beyond

11 November 1918. But, on the other hand, it was also the starting pistol for what we now know followed. And if 1923 was the break between these two worlds, then the bright blast of the Duisburg-Hochfeld bridge bomb might just have been the break within the break, where the first world war ended and the second one began.

On stage 1 of the 1923 Tour, just six days before the bomb, six days before Beeckman's attack, the race had passed through the ruins of Montdidier, just to the south-east of Amiens in the Somme. L.C. Royer, the *envoyé spécial* of *Le Petit Parisien*, described how the organisation had placed a feeding station at the top of a climb on the outskirts of the town. Each rider had a bag with his number on it placed on a table, with ham, chocolate, bread, sugar and cheese. Jean Alavoine reportedly took more than his fair share and apparently stuffed it all into his front pocket, prompting Royer to compare him to a kangaroo. Before setting off, the men all paused briefly to take in the view. From this vantage point the riders of the Tour de France looked down on Montdidier, or what remained of it.

The town was still in a state of partial ruin, with rubble piled high by the roadside, or swept away to reveal an empty lot, an awful absence where a house once stood and a family had once lived. The battle of the Somme had levelled much of it, though the rebuilding had begun. The remaining townsfolk had turned out to see the race pass through for the fourth successive year, but a quarter of Montdidier's pre-war population was missing.

The gun metal was still cooling from the calamity of 1914–18, and Europe's blasted populations had emerged shell-shocked into a cultural and political landscape changed forever and unknowable. With life's foundations blown to bits, and its expectations ruined, any sense of geographical or political permanence must have seemed a rare and precious commodity. Consequently the very notion of the French Republic was being stirred to simmering once more; the notion of France was an exercise in magical thinking.

Henri Desgrange, who called the shots and conducted the orchestra, was himself a kind of visionary. His great race drew on the shared mythology of the eternal place in the world that France saw as its birthright. It existed before 1914. It returned after 1918. Such continuity was potent stuff as Desgrange understood very well and would continue to understand until his final Tour in charge in 1935, and until his death in 1940. He died in Nazi-occupied Paris, never knowing the final outcome. None of us ever do.

So many utopias abounded in the disparate thoughts and writings of 1923, visions of a better world, that it must have been bewildering to have been alive in the middle of them. Some ideas would go on to come terrifyingly to fruition, malformed and mutated into murderous dystopias, while others existed only in the salons of Paris and on the ink-spattered presses of Montparnasse, teeming as it was with the avant-garde.

As the writer, turned war hero, turned politician Jean Giraudoux observed in *Siegfried et le Limousin*, the streets of Paris had always simmered with international life and boundless ambition. He describes once having sat next to Trotsky in 1905, who was dining alone on salt beef in a run-down café, and no one batting an eyelid '... because nobody in the café – in this café alone, and perhaps only in this place in the world – would despair of any uncouth, poor or coarse neighbour to the point of believing that he couldn't one day become a king or a tyrant.'

Paris was a seething melting pot of inexhaustible ideas, and sometimes lunatic pretensions. The absinthe-drinking anteater-walkers were very real, and the only thing made-up about them was themselves. With theoretical physicists busily chipping away at our understanding of reality, artists were engaging in the same process, and reaching ever more bizarre conclusions which they expounded with extreme enthusiasm and even defended with their fists, if need be.

The Americans were also in town. Ernest Hemingway, having returned from the same front line that Ottavio Bottecchia had fought in, was in and out of work, in and out of restaurants and cafés, sharpening his pencil in the corner of bistros, drinking carafes of Fleurie, swallowing oysters, and expounding on the great themes of love and death with his pared-down prose. In and out too of the lives of his fellow exiled literary giants: James Joyce, Ezra Pound, Gertrude Stein and F. Scott Fitzgerald.

What a city, and what a time to be in Paris. The year 1923 perhaps saw the city at its peak, though it's had many of those I suppose. This was, for example, the year of Marc Chagall's return to Paris from Russia, and the advent of his most important work.

In my exaggerated imaginings, I see great artists, thinkers and politicians around every street corner, in the kitchen of every restaurant scrubbing dishes. And on their way home, dropping in on the velodrome to see the racing, or perhaps catch the great Georges Carpentier in action; to see the French boxing world champion lay waste to another plucky rival in the ring.

The roll call of portentous names in Paris in 1923 is almost absurd. A young Ho Chi Minh was a pot-washer, slaving away for a pittance in just such a manner, learning French, making speeches to Socialist meetings, and generally formulating the beliefs with which he would return to Vietnam to such devastating effect. He lived a life of extreme poverty, carrying a brick to work which he placed in the oven. Then he would carry it back to his room in the slums, wrapped in newspaper, to keep away the frost in his bed. From his lonely garret he would publish his thoughts in French newspapers under a bewildering number of different pseudonyms, including Nguyen Tat Thanh. A keen student of boxing, he once published, under the name Thanh, an open letter to Prime Minister Poincaré imploring him to pass a law banning anglicisms in the ring reports of the day. It seemed that, for reasons best known to himself, the communist leader-to-be of Vietnam wanted to keep French boxing vernacular French, and railed against the terms 'le knock-out' and 'le manager'.

Placed under increasingly severe police observation, having been identified as a potential political subversive, Ho Chi Minh took flight, leaving Paris by stealth in June 1923. On 13 June, by now known as Nguyen Ai Quoc, he took a bus out to the suburbs, as a decoy. Immediately, and secretly, he returned to Paris and picked up a fake Chinese passport in the name of Chen Vang. He then took a train to Berlin, thereafter boarding the *Karl Liebknecht* ship which took him from Hamburg to Petrograd, from where he travelled to Moscow in the hope of meeting Lenin, to study at the university and to cement his thinking.

It came as no surprise to me to read that Ho Chi Minh disembarked in the Soviet Union on the very morning that my film was shot; just another razor-sharp detail in the infinite complexity of 30 June 1923.

HEMINGWAY, BOTTECCHIA AND THE LOST GENERATION

Picking over the biographies of so many of the young riders of the age, I was reminded time and again of the turmoil they had somehow navigated to be at the start line. Not one rider in the 1923 Tour de France could possibly have avoided displacement, hardship, mortal danger or bereavement in their young lives. One phrase stuck with me, and I could not shake it off: 'The lost generation'. It was attributed to Gertrude Stein, and had been popularised by Ernest Hemingway, who, as noted, like Stein, was in Paris in 1923.

The year 1923 was a big one for Hemingway, one which saw the publication of his first book, *Three Stories and Ten Poems*. The poems in this slim volume are especially bleak, and are shot through with his still-recent experience of war on the Austro-Italian front in the Dolomites.

He and his then-wife Hadley were renting a little room on the Rue du Cardinal-Lemoine, and were living a hand-to-mouth existence, relying occasionally on the largesse of friends and waiting impatiently for the small payments to be wired from Canada for the newspaper reports he had been filing. In *A Moveable Feast*, Hemingway describes the many afternoons he spent around that time in Stein's famous salon, enjoying her censorious company, talking about art and putting the world to rights. She acted for a long time as some sort of matriarch in the Parisian arts scene, an authoritarian yet indulgent mentor figure not just to Hemingway, but to F. Scott Fitzgerald, Picasso, Pound and Matisse, among others. It was during one such conversation that Stein reportedly said to Hemingway, 'All of you young people who served in the war. You are a lost generation.'

Hemingway, for all his flaws, was a Renaissance man; interested in as wide a range of human activities as he could experience. He was a keen student of politics, passionately engaged in literature, but also in food, horse racing, bullfighting, boxing and deep-sea fishing. When he wasn't working, he would spend days turning an occasional profit at the race tracks of Auteuil and Enghien. And when he wasn't there, you might find him high up in the wooden stands of the Velodrome d'Hiver or the Buffalo, marvelling at the thrill of the track-racing scene; a spectacle of such wonder that he threw his arms up in defeat when attempting to describe it.

Many years later in *A Moveable Feast* he wrote that despite trying numerous times to create stories about cycle racing, he could never write one that captured anything like the experience of witnessing the real thing.

His extensive travels through Europe took him to San Sebastian and into the Basque Country, which would provide the inspiration for his first novel, *The Sun Also Rises*, published in 1926. Towards the end of the tale of debauchery and regret among the 'lost generation' of those young men and women who emerged from the war bereft of purpose, there is an encounter between Hemingway's narrator and the manager of a cycling team competing in the Tour of the Basque Country. During their conversation, the manager actually mentions Bottecchia, stating that the race would have been better had the Italian not dropped out at Pamplona.

This is an eye-catchingly precise detail in Hemingway's fiction. None of the other characters are real people; not Jake Barnes, the melancholic bankrupt anti-hero, nor the young matador Pedro Romero. But Ottavio Bottecchia is *real*; his sudden presence on the page, during the middle of Hemingway's taut, wistful prose is surprising; a true character in the midst of a psychodrama. When I read *The Sun Also Rises*, I am caught out by the realisation that Hemingway must have followed the Tour of the Basque Country to know this detail and opted to drop in the name of the great Italian rider; a pinprick of reality in an imagined world. The two are always coexistent to a lesser or greater extent, because that's how the best stories get told.

This mention anchors the genesis of Hemingway's story precisely to the summer of 1925. I check the facts by searching through the contemporary sporting press. Just two weeks had elapsed since the Italian had won the Tour de France for the second and final time in 1925. Bottecchia had started the Tour of the Basque Country in Bilbao and he crossed the finish line in Pamplona all alone and in sixth place. But that evening Bottecchia had received a telegram to his hotel recalling him to Italy, where he was contracted at the weekend to race in Padua on the track. Apologising to the race organisation, who were disappointed that their biggest attraction was deserting them, he got on a train the following morning and departed for Italy, where he would meet up with, among others, Théo Beeckman. This I found out via a typically worded report in *Sportwereld* from August 1925, which confirmed that both men were there: Beeckman, so they reported, was 'now in the Land of the Macaronis doing three track meetings with Bottecchia'.

Hemingway knew his racing and it's highly likely that the American would have paid close attention to Bottecchia's career. He might also have been aware of Bottecchia's personal history with the Dolomites. Both men, after all, had served in the same war; Bottecchia as a soldier in the Italian Army, Hemingway, five years his junior, as an ambulance driver for the Red Cross. In *A Farewell To Arms*, which Hemingway wrote based on his experiences on the front line, his clipped, sparing voice brings to life the horror – known also to Bottecchia – of being faced with the might of Austria-Hungary across the snowy, starlit peaks, even at one point by helmeted troops on bicycles.

I look again at Bottecchia's distinctive figure in my film, ploughing his lonely, unspeaking furrow on the left through the largely French peloton. According to René Lehmann's short account of the 1923 Tour de France in *La Revue de France*, Bottecchia was 'a thin, pale young man with a hooked nose', who 'rode the entire race with an obstinate passion, silently and melancholically'. If ever there was a standard-bearer for the 'lost generation', then it was probably Ottavio Bottecchia, the man in the yellow jersey in my film.

THE MYSTERY OF OTTAVIO BOTTECCHIA

In Hemingway's *A Farewell to Arms* the narrator converses with a priest in the border town of Gorizia, and talks about morale in the army among the Italian conscripts. He relates in a passage that could have been describing Ottavio Bottecchia, how being so defeated and beaten from the start meant the peasant soldiers were the most likely to succeed.

Named 'Ottavio' because he was the eighth child, born in 1894 to a peasant family in Colle Umberto, not far from Gorizia and the Slovenian border, he was never really schooled, and spent much of his childhood labouring in various ways to help the family get by. When Italy entered the First World War in 1915, both Ottavio and his younger brother Giovanni joined a unit of *Bersagliere* sharpshooters who were equipped with foldable bikes manufactured by the famous Italian bicycle brand Bianchi. Bottecchia distinguished himself in the war, three times escaping from Austrian prisoner-of-war camps. On the last of these three escapes, he got away by jumping 10 metres into a ravine and playing dead, before calmly picking himself up and somehow returning to the front line. He went on to earn the Military Valour medal for his part in the defence of the village of Lestans.

The economic hardships in the immediate aftermath of the war meant that Bottecchia was forced to seek work in France as a bricklayer, helping to reconstruct the shattered neighbouring country which would eventually provide him with his greatest successes. In 1920 he could finally begin his cycling career, already aged 25. These lost years he shared with so many other riders of the 1923 peloton.

Though a relative latecomer to the sport, he rose swiftly through the ranks and turned professional in 1922. His debut at the Tour de France came the very next year, when he was hired at the personal behest of Henri Pélissier to join the great Frenchman as a teammate. Pélissier's Automoto team was determined that this would be the year in which they would finally put an end to a series of seven successive Belgian wins. Pélissier was right of course. But he would have to wait until the Alps to stake his claim, and in the meantime he was outshone by his young Italian teammate.

Bottecchia took a victory on stage 2 into Cherbourg, on just his second day of racing at the Tour de France. Unable to speak a word of French, he searched in vain for the banner across the road bearing the word '*Traguardo*', which he was familiar with from racing in his homeland. In a front group of three riders close to the finish line, but uncertain exactly where it was, he attacked Louis Mottiat and Romain Bellenger as soon as he saw ahead of him on the road that a large crowd had gathered. Assuming that this was the finish, he launched his effort, only to find that the actual line was a further kilometre up the road, and that the crowds extended all the way down the avenue. Somehow, he held on, effectively sprinting for 1,500 metres. France, and Henri Desgrange, now knew they had a future champion at the race.

Between them, Henri Pélissier and Ottavio Bottecchia would win the next three Tours. But both men would be dead before too long; Pélissier was murdered in 1935, but Bottecchia's untimely death came eight years earlier.

In June 1927, as Bottecchia prepared to try and win the Tour de France for a third time he would meet a largely unexplained fate. History, and its recording, would only add to the confusion, as truth receded over the horizon to be replaced by improvisation, conspiracy theory and myth. The fact of the matter is that Bottecchia had returned to Italy at the beginning of June, having left France where he had been training. The Giro d'Italia was underway in his home country. On 2 June he put in a ceremonial appearance at the race as the peloton rolled out of Treviso, close to Bottecchia's family home. The following day he set out on a solo training ride on roads he knew well just north of Venice. Despite his attempts to persuade a number of other riders to join him on the ride, he headed out alone that day, telling the friend he was staying with that he would be back within three hours. But he never returned.

Instead Bottecchia was found lying at the side of the road near an orchard with a fractured skull. He was bleeding from his ears and nose when a group of passing locals picked him up and carried him to the local village. From there he was taken by wagon to hospital in Gemona del Friuli where he died 12 days later. What compounded the tragedy was that Bottecchia's death came only three weeks after a fatal accident had claimed the life of his young brother, Giovanni, on the same roads of Veneto.

This is the point at which the mysteries start to pile up. Bottecchia's life-insurance policy paid out half a million lire to his widow Caterina and their family, but did so only on the basis that the death had been accidental, which according to the coroner's report it had been. And yet, the violence of the injuries (he had also sustained some other broken bones, beside the fractured skull) seemed an unlikely outcome of a simple fall, had there been a fall at all. What allowed for further doubt was that the passers-by who had rescued him testified that his bike was still upright, standing propped up by the side of the road. Again, hardly compatible with a fall.

Still more circumstantial evidence emerged when the backstory of his brother's death had closer attention paid to it. Young Giovanni, to whom Ottavio was extremely close, had been hit and killed by the driver of a car on 23 May while out on a ride in Veneto. That car had belonged to Franco Marinotti, an influential entrepreneur and fascist politician, personally connected to the newly installed prime minister, Benito Mussolini. Il Duce, no doubt seeing his propaganda potential, had been very vocal in his admiration for Ottavio Bottecchia ever since the 1923 Tour when he had carried the yellow jersey as far as Nice. Nevertheless, in 1927 rumours circulated that Marinotti had tried to settle the matter of his brother's killing by offering Bottecchia a compensation of 100,000 lire, but that the Italian star had been insulted by the amount.

Dots were joined. Many, including the priest who administered the last rites to Bottecchia, believed and continued to hold that he had been murdered by a gang of fascists, in part to silence the family's demand for justice, but also as an act of political retribution for Bottecchia's widely publicised sympathies for the socialist cause. Nothing could ever be proved, of course, which gave rise to two further theories, both based on confessions which emerged much later. One theory involved a Mafia hit, in which hired assassins had been contracted to take out both Bottecchia brothers who had been involved in a betting syndicate. This theory came about after it was first reported to have been said by an Italian immigrant on the New York waterfront as he lay dying from stab wounds. The other unusual theory came from the lips of a local farmer whose dying confession detailed his having pelted Bottecchia with stones when he saw the rider stealing fruit from his orchard.

Those are the bare bones of this terrible story, rooted in the age, born of the troubles which swirled around the times – suffocating, lawless, and hard for us to grasp in their sense of loss and violence. Just imagine how much Ottavio Bottecchia saw of the world in his brief 32 years before his head was broken and his film was halted, years filled with the extremes of the human experience.

Now, in my film, even as he weaves between wheels on that filmed stretch somewhere on the dusty road from Lorient to Vannes, an isolated Italian, uncommunicative in the relaxed francophone peloton, he is marked out by his difference. His body rocks just a little from side to side, but far less than many more cumbersome forms around him. His hands are on the drops, as if expecting to attack, or perhaps to repel an attack from a rival. His fingers touch the brakes, just gently, as the bunch pulls up close to the rear bumper of the camera car. He eases off a little and raises his hands to sit on top of the bars, drawing his square shoulders upwards as he does so. The *maillot jaune* of the Tour de France, worn since he took control on stage 2, separated from the others, from his Automoto teammate Henri Pélissier by a few metres of road, by a language, and by upbringing. Pélissier rides wordlessly along the dirt road, parallel to the race leader, his Italian teammate who he only met for the first time some two weeks previously, when he arrived in unfamiliar Paris after a train journey from Milan. Already, on stage 3 to Brest, Bottecchia has been of service to the Frenchman. When both riders had punctured, it was the Italian who had ridden on the front, and who dragged his French team leader back into the race. His nickname in the peloton, and in the press, was 'Macaroni'. His presence in the bunch was exotic, his nationality the source of amusement and mockery, but his status nonetheless was in the ascendancy.

There is little at stake for now, and a long way to go still on this stage. The racing does not start in earnest even when Beeckman attacks before the bridge. After that, some way after Nantes, Bottecchia will temporarily lose the lead of the Tour de France when he punctures. But all this drama is still to come. In my film, they're forever on the road to Vannes, condemned never to reach it, let alone the distant Alps.

NEWS FROM BELGIUM

My research ran along twin tracks, operating at different speeds. When I read around the subject, from Bottecchia to Hemingway and Ho Chi Minh, I could plunge in at my own pace. It was exhilarating, private, entirely self-steered and in my control. But where my enquiries necessitated the cooperation of the real world, things slowed to a maddening trudge. I could not fathom why my correspondents, whom I was pressing for further information, did not engage with the same frantic energy that lit up my journey back in time. I wondered if I would ever get there.

Finally, there was news from the Beeckman family, or at least what remained of it after a succession of marriages had erased the surname. One winter afternoon, the director of the contemporary dance company forwarded on my original email to Charlotte de Lentdecker with an introduction from the director herself. I was copied into the correspondence. Three hours later, I followed it up and introduced myself to Théo Beeckman's great-granddaughter more formally:

> Hi Charlotte,
> I do hope I am talking to the correct person, and that you don't mind me contacting you out of the blue. I would so like to know if Théophile was (as I understand) your great-grandfather and share with you some of the little things I have established about his career.

Then, just after four o'clock in the afternoon that same day, I received a direct reply from Belgium, my first contact with the Beeckman family:

> Hi Ned,
> Nice to e-meet. Very interesting to see you are doing research on Théo Beeckmans [sic] and that you managed to track down his family!
> He is indeed my great-grandfather, on my mother's side.
> It would be great to read more about your research and what you have found out about his career.
> In case you have any questions for me or my family, let me know. Happy to help out if we can.
> All the best,
> Charlotte

It was, I noted straight away, only fitting that Charlotte had opted to spell his name with the rogue additional 's' on the end, thereby continuing the confusion about how exactly his name should be written into a fourth generation.

The email provided a sudden sense of alarm, generating in me a feeling that fluctuated somehow between thrill and panic. All of my research to that point had been solitary, abstract and theoretical. It had all been conducted with the same shadowy strangeness that the film itself plays out across the screen, hinting and teasing at opaque lives rather than flooding them with unambiguous light. This woman emailing me in such perfect English had suddenly elevated the project to a different level, one at which actual human relationships were still invested, and that new reality made me apprehensive.

Shortly after that exchange, Charlotte suggested that we link in her parents, Wim and Thérèse. Her mother, now in her sixties, had been born a few years after Théo's death. But Thérèse was Beeckman's sole living grandchild, and the most direct connection to the man at the centre of the film.

Now looped into the whole remaining family, and hoping that I had their attention, I composed a detailed, almost deranged-sounding account of how I'd stumbled across the footage and how, with the help of the town archives in Ninove, I'd managed to track them down. I uploaded the film to a website so that, with a password, they might be able to view it. Then I sent the email and waited to see how they might respond.

I assumed that they would be as impatient as I was. But after two days, I had heard nothing more. And then my amateur historian's ill-developed sense of deferred gratification, thin at the best of times, broke again:

Hi Charlotte, Wim and Thérèse,
I wonder if you had a chance to see the film yet?

BEECKMAN'S VOICE

I wait for more word from Belgium. I conduct an audit of what I know of Beeckman: that he was small, that he was normally quiet, that he was respected, strong, and that he grew up in modest circumstances. He won certain races, perhaps not as many as he should. He married, he had a daughter, he retired and ran a garage. He died in 1955, aged 59.

It's not much, really.

But, looking at his portrait again, and that mournful expression, I realise that his voice has lodged itself within the story. It's simply a question of getting him to use it, allowing him to talk.

THEATRE, ABSINTHE AND BICYCLES

There are pictures online of the 2011 production of 'Terra', the experimental dance performance in which Théo Beeckman's great-grandaughters, Charlotte and her sister Julie had played their part. According to the rubric, the evening promised an exploration, via the medium of dance, of 'the war for land, fertility and loneliness, danced to exhaustion', featuring 'throat singing' and 'mesmerising music by shamans'. The still images of the production look impressive: dancers forming swirling patterns against a mottled lighting state and a floor cloth painted to invoke a parched earth. I can imagine myself very clearly sitting in the comfort of the De Werf culture centre in Aalst, where it was performed, clutching a programme and enjoying the sights and sounds, warm and cossetted in the plush seats of the sparkling new glass-and-steel venue, as a Flemish winter wind whipped around the darkened streets outside.

I took strange pleasure in the fact that the daughters of the only daughter of Théophile Beeckman's only child still called this little corner of East Flanders home. And I was moved by the fact that decades of peace had allowed them to do what they did, to express themselves in dance. I wondered what their great-grandfather would have made of it all. Perhaps he'd have enjoyed it, perhaps he'd have snuck a furtive glance at his wristwatch from time to time. Perhaps he might have stormed out.

Théo Beeckman had been a month old when, in December 1896, there was a particularly riotous theatrical evening staged at the Nouveau-Théâtre on the Rue Blanche in Paris. It was a seminal night in the history of French theatre, which saw the premiere of an extraordinary, ground-breaking play called *Ubu Roi*. The shock which emanated from its first performance would change theatre forever. In fact, it closed on its opening night, and it would be a long time before it was performed again, except by puppeteers. But it is often credited with being the inspiration for what would become the Dada movement.

Ubu Roi ('King Ubu') was a musical play featuring bizarre characters with oversize bellies and great big puppet heads who acted out some convoluted story about the Russians and the Poles, haunting, revolution and murder. The first word spoken onstage was the made-up word *merdre* that sounds so like *merde* (shit) that you could perhaps conclude *Ubu Roi* was almost designed to offend. With great predictability, the evening ended in a fight among an audience that contained, among others, a mystified W.B. Yeats whose appreciation of the evening was not helped by the fact that he couldn't speak any French. From that moment on, the French language acquired a new adjective; *ubuesque* means 'ludicrous' or 'absurd'. I remember once hearing a French *directeur sportif* of a team at the Tour de France describe a futile attack by one of his riders as '*ubuesque*'. The word has made it into cycling, which would have greatly pleased the playwright.

Ubu was the product of the esoteric mind of Alfred Jarry, born in 1873, so aged 23 at the time of *Ubu Roi*'s premiere. He was also one of France's greatest ever tragic drunks. Jarry was a man whose alcohol intake was the stuff of legend and would probably have stood up comfortably to Hemingway's worst excesses: two litres of wine and three absinthes by midday, wine at lunch, more absinthe followed by brandy and spirits throughout the afternoon, aperitifs and two bottles of wine with dinner. This was according to an eyewitness account by Jarry's great friend, and protegée of Sarah Bernhardt, the novelist and fellow playwright Rachilde (Marguerite Vallette-Eymery), who was at the centre of their mutual circle of Symbolist friends. You get the feeling that everyone knew everyone, really.

Jarry was extremely short, permanently broke, and insanely, if unfathomably, creative. Apart from writing plays that almost nobody understood, he also invented an impenetrable philosophy of science which he dubbed Pataphysics. Perhaps unsurprisingly given his passion for permanent and massive inebriation, Jarry died at the age of 34 and was buried in a pauper's grave. Throughout his short, wonderful and desperate life, and despite the fact that he had a coterie of talented artistic colleagues who felt warmly towards their troubled young friend, his one constant love, apart from alcohol, was the bicycle.

Jarry (pictured above) wrote passionately if confusingly about bicycles and their place alongside humanity, or even as part of the evolving human in a sense which prefigured cyborg culture. He rode with great passion and some considerable talent, too. His own bicycle was a furiously expensive Clément Luxe 96 which he bought 10 days before *Ubu Roi*'s sole performance and just a few weeks after Beeckman's birth. The bike should have cost him 525 francs, except, having purchased it on credit from a bike shop in Laval, he only ever made two repayments of 5 francs. Upon his death in 1907, the bicycle was returned to the store by the administrators of his non-existent estate.

His beautiful Clément Luxe 96 was, he declared, his exoskeleton or exterior organ; as integrated into his biology as his brain was to other flesh-and-blood components of his human body. A bicycle represented for Jarry, and others who followed him, a brave modern future for mankind, a new understanding of what it meant to be human; new possibilities. He concocted bewildering theories about the sport, many of which involved drinking. In his treatise *Perpetual-Motion-Food*, in which he describes riders embarking on an imagined 10,000-mile race, he recommends that their diet should be based for the most part on alcohol, as it is the 'only hygienic drink'. It is not immediately clear why.

One of the happiest spells in Jarry's latter years came in the autumn of 1903 (the year of the first Tour de France) during a spell staying in the Isère mountains trying to dry out at the invitation of one of his dearest friends and colleagues. Out on daily excursions into the endless Alpine climbs, for which, strong though he was, he was not particularly well suited, he nonetheless found the state of mind to fine-tune some of his thinking about what bicycles meant to him. Sitting at the dinner table listening to Jarry expounding on his euphoric discoveries was his host, and collaborator on *Ubu Roi*, the composer Claude Terrasse (pictured below).

It was Terrasse's manor house, the 'Grand-Temps', in which they were both staying while they worked on the libretto for Jarry's adaptation of Rabelais's *Pantagruel*. The operetta was fated only to be performed, much altered in style and substance, some four years after Jarry's premature death.

Six years Jarry's senior, born in 1867, the hugely respected Terrasse was well-known and greatly admired throughout Paris's burgeoning arts scene. He was a composer of light opera, whose music filled the gilt and velvet musical theatres of the pre-war French capital and would continue to do so until his death. They made a strange duo, Jarry being very much an outsider whereas his older friend was firmly part of the establishment.

Claude Terrasse outlived Jarry by sixteen years. He died at home in Paris on 30 June 1923, the day of the film.

The following day, alongside news of stage 4 from the Tour de France, newspapers abounded with fulsome and genuine tributes to a man who had been at the heart of Paris's musical theatre for decades and had ridden the wave from the *Belle Époque* to the febrile creativity of the 1920s. 'His work,' reported *Le Petit Parisien*, 'did not prevent him from being the most obliging and affectionate of friends. In theatrical circles, where others carry with them jealousy and vanity, we never once saw him rejoice in the failure of others.'

The coincidence of Terrasse's death with the day of my film fragment brought the sad and incendiary life of Alfred Jarry into the frame. For a while I became diverted by his writing, in particular, his account of his imagined 10,000-mile bicycle race, which ends with the words, 'no one was able to recount what ever happened to the fantastic rider'.

Jarry's modernity found its expression and liberation in precisely the same way that Théo Beeckman had discovered in his young life; pumping those piston-like legs, engaging with his Sisyphean fate that every cyclist understands and which so fascinated Jarry, with his curious and creative death wish. Though I am not sure what Théo would have made of *Ubu Roi*.

IN THE DARK

THÉO:

I always hated Brest. God knows why they sent us out this far every year. Always I'd sleep badly there in rotten beds with a smell of salt and rain.

The night had been warm and, unusually, so still that I could hear every creak from every bed along the corridor where we all lay, tossing and turning in our rooms. We had eaten early, and then had gone to bed with hope, but not expectation, of deliverance from the pain and discomfort of the race, dreaming of oblivion. But sleep had stayed away. I needed to hear the wind like we got back home in Ninove to sleep, but there was none that night. It was still and noiseless.

A few restless hours later I had stood along with all the others in the pitch dark outside yet another café. We were a miserable lot, dressed in kit that had hardly dried after one day; damp still to the touch, chilly around the waist and neck. Desgrange and Desmarets were there as always standing sentinel inside, like guards. We took a coffee and a sandwich from the women at the café. We knew that they would soon be tucked up in bed once more, as soon as our sorry souls had departed. We knew also that we had 412 kilometres to ride. A race to lose, but hardly a race to win; a day to get through. The morning's slow progress towards dawn felt endless. Everything about that day had been sort of messed up even before we got towards the iron bridge. And when we got there, I don't know . . . I was ready to snap.

When we reached Landerneau, the moon appeared above the river. It was round, almost full. I think we all glanced at it as we rode silently on. There wasn't much to say. I looked around to see where Alfons was. Normally we keep each other company. He's from Ninove, too. He makes me laugh when I need it, talking shit about people back at home. They have no idea what we do when we come here to race this thing.

When Alfons and I came home together in '22, and they played music for us and we marched through the town, I had to look at the ground. Alfons didn't mind all the fuss, in fact I think he was enjoying it. He was already a bit drunk I think. But I would rather have been anywhere else. And besides, I couldn't stop worrying about my bicycle, which someone had said they'd pick up and carry home for me. Too much fuss.

The worst thing about stage 4 is the fact that it is stage 4. We still have almost a thousand kilometres before we get to the first mountains in four days' time. And that's when the race begins.

It was still dark, and I dropped back to be on my own. I don't know how I knew it. But I was about to puncture.

THE BRIDGE OVER THE VILAINE

To be honest, I'd not heard of this particular river before the film brought it to my attention, and despite the fact that over the course of covering nearly 20 Tours, I must have crossed it dozens of times without knowing it. But that was true of so much of France, away from the more obvious, identifiable 'other' landmarks I could close my eyes and imagine: like Albi, with its brick-built cathedral, Mont Ventoux, the humpbacked monster near the Rhône, or St Malo, sheltering from the watery wind behind its grey city walls. This part of the great 'hexagon' had probably slipped anonymously across the side window of our car as I gazed out at the rushing motorway embankment, wishing the kilometres away on the way perhaps to Bordeaux, or north towards the heart of Brittany.

The Vilaine rises from the fertile plain between Fougères and Laval on the border of Brittany and the Pays de Loire. From there it heads west towards the sea, switching direction, gaining in force as it picks up volume from more and more tributaries. It passes through Rennes where it meets the river Ille, funnelling the water along the embankment named after *Ubu Roi*'s creator Alfred Jarry, brushing with a past it knows nothing of.

Then, upon leaving the Breton capital, the Vilaine sets off in a more southerly direction, for a while forming the border between the neighbouring regions, before it switches west again and rushes to join the Atlantic, cutting ever deeper into the surrounding land. By La Roche-Bernard a few dozen kilometres inland from the open coast, it flows past steep, wooded banks on either side, and eventually it runs into the ocean and ceases to be a river at all.

In the nineteenth century, La Roche-Bernard grew in importance. The little town had started to blossom into a thriving dock from which goods were transferred from seafaring craft to barges for transport further upstream and on to Brittany's growing network of canals accessible from the Vilaine; and from there to Paris. These were good years for the town, which fattened at the margins into a notable point on the map.

La Roche-Bernard is at a geographical crossroads. It's where Brittany meets Les Pays de la Loire. North of this midway point lies first Morbihan and then Finistère; territory of increasingly distinct architecture, topography and culture. South of the river Vilaine is Nantes, then the Vendée, a rolling land with a low-lying coast and an introspective population still scarred from the bloody repression of peasant insurrection by the Republican Army at the end of the eighteenth century.

After that, as the race heads south, comes the gaping Amazonian mouth of the Gironde and Bordeaux. Thereafter the slow, hot, straight creep of Les Landes, with their nineteenth-century plantations of pine trees and endless straight roads, celebrated in François Mauriac's 1927 novel *Thérèse Desqueyroux*, in which the forests sigh melancholically in the hot summer wind. This artificial landscape was planted to prevent coastal erosion, throwing up huge dunes as it grew, both inland and out to sea; the very reason why some of the world's most reliable surf can be found along this coast. All the way down the Bay of Biscay, France experiences continuous drift, until, by the time you reach Bayonne in the French Basque Country, you might as well be on a different continent. The fact that the race used to run from Brest to Bayonne (a distance of almost 900 kilometres) in just two giant leaps is still hard to compute for anyone with a feel for the vastness of France.

It would have been longer still, had the bridge over the Vilaine at La Roche-Bernard not existed. The mighty steel and stone construction from the film was in fact the third bridge in a relatively short period of history to have spanned the river at that point. The first one had been a suspension bridge, opened to great fanfare in 1839. That one lasted just 13 years before an October storm blew in up the Vilaine from the Atlantic, causing the bridge to oscillate wildly, destroying the road and snapping some of the suspension cables, which fell into the river below. So, the residents of La Roche-Bernard had to make do with an old barge to get across the river for the next 10 years, until that too sank after a collision.

Working swiftly on an alternative, a wooden gangplank road was erected over the river, supported by the same stone arches on either side of it, left over from the original bridge. This very temporary arrangement endured until it too was destroyed in another storm in 1870, the same year the Franco-Prussian War broke out.

Another makeshift solution was cobbled together out of wood; a temporary bridge that was actually used by the Tour de France on its first ever passage through La Roche-Bernard in 1906, the fourth ever edition of the race. For the first time, the full extent of Brittany would be deployed as the Tour went clockwise around the hexagon, heading for distant Brest after a stage start in Nantes. This temporary structure endured until 1911 when it was removed for the construction of the steel-arch bridge seen in the film. This massive, sturdy bridge was built by Gustave Eiffel's great competitors, the architectural firm Daydé, who had also built the Grand Palais and the Alexandre III bridge in Paris. The steel-arch bridge was therefore a construction of great prestige.

None of this was of the slightest concern to the racers of the Tour de France. Yet, when Théo Beeckman attacked in the mêlée of spectators just before the bridge, he knew what he was doing. He and the bridge had history. Already in 1920 and 1922 he'd raced across it. He would have anticipated the swift descent onto the bridge. He would have known to ride on the pavement on the west side of the bridge to avoid the cobbled road surface and prepare for the 90-degree right-handed bend on the far embankment.

All in all, La Roche-Bernard would be visited annually for 22 consecutive editions, before the race organisers started routinely to skip their traditional jaunt to Brest, preferring to head inland after Nantes and cut out the wilder extent of Brittany. La Roche-Bernard returned to the route map again in 1938 and 1939, during the era when national teams rather than trade teams competed. The year 1939 was the last time that the arched bridge would ever be raced by the peloton of the Tour.

The 1939 race was held on the eve of hostilities in Europe, and boycotted by half of the nationalities, including Italy. This meant that the great Gino Bartali would not be defending his 1938 victory. Germany, for obvious enough reasons, also declined to send riders to France. The Tour was about to pause for seven years while the world fell apart again, and the great arched bridge would bear the weight of armies crossing its span from bank to bank as once more thousands of young men were sent to war.

A REST DAY AT THE SEASIDE

With the summer's evening drawing in, and the sun setting out at sea, 30 June 1923 came softly to an end. The riders of the Tour de France, having washed the dust from their hair and skin, finally bedded down in the holiday resort of Les Sables d'Olonne, some maybe falling straight to sleep, others perhaps lying awake for a while at least, replaying in their mind's eye the images of the day: the long ribbon of chalky white road that led from Brest to this seaside town.

The independent riders, the *touriste-routiers*, in a race of their own and without any team support, would only get to bed that evening at almost midnight. These hardy souls trailed in hours after the race had been won by Albert Dejonghe. Their experience of the Tour was different in so many regards to the star cyclists that they might as well have been in a wholly different event. One such unsupported *touriste-routier*, a Parisian rider called Maurice Guénot, had been spotted earlier in the day succumbing to unbearable thirst. At the sight of a herd of dairy cattle, he'd leapt off his bike, jumped into an adjacent field and, much to the surprise of the dairy maid, set about milking one of the cows, only finishing when his two bottles were full.

The next day, the notional rest day, the *touriste-routiers* were up at 6 o'clock to start work on their bikes, repairing them in time for the early start in the night. Even though, in the final analysis, their presence was of no relevance to the race's outcome, nonetheless their resourcefulness was universally admired. Perhaps because it spoke to the heart of the simple qualities of stoicism and resilience for which the Tour is still held in such regard.

The star riders had it a little easier on the rest day after stage 4. It was a Sunday. Some of them would head out for a stroll along the beach, to idle at cafés, pose for photographs, and mill around with journalists. Others might not leave their room.

I know that Théo Beeckman headed off to the beach that morning, wearing a suit and tie, his Sunday best. The sun was warm that morning, but there was a cooling offshore breeze which must have been a blessed relief; the first and probably last day of that delayed summer which he could really enjoy.

Beeckman was joined by three other riders: Marcel Huot, Arsène Alancourt and Georges Cuvelier, all Frenchmen, a detail which I found surprising to unearth since I had always assumed that Beeckman spoke only Dutch. But that was naïve of me. Ninove is very close to Brussels, and perhaps the cross-pollination of the two languages was always greater than I'd imagined. Not far from Ninove there are villages whose populations are solely French-speaking to this day. The very fact that Théo opted to spend his rest day in Les Sables d'Olonne with three French riders suggested strongly that he must at least have been competent in the language of his hosts. It is very unlikely that the French spoke any Dutch.

The four men, all dressed as if they were heading to church, decided to have a few friendly races on the beach. They sauntered over to where donkeys were being hired for tourists, and, watched by some clutches of amused holidaymakers, promptly rented four of the animals. Then, joined by the double Tour de France champion Firmin Lambot acting as the starter, and Philippe Thys filling in as the finish-line judge, the racing began. Cuvelier won the donkey race and was enthusiastically hailed as a champion by the irrepressibly cheerful Jean Alavoine, who characteristically failed to produce any actual prize money for the win. The usual ribbing about dust collecting in his wallet almost certainly ensued, much to the jollity of a small crowd which had by now gathered to watch the antics. Then the riders moved on to rent four tiny children's bikes, and promptly raced them as well, four abreast along the beach, heads tipped back in laughter, enjoying the glorious silliness of it all, playing like kids in the perfect sun. Huot took the honours in the miniature bicycle race, sprinting for the line with his back hunched over the bars and his legs jutting out at right angles. His next win at the Tour would be in the Parc des Princes on the final stage of the 1928 edition.

An observer noted that they didn't seem tired at all, at least no more than the holidaymakers splashing around in the waves. There was, after all, in the earnest figure of Théo Beeckman a frivolity which could now come to the fore after the frustrations of the previous day. Such *joie de vivre* is not often evident when he is described, but on this occasion, it was there. The laughter subsided, and the riders might eventually have drifted back to their seafront accommodation, a midsummer sun high in a blue sky. After lunch, perhaps they fell into a dreamless and restorative sleep.

A report in *Le Miroir des Sports* on the rest day in Les Sables d'Olonne

REPRISALS AND REPERCUSSIONS; AFTER THE BOMB

On the other side of the country, there was no such peace that Sunday afternoon. The aftershock of the murders on the Rhine were only just starting to be felt.

Investigators, crawling through the mangled railway carriages from which the remains of 10 soldiers had by now been removed, were establishing that the Duisburg-Hochfeld bridge bomb had been detonated by a timer device that had been placed in the toilet on board the rear carriage. That version of events was disputed in every single German newspaper, whether from the left or right of politics. In Germany, it was reported with near total uniformity that it had not been an act of sabotage, but rather the result of a gas canister accidentally exploding. The truth depended on which side of the great European schism you had been born. There was little room for ambiguity in either interpretation.

Aside from the dead, 40 soldiers and civilians had somehow survived the blast with varying degrees of injury, among them a dozen Germans caught up in the carnage. To add to the tensions, when German police were despatched to investigate the scene of the explosion, they were shot at by Belgian troops, provoking further outrage in the local population.

France looked on all this with fatalistic horror. With the bellicose conservative Poincaré setting the direction, pace and tone of foreign policy, there was not a great deal of internal dissent within French political circles. Public opinion in France was generally fully behind the penalisation of Germany and was outraged by the attack, but there was also a large constituency of the population who were simply exhausted by the constant need to threaten or be threatened. The violence of a decade had inured many to its shock of further bloodshed. Parts of the left in France were bitterly opposed to the occupation of the Rhine and its extension to the Ruhr. The socialist daily *L'Humanité* stuck to their oppositional line by suggesting that the dead had simply become 10 further victims to France's ruinous policy of waging this illegal 'War in the Ruhr'.

News of the attack had been wired in the early hours of Saturday morning to General Louis Rucquoy, the commander-in-chief of the Belgian occupying forces. The general had been woken and informed of the single biggest loss of Belgian soldiers' lives since the guns had been silenced in November 1918. By Sunday, he had started to impose his authority on the German population, taking the measures he deemed necessary to restore order in his territory.

Rucquoy, a brusque Belgian war veteran of 62 years with heavy eyes, a flat-top crew cut, and a thick, extravagantly tapered moustache, had been the Lieutenant Colonel of the 3rd Light Infantry Regiment (*chasseurs à pied*) when war broke out in 1914. Shot twice during the chaotic evacuation of Antwerp, the key battle after the fall of Liège, he then oversaw the retreat of his troops to the tiny portion of Belgium along the river Yser which they defended after the German army had swept in. His only son, Pierre, who had served in his regiment, was killed in the trenches on Boxing Day 1916 in Boezinge, in the Ypres Salient.

Just nine days after his son's death, Rucquoy had been promoted to Chief of Staff in the Belgian Army, and led his troops into the Battle of Passchendaele. Fiercely francophone, he was no natural friend of the Dutch-speaking Flemings over whom he now presided and declared that he would 'break . . . anyone who took part in this linguistic movement'. With that set of values towards his fellow Belgians, one could only guess at his attitude towards the German-speaking population now under his command.

By lunchtime on the day of the bomb attack, General Rucquoy had already contacted Brussels and received from the Belgian capital full authority to take whatever measures he deemed necessary and mete out the most severe punishments. As the hunt for the saboteurs got underway, Rucquoy placed the occupied zone into a state of total lockdown. With immediate effect, all cafés, theatres and other public buildings were to close. All trams were to cease running, all traffic was to stop. Pedestrians were not to be seen on the street from the hours of 10 o'clock at night to 5 in the morning until further notice, and no travel permits across into unoccupied Germany were to be issued. In addition, 10 notable local German individuals were to be rounded up and arrested, effectively kept as hostages until the perpetrators of the sabotage were apprehended. Germany's influential opinion formers erupted with outrage and fury.

But this violence had not come out of nowhere. Shootings and explosions were commonplace occurrences in 1923, as resistance to the French and Belgian occupation multiplied. In reprisal, the dossiers of the *Haute Commission Interalliée des Territoires Rhénais* show the extent of the measures taken against the civilian population. The previous day, six German newspapers had been ordered to close and French troops had extended their area of control by simply marching into Eschborn, Limburg and Langen. On that one day alone, hundreds of German officials and workers were expelled under suspicion of seditious activities. Over the months of occupation, a total in excess of 70,000 expulsions were enforced under the authority of the High Commission. The military court established by the French in Mainz ('Mayence', to give it its French name) was regularly handing down the most punitive sentences, including death, often on flimsy evidence.

For a few months the situation had been deteriorating steadily. The atmosphere of crackdowns and reprisals set in motion a deadly inevitability and seeded in the minds of the newly mobilising Nazis a genuine and new sense of national grievance, which rode a wave synchronous with hyperinflation in the German economy.

Six months previously in the winter of 1922/23, a young and little-known Ernest Hemingway, working out of Paris for the *Toronto Daily Star*, had crossed into the occupied Rhineland to see for himself what the reported economic collapse and associated descent into lawlessness looked like. It was a bleak column, for which he was paid 30 desperately needed francs. He wired the copy back to Canada. His words recounted his having witnessed a policeman trying to disperse a riot on the Hohenzollern bridge over the Rhine in Cologne. A rioting crowd had been vandalising the statue of Wilhelm I. Then they'd turned on a German policeman and had thrown him over the railings. The policeman managed to cling onto the stonework of the bridge. Hemingway watched what happened next. He described the horror of the scene before him whereby the policeman's fingers were chopped loose and he plunged into the current below.

GERMAN MARTYRDOM

Violence was part of the rhythm of 1923. Night after night, in the days leading up to the Duisburg-Hochfeld explosion, there had been a steady stream of reports coming out of occupied Germany that indicated a distinct heightening of the tensions. Only the day before the bomb, as the riders had been enjoying their rest day in Brest, there had been four separate incidents of shots being fired by German resistance activists at checkpoints or outside barracks. In the much smaller British-controlled zone, another bomb had gone off on a railway track in an unsuccessful attempt to derail an express train. On the same day a huge depot of coal owned by the steel giant Krupp was simply confiscated when French troops had moved in and taken control of the mighty industrial plant. In such a tense atmosphere, nerves were of course fraying. A French infantryman from the 67th Regiment accidentally fired on his captain and shot him dead. Five years of peace had led to this point.

Just a few weeks before the explosion on the Rhine, at the beginning of May, a high-profile German saboteur called Albert Leo Schlageter had been arrested, seemingly after a tip-off from an informer. Schlageter was a veteran of Passchendaele, like Pierre Rucquoy but on the other side. By 1923 he had become a major agitator in the ranks of the illegal German Freikorps, who were fighting with uncompromising methods against the communist revolutionaries in both the failed 'Kapp Putsch' of 1920 and the Silesian Uprisings in 1921. During the spring of 1923, Schlageter and his accomplices had managed to derail a number of trains in the occupied Rhineland, disrupting French and Belgian supply lines carrying coal and steel back over the borders.

In March, Schlageter had killed a German policeman in Essen who was suspected of passing on information to the French. Sometime later he dynamited a bridge near Düsseldorf. He was a prize asset when the French police finally caught up with him heading away from the bar in the hotel he was staying in late April 1923. By mid-May he had been tried, convicted and executed by firing squad. Ten years after his shooting, in 1933, Hermann Göring would organise a massive rally in his honour, attended by enormous crowds – hundreds of thousands. In death, Schlageter had become a Nazi martyr.

Nor did the immediate ramifications of his story stop there. A few days after Schlageter's execution, on 31 May 1923, a schoolteacher called Walther Kadow was dragged out of an inn in a small town in Mecklenburg, beaten, loaded onto a wagon, driven out into the woods and tortured before having his throat cut and a bullet shot through his head. His crime was that he was suspected of having betrayed Schlageter, who, incidentally, had handed over the identities of 10 of his accomplices during his trial, many of whom were also executed.

Kadow's murderers were Martin Bormann, who would become Hitler's private secretary, and Rudolf Höss, who was appointed Commandant of Auschwitz in April 1940. Höss too would be executed for his crimes, hanged from gallows specially erected by the crematorium of Auschwitz I. The tentacles of 1923's violent summer reached far into the future, as well as back into the past.

HITLER

The year 1923 would prove to be the one in which the Nazis made giant strides. Far to the south of the occupied Rhine, in Bavaria, all the grievances were being used to great effect by Adolf Hitler. Indeed, as Karl Dietrich Bracher notes in *The German Dictatorship*, 'the battle of the Ruhr gave Hitler his first great opportunity'. Now 'a "fascist wave" was sweeping Europe', moving with extreme severity and building on the radical events in Italy, Bulgaria and Turkey, where sudden and profound change had occurred, just as the Russian Civil War was reaching its bloody end in 1923. Most significantly perhaps, less than a year had passed since Kemal Atatürk's massacre of Greeks and Armenians at Smyrna, and the infamous March on Rome by Mussolini's forces. Inspired by 'il Duce', as well as the rushed ascent to power of Atatürk, who would become the first president of the new Republic of Turkey in 1923, Hitler was literally planning his own coup d'état.

Just weeks before the series of ever-escalating bloodshed in the Ruhr led to the bombing of the Duisburg-Hochfeld bridge, Hitler had addressed a crowd of 4,000 seated in the wooden stands of the Krone Circus hall in Munich with, according to Bracher, an 'aggressive, radical, rousing speech'. Rumours of a potential power grab by Hitler became ever louder, until it was more a matter of when rather than if. The cult of Nazism started to find its peculiarly visible identity among its flags, uniforms and pendants. Now for the first time swastika standards were being mass-manufactured in large numbers and distributed, such was the increased demand. Parades were organised, as well as numerous, simultaneous mass meetings in the famous Augustiner and Löwenbräu beer cellars.

The tone of the rhetoric reached fever pitch on 8 November 1923 when Hitler, accompanied by Göring, marched into a meeting of Nationalists in the Bürgerbräu Bierkeller and fired a shot at the ceiling to signal the start of the 'national revolution'. Thousands of armed Nazi militias marched on the Marienplatz in an attempt to seize power from the Bavarian government, a march that left dozens dead and Hitler wounded (he dislocated his shoulder in the struggle). The Nazi leader fled to Austria, only to be arrested in his pyjamas, to which he had affixed his Iron Cross from the Great War. It was while Hitler was in prison in 1923, awaiting his sensational trial the following year, that he began to write *Mein Kampf.*

FIRES AND MAPS

In the evenings, my family and I would gather in the living room. As winter drew in, we'd light a fire from time to time, guiltily watching the smoke rise up the chimney, imagining it dissipating over the slate roof into London's frigid night sky.

On such occasions, we'd try to avoid making one another more anxious for the future than was necessary. But the present felt like such an inviable place to be that it was a soothing relief when night fell, and the world outside our windows grew dark.

I'd watch the flames lick and curl at the back of the hearth and think about the day's discoveries I had made. Often, I bit my tongue, fighting the impulse to open up and talk, perhaps until the fire went out, about Germany in 1923. Instead, I'd turn my gaze to the colossal map that hangs on our living-room wall, a gift from our neighbours many years ago. Printed on heavy material, it is a leftover from a West German schoolroom of the 1950s. It depicts the patchwork of tiny duchies, kingdoms and city states that made up the insane complexity of the Holy Roman Empire in the seventeenth century, long before Germany was any more than a vague notion. Long before Hitler.

I had spent three or four years living in Germany as a young man, floundering around in Hamburg at the time of reunification, after the fall of the Berlin Wall. Back then, agog at the fast-moving present, I had neglected to consider the past; how the new nation had arisen from this intricate pattern of tiny fiefdoms to become the central power at the heart of western Europe. I started to think that history should always be taught in reverse. It should start in the present tense. This is where we are now . . . but how did we arrive here?

We switch the news on. One of the cats slinks out of the room.

THE PYRENEES AND THE DEATH OF DADA

We leap forward to stage 7. It's now 6 July 1923. After holding a southwards trajectory along the western coast of France, the Tour had reached Luchon in the Pyrenees.

Beeckman has been dropped and has fallen out of contention. Jean Alavoine is at the same time close to the top of the Col de Peyresourde in the Pyrenees. It is the fifth massive mountain he has been over that day. He gets to the top of the Peyresourde and then flies 'towards Luchon on that terrible descent' according to L.C. Royer, 'at a speed which is almost miraculous'.

It was the same descent that many years later Chris Froome had used to launch an attack that would effectively win the 2016 Tour de France. On that occasion, Froome had been racing for just under five hours. In 1923 Alavoine had been racing for just over 16 hours when he won the stage into Luchon for the second year in succession. He'd set off from Bayonne at 2 o'clock in the morning. He finished the brutal race in the early evening. It was now 18.05 in both Luchon and Paris.

At the Théâtre Michel in Paris, dancers would have been clambering into their unwieldy costumes. Man Ray might have been trying to thread his film into the projector. The crowd would soon be there. In

Paris, just as in Luchon, human beings were living their extraordinary lives. That day the race would finish an hour or two before the curtain went up on another theatrical performance in Paris. The chaotic evening that followed would come to be recognised as the last act of Dadaism, a movement which traced its origins back to the scandalous premiere of *Ubu Roi*, performed 27 years previously. As with Alfred Jarry's controversial premiere, this evening, too, was destined to end in a punch-up between furious artists of the avant-garde.

The bizarre evening's entertainment was the brainchild of the Parisian ex-Romanian Dadaist playwright Tristan Tzara whose play *Le Coeur à Gaz* ('The Gas Heart') featured six characters, all of whom were representative of parts of the human anatomy: Nose, Ear, Mouth, Neck, Eyebrow and Eye. These characters talked in non-sequiturs for an hour or so before the piece ended with a curious ballet. The play's second-ever staging was part of a whole evening of Dadaist art called *Le Coeur à Barbe* ('The Bearded Heart') and was hosted at the Théâtre Michel in the 8th arrondissement, in the heart of Baron Haussmann's Paris. It must have been an amazing evening to attend.

Overreaching perhaps, the ever-ambitious Tzara had also pre-announced that the American artist Man Ray would be premiering a new film that evening. He made the bold proclamation despite the fact that no such film existed and that Man Ray had never actually made a film in his entire life. Undaunted by such a glaring absence in his CV, Man Ray set about creating *Retour à la Raison* ('Return to Reason'), a silent film (by happy coincidence an almost identical length to my silent fragment from the 1923 Tour) in which a sequence of patterns and light textures play out on the screen, before ending on a close-up of the naked torso and breasts of Man Ray's (and almost every Parisian artist's) muse, Kiki of Montparnasse, otherwise known as Alice Prin. Nowadays the film is considered a triumph, of sorts. But back then, it was less fulsomely appreciated.

The evening did not go well. For a start, the projector broke twice, and, when it was up and running, Man Ray's landmark film was roundly booed. After the film, things descended into total chaos, as the writer André Breton stormed in a fury onto the stage during the closing ballet sequence of *Le Coeur à Gaz* and started to chase the dancers around, beating them with a stick, and in the process breaking a poet's arm.

The police were called, probably by now weary of having to break up violent Parisian aesthetes who disagreed about the nature of symbolism and reality. Breton flounced off to co-found Surrealism and do very nicely for himself by teaming up with Salvador Dalí. Tzara's Dada movement however was falling apart. Eventually, he'd go on to play a considerable and brave role in the French Resistance in Vichy France, but for now his war of words was over. Man Ray, born Emmanuel Radnitzky, was just hitting his stride. His remarkable legacy as a photographer would endure until his death at the age of 86 in 1976 and far beyond. He only left Paris under duress in 1940 and returned in 1951. All that history to be written was unknown to both men as they prepared to welcome the elite of Paris's vibrant art scene to their soirée.

And earlier that day, in occupied Germany, a resistance fighter had shot a Belgian soldier on the streets of Duisburg. The German's actions were roundly praised by Adolf Hitler. That gunshot in the Ruhr might have been inaudible in the Pyrenees, and been totally ignored by the surrealists of Paris, but that didn't stop it from ending another life.

IN THE DUST

THÉO

The sun came up just after Quimper, and the mist started to clear, thank God. It was the same scene as every year, the same as every day on the race: with the sunrise comes a change of heart. I could tell as that giant oaf Desmarets shot his arm out and set us off on our calvary once more that the French would start again to joke around and shout at us in their half-joking, half-threatening way.

On the road to Vannes, one of those film cameras drove ahead of us for a while as we rolled along. All the French riders charged to the front waving their arms and horsing around. I just wanted the camera car gone. It was kicking still more dust in our faces, as if we hadn't had enough of it already. I tried to avoid riding near either of the Pélissier brothers: Francis, I didn't like. Hénri, I didn't really trust. Even Alavoine, for all the constant drivel that came out of his mouth, would leave you for dead in a ditch if he could. I kept my eyes on the road, sometimes riding alongside Bottecchia. He was quiet, and I can't speak Italian.

But, God, Brittany. Nothing but stone roads and fields. I didn't know where we were, really. Does it matter? If the race had disappeared, if all the riders around me had suddenly vanished and all the cars in the convoy had driven over the shimmering horizon and left me all alone, I would have been lost for days on end. I'm sure of that.

I remembered that bridge, though, with its high riverbanks on either side and its thundering steel arches casting its cool shadow over the road and I tried to think how much further it might be along this endless rutted road, before we crossed it and struggled up the other side of the bridge and into that little town with the big name. I forget it.

Sometimes a glimpse of the sea, and then fields full of . . . God knows. At home you can see what it is that they are growing, the cabbages plump and unmistakable, the potatoes tall already in June, by which time some of the worry would be over that they might not make a crop. The sugar beet, stacked up in big piles before winter sweeps in, getting soaked in the autumn rain. The farmers were always bitching about something or other. I tried to stay out of their way, to be honest, especially out to the west, where they really had nothing.

But here? I wasn't so sure what the green little things in the arid fields were all about, and I didn't really care. The dust was all I cared about. I couldn't think of anything else for days on end.

Sometimes we'd read about the dust in the papers. I mean, the others would read aloud, hesitating over words they couldn't understand, which were a lot. I think sometimes they made up the stories they pretended to translate. Other times some French journalist would call me by my name, ask me over and offer to buy me a beer, but I normally refused. I never knew what to say and they didn't seem to know what to ask me. So that was okay. But the other boys would always talk to them, and knew them by name. Then they'd read what had been written, picking things out for me, and laughing. Always the writers were complaining about the dust. As if they could possibly know the dust like we knew it.

And then I punctured, yet again. That familiar sudden feeling of riding with an invisible hand tugging you back. I felt once more the slow, then sudden dread of being deserted on the open road. I fell back from the race, cursing that no one had noticed me drop away. I would have to chase back on and it was going to hurt.

As I came to a halt, I dismounted, dropped my bike to the ground and stood all alone for a second or two, hearing nothing but the insects in the fields, and the blood in my veins.

I don't think a single thought passed through my head.

THE NEARLY MAN OF 1923, 'GARS JEAN'

I spend long hours spooling back and forth on the film looking at one rider in particular. The longer it goes on, the more I start to get a hunch that I know who he is. The facial expressions, bike configuration, clothing, the body shape of the man. In the film he is the one who waves at the camera on the road to Vannes, and who appears to be having fun.

I move his digital shape onward, using the arrow button on my keyboard. Frame by isolated frame, the rider judders forward. But it's an infuriating distortion; the individual images are maddeningly indistinct, and only make their partial and limited sense when joined together and moving at real speed. Sometimes his hand is clear, as it grips the bar, or the light catches one of his bidons. A foot comes into focus as the pedal stroke revolves, or the tip of his nose, as it emerges from the dark shadow cast by the brim of his casquette. He removes his goggles, raises a hand, sits back and smiles. I shuttle back. He frowns, sits forward, his hand drops back, he replaces the goggles so that they cover his eyes once again and mask his identity. The harder you try to see him clearly, the more he seems to emerge from the sepia fug of a century past.

He seemed to separate himself from the mass of others, to come forward in his individuality and almost demand to be known, which is, in the end, what I think happened.

My suspicions that I knew who he might be were first piqued by reading Albert Londres in *Les Forçats de la Route*. Londres has a light narrative style, full of humour and wry implications. His sentences, a bit like his fellow Parisian, Ernest Hemingway, are short and clipped (though with a good deal more humour). Each single observation is hardly elaborated before the next one supersedes it. The dialogue flows in a similar vein: staccato, unevolved, sparing.

And often it's the voice of Jean Alavoine which is being transcribed by Londres; a voice to which the correspondent of the *Petit Parisien* seems particularly drawn. In fact, Alavoine acts almost as Londres' muse, performing a constant choric refrain of wit and sarcasm throughout the short account. Later, Londres would half-jokingly suggest that Alavoine be nominated for the Académie Française.

Small wonder, he was so highly thought of. Alavoine had already captivated the nation in 1922 and would again in 1923. By 1924, Londres was writing about a man, in Jean Alavoine, who had been elevated to something close to national-treasure status. Ever present at the Tour since his debut on the race as French National Champion in 1909, his big, slightly ungainly presence had been a touchstone of the race. Supporting the great Luxembourg champion François Faber, Alavoine would sometimes end up spooking his team leader by demonstrating just how strong he was, eclipsing him on occasion. He won two stages on his debut in 1909, including the final one into Paris, and finished third on GC (General Classification). He would go on to win 17 stages in a total of 11 Tours and over a 14-year period; a winning time span that even Mark Cavendish might be proud of.

Alavoine was born in 1888 into a working-class family on the outskirts of Paris, near Versailles. Perhaps fittingly, his unplanned birth came about while his mother was in Roubaix; then, as now, one of western Europe's most economically deprived towns, and soon to be the finish line for perhaps the most famous and gruelling one-day race in the world. From a very young age Alavoine only had eyes for racing bikes. As a journalist from the socialist daily *Le Populaire* would characterise his childhood, 'charms and works of art did not detain him for long'. Employed as an apprentice mechanic for the all-conquering Alcyon brand, he soon found himself racing in their famous sky-blue colours. By the age of 15 he had started to compete against the best. That was in 1903, the year the Tour de France came into existence.

During those pre-war years, he established himself as something of a marauding rouleur-cum-sprinter; ever willing, always smiling, more often than not on the attack. A larger-than-life presence at the best of times, he was seldom to be found *not* talking to someone or other about something or other. His roommate and teammate-to-be Honoré Barthélemy would recall how 'you'd often see him riding alongside Desgrange's car and telling the boss "I've punctured five times!" He was a great guy, but he did exaggerate a little.'

Then came the war, during which Alavoine served as an aviator and made it through. His brother Henri, also a professional racer, was not so lucky. He was killed in July 1916, when his aeroplane crashed close to Pau, near the foothills of the Pyrenees.

In 1922 Alavoine won stage 5 into Bayonne. After that, he went on to take the first mountain stage to Luchon and the next to Perpignan; a hat-trick of victories which enabled him finally to prise the *maillot jaune* from the shoulders of the great Eugène Christophe, France's main hope. However, it was not the decisive move on General Classification that year. In the end, neither Frenchman had been able to prevent yet another 'bulldog' Belgian winning, this time Firmin Lambot, repeating his success of 1919. But Alavoine finished second into Paris in 1922, a lone French tricolour by his name in the record books, surrounded by the black, yellow and red of Belgian riders.

The following summer of 1923 hopes ran high for the big-hearted rider from Versailles. *Le Populaire* declared him to be 'more than capable of taking first place and winning the "Derby of the Road" [an unusual nickname for the Tour de France]'. With a hundred years of hindsight, it seems to me now that Jean Alavoine should have won the 1923 Tour de France outright. He was dominant on three-quarters of all the bona fide mountain stages. The man from Versailles might well have got to Paris first, ahead of Henri Pélissier, had he not crashed in the Alps.

His race had started so well: after they rode away from Bayonne on stage 6 into the Pyrenees, he set off in pursuit of glory there, just as he had in the previous year. Near the top of the last of three huge climbs, the Col de Peyresourde, he was closing on the lone leader Robert Jacquinot. Jacquinot was Alavoine's teammate, a rider who will perhaps best be remembered as the subject of a remarkable photographic portrait which has become a totem for the privations of the early Tours de France.

In the much-fetishised black-and-white image, Jacquinot is seen spooning soup into his mouth in a dingy cottage kitchen, his mud-caked legs folded and his bike propped against the table, and a curious, comical onlooker poking his head through a window behind him. Jacquinot was also a renowned sprinter who had won stage 1 and the interminable slog of stage 5 already, and had attacked with a foolhardy sense of adventure on the hardest mountain day, hoping somehow to snatch back the yellow jersey he'd worn on stage 2.

But Jean Alavoine was by now something of a transformed rider. He had become a specialist climber with reserves of endurance that were only just beginning to be tapped. He pegged Jacquinot back metre for metre, hairpin for hairpin. Near the top of the endless Peyresourde, Alavoine drew level with Jacquinot who had collapsed into a ditch through exhaustion. Accounts of the exchange that ensued between the two men vary according to which newspaper you read, or which homespun website's additional distortions you choose to believe. But it seems clear that, as Alavoine passed his stricken teammate, the good-natured rider enquired after his friend's well-being.

'*Alors, quoi, Robert, ça va pas?*' was how one chronicler recounted Alavoine's question. To which Robert Jacquinot raised his cap in greeting and told his friend that it wasn't his day. '*Je te salue, gars Jean!*' 'Gars Jean' was Alavoine's affectionate and widely used nickname. It best translates as 'Johnny Boy'.

Another version of Jacquinot's famously valiant reply comes from the vibrant pen of *L'Auto*'s chief correspondent in 1923, Henri Decoin. He claims that, as Jacquinot lay exhausted in the ditch and watched Alavoine pass, he called out, '*Jean, je me découvre devant toi!*' This is a tantalisingly ambiguous phrase that could mean a number of different things from 'I discover myself in front of you' or even 'I am unmasked in front of you'. Either way, Alavoine won the stage (Jacquinot regaining his equilibrium to finish a creditable second). Before most of the other riders had finished, Alavoine was spotted parading outside his hotel in the elegant spa town of Luchon having already washed, shaved, and carefully coiffured his foppish locks, treating them to enough hair oil to be worn in the style '*of an Argentine dancer*'.

Jean Alavoine

Then he won the next stage to Perpignan. After a flat transitional stage, they reached the Alps and Alavoine duly won again; a third success already that year! But on stage 10 on 12 July he came unstuck. It was the stage to Briançon which saw Henri Pélissier ruthlessly exploit Ottavio Bottecchia's lack of experience to take the race lead. In second place on General Classification, descending from the Col d'Izoard, 'Gars Jean' crashed and injured his arm. Though he clung on to fifth place on the stage, he lost nearly half an hour to Pélissier, and with that any realistic chance of winning the Tour. Decoin, the ghoul, was on hand to report on his misery.

'*He cries, "gars Jean"!*' writes the creative reporter on the pages of *L'Auto*. '*Not because of any pain. He cries because it is all over! He cries because his hopes have been dashed on the cruel and soulless road. "I'll never win a Tour, now!"*'

Decoin was correct. Already 35 years old, Jean Alavoine had enough self-awareness to realise that his moment of great opportunity had flickered and gone out. A few days later, he put in an appearance at the Parc des Princes to cheer home Henri Pélissier. When Alavoine was introduced to the crowd, he was treated to an ovation almost as great as that which accompanied the arrival of the final stage winner, Félix Goethals.

He was at the start line of the Tour de France for the last time in 1924. A crowd of children spotted him on stage 1 in Amiens as the peloton rode past. '*Vas-y, Gars Jean!*' they called out, according to Albert Londres. By Le Havre, the bad luck that plagued Alavoine was back once more (as perhaps was that famous penchant for exaggeration) 'I've punctured five times!' he was heard to cry, not for the first time.

On stage 4, a year on from the last time he raced from Brest to Les Sables d'Olonne, he complains bitterly as the peloton takes on the road to Vannes. It is the same stretch of road on which, 12 months previously, he is seen to be horsing around for the camera in my film, waving it away. In 1924, the weather is by all accounts similar to that in 1923, dry but hotter still. As the sun starts to work its way up in the sky and they ride south-east, it starts to blind them. 'No way of riding with the good Lord's button right in your eye!' quips Alavoine to Londres. The famous journalist has something of a keen ear for the aphorisms of 'Gars Jean'.

On reaching the feed zone at Vannes, the riders fall on the food bags like wild animals, prompting a commissaire to tell them all to calm down. 'You've got three minutes!' he reminds them.

'It's not that I'm in a hurry,' replies Alavoine. 'It's just that my masseur is waiting for me two hundred kilometres away to push my heart back into place.'

A bit further down the road, he wipes the dust from his eyes and says to Londres, 'I think my mother-in-law has been out powdering the road, today!'

'Is it hard?' asks Londres.

'It's hard for us, but it'll amuse your readers . . .' replies Alavoine.

'Always,' writes Londres, and 'as to who cracks the jokes more and more, it's obviously Alavoine'.

On the first day in the Pyrenees in 1924, which had for the last two years belonged exclusively to him, 'Gars Jean' launches a violent attack, riding off the front and into the virtual race lead, before Ottavio Bottecchia reels him in en route to a stage win and to overall victory.

'When I'm going well, my tyres burst,' he complains. 'And when my tyres don't puncture, it's me instead who bursts!'

'For the first time in the race,' writes Albert Londres, 'I noticed that he was wearing the number 13.'

Londres' celebrated account of the 1924 race, which was to be Alavoine's final Tour, ends with a quote from the man who had ridden to 17 stage wins yet never tasted overall victory. As the riders approach the finish line in the Parc des Princes, where Ottavio Bottecchia for the first time in his career is about to claim the win, 'Alavoine lets his head drop and does not look up.'

'Yes, it's sad indeed,' he tells Londres, 'after fifteen years of conscientious graft, to unhitch from the train, like an old goat, in the dust of the victor.'

The words may have been embellished, but the sentiment certainly seems perfectly expressed in summary of a man who had come to the end of the only journey he'd ever really known. I look back for the umpteenth time on the figure on the bike in the dust of the road to Vannes, his hand drifting upwards and waving as his features break into a smile. I press pause on the clearest frame, as I have so often done. It's at exactly 1:09:11 in the film's timecode along the bottom of the screen. He sits back on his saddle, left hand on the bars, right arm on its way up. He is looking directly into the camera, breaking the fourth wall, and grinning.

On another screen, I call up the images which I have used dozens of times to establish Jean Alavoine's identity for sure. There are precious few of them: a portrait or two, a few posed shots on track bikes, a blurry newspaper picture of Alavoine surrounded by dignitaries at the end of some race or other. And, the key photograph from 1923: a dramatically composed shot of Alavoine attacking in the Pyrenees, looking ahead as he passes through a switchback, with the *maillot jaune*, Ottavio Bottecchia, straining his every sinew on his heels.

This last time, but now with a degree of certainty, I cross-reference the details which create the match: the pattern on his socks, the length of his shorts, the hunch of his shoulders and musculature of his biceps, the shape of his head. And his big left hand, how it grips the bars with enlarged knuckles on his index finger. This is Gars Jean, I am sure of it. Somehow, I know.

PARIS, 1943

A jump forward in time, something this journey often asks of me. The first stopping-off point is once again the 20-year leap which lands me firmly in Nazi-occupied Paris of 1943. Jean Alavoine has long since retired; in fact, he's 55 now.

For the second time in its short history, the Tour de France has been suspended for the war years, Henri Desgrange having died in 1940 shortly after Paris fell. His successor, Jacques Goddet, argued that the Tour should continue, under the notion that sport should remain neutral, and the German occupiers as well as the Vichy government wanted the race and its accompanying outward semblance of normality to prevail. A deeply compromised and curtailed parody of the Tour, in which a mere 69 riders participated, was held in the autumn of 1942; the Circuit de France. But it didn't return in 1943. Instead, the Tour de France modestly celebrated its 40th anniversary with a ceremony to coincide with the Grand Prix de Paris bicycle race. Jean Alavoine, among other founding figures from its already long past, was invited as a guest of honour, posing for a picture with Maurice Ville (the third of the 'mutineers', along with the Pélissier brothers, from 1924). But a couple of weeks later, in July 1943, Alavoine was dead.

Typically enough, for a man whose passion for the sport never left him, his demise involved a bicycle race. Competing in a veterans' criterium in Sannois, to the north-west of Paris, he collapsed in the middle of the race, was rushed to Argenteuil hospital where he died shortly after from a brain aneurysm. Deeply Protestant, Alavoine's funeral was held at a church near his adopted home in Versailles, and was attended by Francis Pélissier, among a host of others; Alavoine's evident popularity left a deep impression upon his widow. Less than two weeks after his death, a 100-kilometre race was run off in his honour: the Grand Prix Jean Alavoine. He was subsequently laid to rest in Roubaix.

Alavoine always believed, according to his own partially recorded legend, that a 'good smile' was your 'best defence against weakness'. And still he smiles from the screen of my laptop. An innocent face, whose passage through the race and across the unmade roads of France was often troubled, but whose loyalty not so much to his country, but to the self-destructive ritual act of racing a bike, made any other kind of life unimaginable, and ultimately unliveable.

I hunt for a sign, a digital arrow pointing out the location of his grave in Roubaix, as I'd like one day to visit it on my way to or from Belgium. But I find no trace and start to doubt that he's even buried there. His is a life that is clinging onto history by the fingertips. I fear that Théo Beeckman's life fell long ago into the void and can only be glimpsed weakly signalling.

HOLDING HANDS AT THE GRAVESIDE

The winter of 2020 brought further upset. What might have promised a Christmas in which families could once again share time and space together proved to be the opposite. The world pulled apart again. Because of a new and more infectious strain of Covid-19 which had first been identified in England, President Macron of France, himself suffering from infection, had closed his borders to the British. Taking his lead, the rest of the European Union, from which the United Kingdom was finally negotiating to take its definitive leave, followed suit.

Britain had been effectively placed in quarantine, quite cut off from the continent. It was a desolate, drawn-out moment, perfectly matched by the dark, wet winter weather which had been sweeping over the islands for days. It was some time during those weeks of quiet reading that I stumbled across a line from Jean Giraudoux's *Siegfried et le Limousin*:

> *Like all French people, for fear of water, my thoughts lean voluntarily in towards the continent.*

The words of the narrator serve as a reminder to me that France has always looked to its eastern margin for its destiny and sense of self, not across the water to Britain. Napoleon, though born on an island, once he had his feet on continental soil, always sought to march his armies east, setting in train the domino effect of defeat and reprisal which would define France and Germany's mutual loathing for a hundred years and more. The French nationalist soul gazed away from the water's edge. It looked to the distant centre inland, far from the bridge over the Vilaine, or the Café Gloux in Lorient with its bustling waitresses and patiently attentive crowds. The hidden forces which were prising the pieces in the film apart lay a long way from the Tour, but still exerted a pull. Eventually, over a week later, the riders would reach the generationally disputed land of Alsace-Lorraine, drawn there by the tug of history and the strength of feeling.

In the film, in Brittany, the peloton can still smile and wave at the camera as it rolls along the dusty coastal road between Lorient and Vannes. It is made up of the flags of half a dozen nation states that have emerged blinking into the sunshine of a ravaged landscape. But there are no German riders at all, no Austrians, no Dutch. The peloton is a one-eyed misrepresentation of a still bellicose continent. Between them, the riders come from no further east than the central slice of Europe, from the mouth of the Rhine to the Alps and Piedmont.

Perhaps if there had been a clear mountain range running down the spine of the continent, this difficulty might never have existed. But there isn't, so the historical and legal ambiguities of ownership and birthright in these disputed lands have always had space to multiply and replicate. This difficult central portion of the continent, either side of a jagged and variable line running from Belgium downwards like an unpeeling zip, was ceded to Lothair I under the terms of the Treaty of Verdun in 843, sowing the seeds of the almighty destruction that would be visited upon that very city over a thousand years later, by which time ballistics had been invented, industrialised and merged with medieval siege tactics to create the killing fields of the Great War. It was at the battle of Verdun that the German General Erich von Falkenhayn promised to 'bleed France white'; an unholy aim in which he very nearly succeeded.

Years previously, I had read in Simon Winder's brilliant account of central western Europe, *Lotharingia*, how this central belt had come to be. My dim remembrance of his argument went something like this: After Charlemagne's death in 814, western Europe was split into three massively unequal chunks. 'West Francia' (for simplicity's sake, France) was the inheritance of Charles the Bald. 'East Francia' (Germany, in a way) went to Louis the German. And 'Middle Francia' (the bit in the middle into which Alsace-Lorraine can be placed) fell to Lothair I.

Broadly speaking, western Europe remained thus divided in myriad complicated ways, its fractured soul somehow surviving the attentions of the Ottoman empire, until Napoleon decided he wanted everything for 'West Francia', and the blood-soaked, decade-sized dominos started to tumble on top of one another, first in one direction, then in its opposite.

I'm seized by a sudden memory. A black-and-white photograph fills my computer screen. Rather than coming from a time which pre-dates my experience and exists only in my imagination, this is a part of my personal recollection. One day it was printed in a Sunday paper, all across the front page. The paper was spread out on the dining-room table, where my mum and dad would tend to read it with a mug of tea, or a cup of coffee.

I was 14, maybe 15. Even at the time, I'd been struck by the gesture, though its profound significance eluded me entirely. Helmut Kohl, tall, broad-shouldered, grey. And François Mitterrand, gaunt, severe, and already hiding the cancer that would eventually kill him. The two men are holding hands, but at such a distance that they have to reach across the gap between them. They face two military wreaths, and a coffin over which is symbolically draped a West German flag and a French tricolour. Behind that, the towering edifice of the Douaumont Ossuary. It's 1984.

Perhaps it took these two men to hold hands for the bigger picture of peace and prosperity to act as a final balm to the sting of wounded pride on either side of the Maginot Line. Whenever the race passes nearby on the modern Tour de France, we are served up aerial shots of Douaumont and reminded that each nation has its own traumas.

MERCURY RISING

As the 1923 Tour ground on, rattling over the stony paths cut into the Pyrenees and dropping down again into the flat plains of the Camargue, so a typical *canicule*, a July heatwave, started to build. After three or four days of inexorably rising temperatures, the humidity and the strength of the high summer sun became so oppressive that the heat started to make headlines of its own, printed alongside the grave news of the day, and the many personal tragedies that unfolded on 8 July 1923. Across the nation, as often happens during the hottest, maddening days of summer, strange and ugly accidents abounded. All this, on one day alone:

*In Argenteuil, a four-year-old boy was killed as he played outside his grandmother's house. A car was driven over him, fracturing his skull.

*In Le Havre, a military biplane took off, caught fire and then exploded, incinerating its pilot.

*In Montoire, in the Loir, a salesman emptied five bullets from a revolver into his father, killing him instantly.

*In Nantes, a lady called Christine Bacante stepped off a train from Paris and into a waiting taxi. No sooner had she sat down than she pulled from her purse a pistol and shot herself twice in the stomach. The motive for her suicide was never established.

*At a concert hall in Dijon, there were multiple injuries when a section of a glass dome dropped 12 metres into the orchestra pit. A worker had been trying to open a panel to allow some ventilation on a stifling evening.

*In the Boulevard Barbès near Montmartre in Paris a public meeting was held to debate the 'Occupation of the Ruhr in the light of public opinion'.

*And in Brussels, a delegation of bereaved relatives of the dead soldiers from the Duisburg-Hochfeld bridge train bomb petitioned King Albert I of Belgium, demanding that the young Belgian conscripts in the Ruhr be protected from the 'implacable hatred of an enemy who has yet to be convinced of his own defeat'.

And all the while, the heatwave held sway. By this given day, 8 July, it had truly started to become unbearable, and nowhere was it worse than in the south of the country, where the race had just arrived.

The Tour set out that day from Perpignan, heading for distant Toulon, along flat roads fringed with fields singing with cicadas. The peloton, many of whom knew this stage from previous editions and all of whom were struggling after two hard days in the mountains, appeared to sign off on an unspoken pact to take the day off, in terms of racing. Besides, in the battle for the General Classification, the featureless route of stage 8 did not present an opportunity to strike.

They reached Saint-Martin-de-Grau, passed through the little town, and hit the straight road towards Salon-de-Provence, with the sun now *'beating down on their skulls like a blacksmith working on a red-hot iron.'* according to Henri Decoin, writing for *L'Auto*. As they approached the next waypoint, thoughts turned to what many riders in the bunch knew they would encounter in the centre of Salon: a series of refreshing water fountains, including the famous Fontaine Moussue, or 'mossy fountain'. Once in Salon, riders leapt off their bikes and plunged their burning legs and feet into the cool waters, filling water bottles and cascading their chilled contents over their heads. Every rider, that is, save for one: the Belgian Lucien Buysse.

Seizing his moment, and risking dehydration, Buysse eschewed the opportunity to fill the two bidons held in bottle cages across his handlebars. Without stopping, he stamped on the pedals and attacked the peloton of the Tour de France as they flopped around in the water. Before they knew what had happened, he had gone. By Aix, he'd built up a lead of 7½ minutes. At La Ciotat, he led them by 13 minutes, and at the finish line he won the stage by more than 15 minutes. What made this victory still more impressive was that barely two days previously, after suffering like a dog in the Pyrenees, Buysse had talked about abandoning the race. His young compatriot, Théo Beeckman, finished stage 8 in 15th place, in a group of four riders including Jean Alavoine. But, in one fell swoop, Buysse had moved himself up to 14th place in the General Classification, now four minutes behind Beeckman in 13th place. It was the first of Buysse's total of five career stage wins at the Tour.

The following year, Buysse would be employed solely in the service of Ottavio Bottecchia, partly on the strength of what the Italian had seen of him on that hot day into Toulon. By riding with Bottecchia on his wheel in 1924, Buysse thereby became by common consent the first unambiguous 'domestique' in Tour de France history. But two years later, in 1926, he won the race outright.

His fleshy features, sad eyes and hangdog expression endure in a sequence of photographic portraits of the age and testify to the endless suffering of the riders. There are few shots that I could find of him winning and smiling, save for one, from the year of his overall victory in 1926, in which he is brandishing a champagne glass and grinning with absolute delight. Buysse got further than Beeckman in his career, and it started that day when the race passed through Salon.

He would live far longer than Beeckman, too, only dying in 1980, at the age of 87.

THE TOUR DE FRANCE BEFORE THE TOUR DE FRANCE

Long before the Tour de France had been dreamt up, a bestselling writer, a philosopher's widow, had imagined an even greater journey, one which would never end. In her way, she had been one of the most influential writers of, and in, French history. Augustine Tuillerie was 89 years old when she died on 8 July, the same day the race reached Toulon on stage 8 of the 1923 Tour.

Writing under the pen name of G. Bruno (in homage to the sixteenth-century Italian philosopher Giordano Bruno), Tuillerie was famous throughout the land, known and cherished far beyond the salons of literary Paris. She was the author of a book that had been read by almost every French citizen of a certain age, *Le Tour de France par Deux Enfants*.

Published in 1877 to substantial acclaim, it had sold over seven million copies by the outbreak of the First World War. There was scarcely a schoolchild alive who had not been taught it in the schoolrooms of the Third Republic. Her work is still well known throughout France; it was used continuously in French schools, survived two world wars, and was being read long after the guns had fallen silent in 1945. By 1968, for example, it was still in print, and had gone into its 411th edition.

In 1923, the year of her death, Pathé Cinema France was actually in the process of making a film of the book, the first of many adaptations for the screen of *Le Tour de France par Deux Enfants*. The 1923 film was not particularly well received and fell out of circulation soon after its completion. Try as I might, I could not find a copy of it available anywhere. In a curious way, this was the same historical fate that awaited my fragment of film, another Pathé product of 1923. All trace of both films had almost been extinguished.

Le Tour de France par Deux Enfants tells the story of two young brothers, André and Julien, and their clockwise journey around France from the Alsace to Orléans, via all the compass points on the map. It was a journey that in many ways resembled a route map of an early *Tour de France Cycliste*, save for the detail that the boys did a good half of the journey by boat from the Gironde river, via Brest, to Dunkirk.

The story opens with the German army's siege of Phalsbourg (or Pfalzburg as it became known until the Germans were evicted again in 1918). The boys' father, Michel, who had been wounded in the war of 1870, when the Prussian army swept into Alsace-Lorraine, is on his deathbed. As he lies dying, he beseeches his two sons to escape German occupation into France and keep alive in their hearts the notion of their great *Patrie*. Michel's last word, predictably enough perhaps, is 'France'. And with that, he dies. 'His eyes turned towards the open window in whose corner he could see a big blue sky. He seemed to be looking beyond the horizon to the distant frontier of his beloved homeland where he now no longer would be going, but where his two sons had promised to go instead.'

What follows is a sentimental, extremely patriotic, always earnest and sometimes enlightening immersion into selective moments from French history. It also contains a detailed appreciation of the huge variety of France's landscapes, agriculture and cuisine, as the boys tour their nation in search of their uncle, in a wildly over-dramatised series of chance encounters and adventures. At one point in the English Channel they are even shipwrecked, but survive. They eventually settle down in a farmstead, marry and raise families according to the spirit and the obligations of another holy trinity of French values: *Devoir, Patrie, Humanité* (Duty, Country, Humanity).

Augustine Tuillerie was born in Laval, 50 years before the playwright Alfred Jarry would go to school there. Their shared association with the little town of Laval is an intriguing coincidence that speaks of the changes which rushed up on certain strands of French society as one century grew old and another one was just around the corner. If Jarry was a wildly uncontrollable free spirit, then Tuillerie was his exact opposite. Save for their twin association with Laval, they would almost have had nothing in common, in life as in death. The very bare bones of their two biographies spell out some of the differences: Tuillerie outlived Jarry by 14 years, despite having had a 40-year head start on being born. Whereas Jarry would die at just 34 in penury, Tuillerie spent her extended latter years in luxurious surroundings. Having managed to escape an abusive relationship with an industrialist called Jean Guyau, she eventually married the philosopher Alfred Fouillée and the pair would go on to settle in a beautiful landmark villa in Menton, 'Les Colombières', overlooking the Mediterranean. Every year, including 1923, the *Tour de France Cycliste* came almost directly past the house.

There, on the Côte d'Azur, she continued to write. After her husband Fouillée's untimely death in 1912 she remained in her marital home, now into her eighties, composing a dark sequel to *Le Tour de France par Deux Enfants*. In 1916, just as the battle of the Somme was raging in Picardy, she published a continuation of her saga under the title *Le Tour d'Europe Pendant La Guerre*. Following a similar theme to her highly successful debut book, this volume was also designed to educate children on the national characteristics of France's European neighbours, at a time when scarcely one of them wasn't embroiled in some way or another in the conflagration of the Great War.

The book is a litany of prejudices; some timeless, others contemporaneous. Picking up on the themes of honour and patriotism, the narration comes this time from a wounded soldier, Jean, returning home from the front line. Jean sets about educating his younger siblings on the justified reasons for the war (French ones are honourable, German ones are despicable). Jean's father is Julien, the younger of the two boys in the first book, and therefore he is the grandson of the original patriot of the series, Michel; another French soldier wounded by the Germans at another time in a history which seems predestined to repeat itself ad infinitum.

The messaging about continuity, bloodlines and lineage could hardly have been clearer, nor the etymology of the word *Patrie* more obvious. Fatherhood is everything for Tuillerie's conception of French society. The central premise of the work is to make this point: the roots of the German aggression of 1914 lie in the unfinished business of 1870. Yet Tuillerie's language has become darker in the 39 years that separate the two works. Her condemnation of German barbarity has sharpened to a point of bitterness. While her first book somehow strikes a sunnier, if by today's standards an uncomfortably chauvinistic tone, this volume is full of vituperative judgements about the violent German race over the border. 'It will doubtless take several generations,' she writes, 'to rebuild a sense of morality which has sunk so low. This people has become Europe's disgrace and her greatest danger.'

Five years after the end of the war, as Tuillerie lay dying in Paris on 8 July 1923, the mood in the country could still be as dark as ever, as the distant rumbles from the Ruhr valley were heard across the land. On that same Sunday the Socialist president, Alexandre Millerand, made a speech to a massed crowd in Clermont-Ferrand in which he invoked the spectre of the inordinate sacrifices made by France to save 'herself and civilisation itself', and that her debt must be repaid. In reference to Germany he declaimed, 'We may have won the battle, but the fight goes on!'

On the same day, four German residents of Paris were taken into custody by the authorities. They had committed no crime whatsoever, nor were they charged with any offence. They were quite simply hostages to be exchanged for the release of a Frenchman in Mannheim; a certain Edmund Schuldes, who had been arrested apparently on trumped-up charges. The name Schuldes, incidentally, is derived from the German word 'Schuld', which means both 'guilt' and 'debt'.

'Fatigue, fatigue' were the words that the writer Jean Giraudoux chose to paint a picture of the national mood in 1923. Certainly France had turned out to become a very different place to the vision Tuillerie had summoned up in her much-celebrated work of half a century previously. She died before she could know what was still to come.

THE FIRST GREAT BICYCLE DREAM

Back in the velvety twilight Belle Époque of Tuillerie's France, on 21 December 1889 the Grand Véfour restaurant in the Palais Royal was a sight to behold. Its golden carvings and ornate frescos plastered from ceiling to floor were lit by constellations of chandeliers whose reflected light twinkled in the pink marble of the tables. The atmosphere inside was heavy with lively debate; the great themes of the age found themselves expounded upon in closed air that carried with it, among the smells from the kitchen, an opulence and optimism befitting the times. This was where Paris thought, chewed, laughed, argued and drank, and all was well in the world, as long as you could afford your place at the table.

It was to here that major figures of the political, social and artistic scene of fin-de-siècle Paris would flock for lunch. It was at these tables that they would choose to be seen at dinner time; one eye on the eclectic menu, another trained on the comings and goings of the other diners. The great Victor Hugo, whose colossal presence on the Parisian scene seemed to act as a touchstone for all matters of weight and heft, would often be seen here, dining alone or in company, but always eating his favourite dish of belly of mutton with haricots and vermicelli.

On that particular night the salon was closed to the public for a private function. Every place at every table was taken. With the fillets of sole, the pheasant, the partridge and the fillet of beef already served and the plates carried away to kitchens, crystal glasses were charged with the vin de Bourgogne placed at each table in carafes. The dining hall had fallen silent, save for the voice of one well turned-out man in his forties who had risen to his feet and was making a speech to which the assembled collection of diners was paying the closest attention.

Monsieur Champel, an official of the Union Vélocipédique de France (UVF), was recalling his experience of the Franco-Prussian War of 1870 in which he had served with the French Army. Most members of his audience in the salon were too young to have any memory of the French Army's chastening capitulation at the hands of the Prussians, the subsequent bombardment and encirclement of Paris, the exhilarating, terrible chaos of the Paris Commune, and the widespread fears of the time. But they were hanging on his words as he described the rout and humiliation of Alsace-Lorraine.

Champel was telling his audience of cyclists in detail about the time when two divisions of the French Army were sent off in pursuit of the enemy, working on the basis of completely contradictory intelligence. This was happening in a dynamic theatre of war whose front line was moving fast. Instead of marching towards the Prussian forces who were pushing ever deeper into French territory, the two divisions were instead moving on each other, with the enemy nowhere to be seen. The war, Champel recalled, had been a farce. The shame of 1870, even 19 years later, sat deep.

But he was addressing a very specific audience; one which was universally forward-thinking, optimistic, and open to innovation. The UVF, only eight years old at the time, represented a growing movement of cycling devotees and organisers of ever more ambitious group rides and international cooperation. And the object of their enthusiasm, the bicycle, was busy literally opening up new horizons to rural and urban populations across the world. It was a powerful tool, and in the right hands, a force for great social progress. Though growing in popularity, its philosophical and political appeal was still niche and those exponents and devotees of the bicycle were often considered eccentric. It is for example in the same year, 1889, that the name Alfred Jarry appears in the records of the Laval section of the Vélocipède-Club's lists of enrolled members. The forefather of Dada and Surrealism was just 15 years of age at the time. But he understood the potency of two wheels very well.

'If only our front lines had been equipped with cyclists to convey exact information quickly, who knows?' continued the venerable Monsieur Champel. 'Perhaps we might not have lost Alsace-Lorraine?' It was a bold claim. There was a murmur of agreement around the room. But nothing like the storm of applause he would receive when he concluded his speech.

'I finish by saying this: We are counting on you! Be prepared. Hold yourselves in readiness. Because when the day comes, you must prove yourselves to be excellent pioneers, worthy of the esteem of your country!' The Great War was still 25 years away, but fast approaching.

These extraordinary decades towards the end of the nineteenth century would often be referred to as the 'heroic' age of French cycling. It was these years which directly forged the character of Henri Desgrange, who would have been just 24 years old on the occasion of the banquet (he may even have been there, though I could not prove this), and in the prime of his racing career. A few years later Desgrange set the first recognised hour record at the Vélodrome Buffalo, before becoming the pivotal figure in sports journalism, a man at the heart of a certain tradition of French enlightenment, and the creator of the cultural juggernaut that still holds sway to this day: the Tour de France. This generation were the true pioneers.

Another man, Christian Breyer, was listening on with great intent. The Belgravia-born patriarch of a dynasty of like-minded sons, his presence in the hall carried weight. Seated among the guests of honour, Breyer was a stalwart of the nascent cycling scene, whose jovial presence on organised cycling 'promenades' was familiar to many a Parisian rider. He was a respectable member of Levallois society; the same suburb of Paris in which Henri Pélissier had just been born that very year into poverty.

Christian Breyer was the owner of a villa in which he and his English wife Emma lived with their four sons, who were also in attendance at the UVF dinner that evening. The entire Anglo-French Breyer family maintained close connections with England and were friendly with a section of the English community in Paris. They also occupied centre stage as French cycling culture was gathering momentum.

Charles Breyer, just 22, was one of his sons. He was seated with the press that evening. Like his father, he was known by all and sundry in the salon Grand Véfour. Charles was a hugely talented racer with notable wins to his name on all of the proliferation of brand-new velodromes which had emerged. But prowess on the bike was not the only string to his bow. He was also the rising star of French cycling journalism, writing for the Rouen-based publication *Revue du Sport Vélocipédique* and the *Cycliste* journal from St Étienne. As was often the tradition in the sports press of the era, Charles assumed a *nom de plume*. Sometimes he was 'Nick' and at other times 'd'Homino' and 'Marcellus'.

But Charles was to die tragically young. Less than eight months later, having returned from an international track meeting in London in which he had represented France, Charles contracted a fever. Within two weeks, he had succumbed, and died surrounded by his brothers and his family at home in Levallois. The esteem in which he was held as a writer became obvious in the welter of obituaries that appeared.

There had been an outpouring of grief in the French cycling press for their lost colleague. '*Adieu cher et bon camarade*' lamented one friend. And another of his journalist peers simply wrote in English, 'Poor Charlee' (sic), in playful recognition of Charles's English family roots. On the day of his burial Charles's two surviving older brothers, Emile and Christian, as well as the youngest of the family, Victor, were to be seen at the front of the funeral cortege which numbered over 200 cyclists.

Despite the impact that Charles's brief life had on the cycling world, it would be Victor's contribution that would endure the longest of them all. The name Victor Breyer would cross timelines repeatedly with so many of the other characters from the future course of cycling, including those names of note from the 1923 Tour de France – which included the two Henris, Desgrange and Pélissier.

And Théo Beeckman.

VICTOR BREYER

Victor Breyer's star was in the ascendency in the firmament that I was populating in my imagination. The more I delved, the deeper I went, the more often his name cropped up in intriguing associations. I was either reading words written by him, or about him. If the story of 1923 resembled the ornate inner workings of an antique fob-watch, Breyer's finely machined presence lay close to the centre; one of the fine cogs which ticked round, touching the other moving parts and delicately altering their course.

Born in Southwold, Suffolk, after his father had met his future wife in London, Victor Breyer nevertheless transferred to Paris in childhood when the family moved there permanently, though he always maintained strong ties to Britain. Growing up in France as a teenager, he would join his older brothers on organised rides such as the 'promenade officielle' organised by the army and the *Sport Vélocipédique Parisien* (SVP) on Bastille Day 1887. Hundreds of riders criss-crossed Paris, stopping for lunch, and generally noisily celebrating their freedom of movement.

Victor was certainly there on the SVP ride around the Parisian suburb of Pointoise, during which his father had stopped off to visit the magnificent Nôtre-Dame church without telling anyone. He was gone for hours, as the other riders fanned out to find him. Eventually the police were called, before Breyer senior sheepishly reappeared wondering what all the fuss was about. Everyone fell about laughing. Reading the accounts of these pioneering cycle rides, it's clear that a certain high-spirited recklessness, optimism and bonhomie was at the heart of what their participants took the bicycle to represent. That spirit was something that ignited the great road races which were still to be dreamt up in a sport that was, for now, largely restricted to the confines of the velodromes.

The more I read of this heroic age of cycling, the more I am given to understand its sheer joy. Victor Breyer was very likely also to have been a part of the 1887 *Promenade de la Pentacôte*, in which the famous Pickwick Club of London crossed the Channel to land in Dieppe. The Pickwick Bicycle Club is still very much thriving, and has a membership limited to the number of male characters who appear in Charles Dickens's eponymous novel, soubriquets which the members then assume, such as Martin The Surly Coachman, Augustus Snodgrass and Mr Winkle, Senior. Once across the water, this idiosyncratic exclusively male club were met by a band of similarly cycling-obsessed enthusiasts. What followed was, by all accounts, a gigantic drinking session which ended in a raucous dinner in Beauvais, a cycling tradition I myself have continued when I rode with a British cycling group from London to Paris in 2014. We, too, stopped in Beauvais and got drunk, more than a hundred years later. Though on this occasion there were plenty of women too.

Victor was not a racer, at least not to the same degree as his older brother Charles had been. But, like Charles, he was drawn to journalism, and through journalism, to money and influence. Writing at first for *Véloce-Sport* under the mysterious pen name '*Veston-Gris*' (Grey Jacket), Breyer quickly established a reputation, and was hired by *Le Vélo*, France's sole sporting daily paper with a circulation of 80,000.

Now, here's where it starts, where it started to intrigue me. The conventional narrative about the birth of the Tour de France was something I'd never challenged, because I'd never looked into it with any attention to detail. But stumbling into Victor Breyer's timeline slowly gave me to understand that there were more forces in play than just Henri Desgrange, *L'Auto*, and a bold idea.

In fact, as I discovered, *Le Vélo* should probably be credited with inventing the model for professional road racing, for forging the path which led to the creation of the Tour de France by *L'Auto*. It was *Le Vélo* which first hit upon the idea of creating bicycle races of their own as an exercise in publicity. *Le Vélo* sponsored Paris-Brest-Paris, as well as Paris-Bordeaux. *Le Vélo* also shepherded Paris-Roubaix into existence, the extraordinary and enduringly admired race over narrow, roughly cobbled farm tracks close to the French border with Flanders.

Indeed, it was Victor Breyer himself who, at the behest of the director of *Le Vélo*, Paul Rousseau, was driven by a friend in a car to Amiens (the first ride of his life in an automobile) with his bicycle strapped to the back. The next day Breyer went on a reconnaissance ride over the fabled cobbled roads which still define the particular savagery of this great race. It was he who declared, upon reaching the Roubaix velodrome freezing cold and shattered, and only after a bath and a restorative meal, that they were onto something. And in 1896 (the year of Beeckman's birth, and Jarry's ill-fated premiere of *Ubu Roi*), Paris-Roubaix was waved off for the first time, seven years before the Tour de France.

DREYFUS AND DESGRANGE

As ever, cycling and politics were jostling up against one another, mostly because that's been the story of cycling ever since it was dreamt up. The Dreyfus Affair, splitting the nation down the middle, had exercised an unforeseeable influence on the development of cycling. Victor Breyer's editor, Pierre Giffard at *Le Vélo*, was a left-wing Dreyfus supporter whose contrarian politics had made many an enemy within the French media.

As a result of the divisions thrown up by the toxic mixture of nationalism, patriotism, anti-Semitism and xenophobia, a bitter rival of Giffard's, the fiercely nationalistic Comte Dion, backed by a syndicate of like-minded bicycle brands (the advertisers), set up a rival paper in direct competition to *Le Vélo* called *L'Auto-Vélo*, soon to become simply *L'Auto* when Giffard sued them and won his case.

Henri Desgrange was chosen as the editor of the new venture, with Géo Lefèvre as his assistant. But while Breyer would go on to have his differences with Desgrange, the same could not be said for Breyer's friendship with Lefèvre, with whom he had previously worked at *Le Vélo*. In fact, Géo Lefèvre was also listed as having been a guest at Victor Breyer's wedding to Marguerite Hendry in 1901, where Desgrange was markedly absent.

It was after *Le Vélo* was wound up in 1904 that Breyer moved across to write for Desgrange and Lefèvre's *L'Auto*. The new race known as the Tour de France, which had been waved off from outside Café Réveil Matin in Montegron in 1903, had had an immediate effect on the fortunes of the two newspapers. Desgrange's title had won the battle, and in Breyer he had acquired a man of increasing influence in the world of sport.

Breyer was still there with *L'Auto* in 1910, standing in for Henri Desgrange who had taken sick, on the day that the mighty Pyrenean Col d'Aubisque was introduced for the first time to the Tour de France. This was the infamous and quite unverifiable occasion where Octave Lapize, cresting the climb in a state of complete exhaustion, reportedly yelled at the organisers standing at the side of the road, '*Assassins! Vous êtes des assassins!*', a phrase which, once uttered, would never leave cycling folklore, and would be repeated in every history of the Tour de France, even if its veracity is questionable.

But it was Breyer who was there to hear those mythical words. Not Desgrange.

BREYER: DESGRANGE AND WAR

By the middle of March 1914, Breyer had left *L'Auto*, eventually to become the editor of *L'Echo des Sports*, the latest rival publication to the Desgrange project. And it was the outbreak of hostilities later that year which was to cast into the sharpest contrast the differing approaches of Breyer and his former boss Desgrange, only five years his senior.

The contrast between the two men's world views was stark: Desgrange's editorial on the eve of war was full of warlike bombast: 'the Prussians are bastards . . . when your rifle is aimed at their chests, they will beg for mercy. Do not show them any. Shoot them down without mercy.' Breyer was taking a more sanguine, though equally patriotic, tone, as if grieving for the losses about to be inflicted yet again on a generation. The day before he temporarily suspended the printing presses of *L'Echo des Sports*, he wrote of this 'gigantic conflict which will pitch ten million men against one another and return us to the dark ages of barbarism.' In particular, Breyer would later criticise Desgrange for describing the war as '*un grand match*'. 'I was close enough to the front line,' Breyer asserted, 'to know that war is not a sport.'

Both men served in the war. Although he was in his mid-forties, Victor Breyer, conscious of the need to make use of his bilingual upbringing, volunteered to join the war effort as an interpreter for the British Army, relaying messages between the Allies. He was stationed in

Ypres, which he described as 'Ypres The Dead'. In 1917 he published an extraordinary and very factual account of his experiences there, which involved everyday horrors, such as a Scottish soldier's face being hit by shrapnel right in front of him. He'd been particularly impressed by the terribly injured Scotsman being able to utter, 'Well, it's a souvenir.'

His book attracted the attention of the French literary set, even receiving favourable reviews for its restrained style in the Desgrange-owned arts paper *Comoedia* as well as *L'Auto* itself: *'25 years of working in the press provide a writer with an unimprovable schooling in reliable, timely and accurate powers of observation.'*

After the war, Breyer and the Tour de France star Eugène Christophe went to reconnoitre the race route of Paris-Roubaix before its restart in 1919. The landscape had of course been blown to pieces by the artillery. He famously described what he'd seen during the ride as being *'L'Enfer du Nord'*. To this day, Paris-Roubaix is known as the 'Hell of the North'. It was Victor Breyer's phrase.

Breyer would become an important figure in Parisian life in the years following the war. In 1925, for example, the names of both Breyer and Desgrange appeared on the panel of judges for a sports journalism prize (worth 6,000 francs to the winner) established by *Le Figaro*. In 1927, Breyer would be awarded the Légion d'Honneur. His journalism was greatly admired. His stewardship of the increasingly popular *L'Echo des Sports*, with its emphasis on photography as well as first-class writing, posed a substantial threat to the media empire and portfolio of sporting events over which Desgrange presided.

Breyer had an astonishingly wide range of interests. He took directorships at several of Paris's velodromes, again pitting his business wits against Desgrange who had much the same vested interests. Even before the war, Breyer had organised track meetings. He had managed the interests of visiting superstars like Major Taylor, the black American champion who drew huge crowds on his many lucrative trips to Europe to race. Breyer was also a founding member of the Union Cycliste Internationale (UCI) in 1900, which to this day is the sport's governing body. But Breyer's interests extended beyond cycling into other sports, in which he played a significant role.

He met the Wright brothers and wrote extensively about their aviation feats. He was a passionate motoring enthusiast and used to report on all the great motoring events (Paris-Vienna, Paris-Berlin, Paris-Madrid) that in many ways were the precursor to the Tour de France. He was a familiar figure at such races, always on his bicycle, jumping on and off trains. He was a close friend of Marcel Renault, one of the two Renault brothers who founded the famous car maker.

Breyer had met Renault in London in the late 1890s when they were both living there, Victor through his family connections, and Marcel in order to learn English. They became close friends, partly through a shared passion for engineering and mechanics, but also through cycling. They used to ride on the track at Paddington, Marcel on a tricycle and Victor on a bicycle. Breyer was devastated when Marcel Renault was killed in 1903 racing his car near Bordeaux. Renault had lost control of his self-built vehicle on a hairpin bend he'd not seen coming on account of the dust kicked up by the car ahead of him. He wasn't the only casualty that day: four other racers died as well as three roadside spectators. In fact, such was the death toll on that 1903 edition of Paris-Madrid that the Minister of the Interior, Georges Clemenceau, was to order all such activities to cease. Motor racing on open roads was paused for over 20 years from 1903 onwards. It was the same year that the Tour de France started.

Boxing was another of Breyer's passions. Drawing on his affection for England no doubt, he started the *Société Française de Propagation de la Boxe Anglaise*. He opened the Wonderland club in Paris, a direct copy of Whitechapel's famous Wonderland boxing hall in the East End of London, which he had often visited. He was one of the founding fathers of the French Boxing Federation, as well as the International Boxing Union. He was a boxing judge, too. And on 24 September 1922 he presided over one of the most extraordinary sporting events in French history, and one I knew nothing about before the fortuitous surfacing of Lot 212 led me to it through a succession of discoveries.

Indeed, I was only alerted to the existence of this fight when I received an email from a curator of the Southwold Museum in Suffolk, with whom I had been communicating in the forlorn hope of trying to find some information about the Breyer family connection to the town, other than it being the birthplace of Victor's mother Emma Magub.

The museum curator couldn't unfortunately supply any more background than that, but she did want to tell me about her own older cousin, Enid Barber. Enid had been a pioneer boxing journalist in

Scotland during the 1930s, writing for boxing magazines as a 22-year-old, which must have been beyond trailblazing. She seemed to think that Enid would almost certainly have met Victor Breyer during the course of her work, which had often taken her to Paris.

'I see that in 1922 Victor refereed the spectacular boxing match between Georges Carpentier and Battling Siki,' she wrote to me in an email. 'On 11 January 1939, on the eve of his 44th birthday, Enid met Georges Carpentier at his cocktail bar "Annotation", which was just off the Champs-Elysées.'

This fascinated me, partly because I had not realised up until this point that Victor Breyer, this significant figure in the cycling world, had any connection to boxing, let alone as a referee (he was actually not the referee, but a judge). But also because of the match itself. Carpentier's name was partially familiar to me, but Battling Siki?

Who on earth was he?

LIVING, FIGHTING AND DYING; BATTLING SIKI

One hot July evening in Paris in 1923 two heavyweight boxers stepped into the ring to fight. It was the same day that the Tour de France reached Luchon. There was wild cheering from the raucous, overheated crowd in the newly rebuilt Stade Buffalo. The heatwave had sweat running off the fighters before they had even faced off.

One man was a former French champion called Marcel Nilles, who enjoyed the loud support of the home crowd, out for revenge of sorts. After all, his opponent had, less than a year ago, beaten the greatest French boxer of all time, Georges Carpentier. The other fighter in the ring was one of the most mysterious, controversial characters in the history of boxing. He was 'Battling Siki'. Nilles never stood a chance, according to the American boxing writer Peter Benson. It was all over within five astonishingly violent minutes:

Nilles hesitates at the wrong instant, and before you can blink, Siki snaps a left hook, followed by a huge right-hand swing that cuts the air like a whip, sending his towering foe crashing to the canvas.

Battling Siki was 25 years of age in 1923. Within two years of the fight against Nilles, he would be found mortally wounded on a backstreet in Hell's Kitchen in New York, shot dead with a .32 pistol at close range by unknown assailants. No one knows who killed him, or why, nor how his life unravelled quite as quickly as it did. His was a brief, but intensely rich existence; unimaginably so, in fact.

'Siki' was born Amadou M'Barick Louis Fall on the island of Saint-Louis off the coast of Senegal, a wild strip of land in the mouth of the mighty River Senegal, battered by wind and Atlantic breakers. How he ended up in France is the subject of great conjecture; various differing versions of the same story coalesce around an account of an 11-year-old boy diving for pennies thrown overboard by an ocean liner about to set sail from the desolate colonial outpost for France.

Some claim he was taken into service, others as a lover, by an unnamed French lady. Other accounts suggest that the woman in question was Dutch, and even German. While the details are vague, what is known is that Fall landed in Marseille in 1908 and began a six-year emergence from his childhood, working as an itinerant labourer in Nice, Marseille, Bordeaux and Toulon, dedicating his spare time to building a career as a boxer. This he did, until war was declared.

Fall, a year younger than Beeckman, was a long way from the land of his birth and about to be caught up in the net of the French Army, as it toured the worst possible slaughter fields of Europe. Through all the chaos, his life in service has been remarkably well documented. To edit a four-year continuous trauma into a few sentences, it appears that Fall joined the ranks not of the racially segregated *tirailleurs sénégalais*, but as a black soldier in the predominantly white 8th Colonial Regiment of Toulon, a *marsouin* ('porpoise'), as such colonial regiments were known. He saw a bit of everything that the Great War had to offer by way of hardship. Barely 17 years old when he enlisted, Fall saw action in November 1914 during the first winter of the German offensive, dodging whistling shrapnel on the frozen chalky ground and mud-filled trenches of Champagne, near the forest of Argonne. Here his regiment remained, pinned down by German artillery near the town of Massiges, as the war rusted up into a stasis of destruction.

In 1915 he found himself in the Dardanelles straits, where his regiment scrambled aground, then advanced along a dry riverbed deploying flag-wavers and drummers in the French military tradition. Their task had been to take the town of Krithia, supported by a British landing party. It didn't work. The Turkish forces counter-attacked, and the Senegalese *marsouins*, sent forward ahead of their white counterparts, were slaughtered in their hundreds. Fall somehow escaped death, but by the end of the disastrous campaign, his regiment had lost 9,000 of its 14,000 men, including 200 officers.

Fall then survived the battle of the Somme, but left the war with a head injury, a long scar bearing testament, he would say, to an attack from a rifle butt. He also emerged with the *Médaille Militaire* and the *Croix de Guerre* for bravery, though what exactly he did to merit them is unclear; stories often centre around a solo attack on a machine-gun nest, accounts which have no real evidence to back them up, but might nonetheless be true. After the war was over, Fall washed dishes in Toulouse, then decamped to Marseille, where he changed his name to Siki, trained hard, and started to build a boxing career which would lead him eventually to Paris and a first professional bout in 1920.

Attitudes in Paris towards the growing black population were full of misunderstanding and ambiguity; a strange mixture of open racist hostility, which was often expressed in particular by the large numbers of white Americans in the city, and a curious fetishisation of African culture. The ugly term 'negrophilia' was in common usage at the time. So, Siki's place in all of this was complex, to say the least.

His life outside of the ring was as eccentric and full of wild excess as many a surrealist poet or Dadaist filmmaker: He once caused panic in a theatre by firing a starting pistol in the air. He was often seen dressed in fine clothes and under the influence of absinthe, which he force-fed to his lion cubs that he took out for walks.

In the ring, he racked up the victories. His style was unconventional, but his ability undoubted. In 1922 he got a shot at the big one. He faced the great French Light Heavyweight Champion of the World, Georges Carpentier, in a title fight at Victor Breyer's Stade Buffalo, which had only just re-opened after the war. Siki would win this fight – but then lose his life. And Breyer was once again at the heart of the issue.

CHAMPION AND CHALLENGER, JUSTICE AND FATE

Georges Carpentier was France's greatest ever boxer; a national and European champion across a number of weights. He became the White Heavyweight Champion of the World, a bizarre title born of the fact that no white boxer could get the better of the 'Galveston Giant' Jack Johnson, an African American. During the war Carpentier won two military medals for bravery as an aviator in the service of the French Air Force.

When his big heavyweight world title shot came, however, in July 1921 in Jersey City, he was soundly beaten by the incumbent Jack Demspey in a famous fight whose purse totalled an unimaginable $1 million for the first time in boxing history. Then came the challenge from 'Battling Siki', the unschooled, unorthodox Senegalese scrapper whose allegedly dissolute lifestyle drew contemptuous comment from the French boxing scene. Siki was to fight the great French hero Georges Carpentier in front of a crowd in excess of 50,000 at the Stade Buffalo in Paris, with the world light heavyweight title at stake.

It was a culture clash in all sorts of unsavoury ways. Not least, in terms of boxing style. Carpentier was a stylist, classically trained. Siki was all over the place, unpredictable, but dangerous. In the sixth round Carpentier succumbed to a succession of blows to the head, and on his way down onto the canvas, his legs briefly tangled with Siki's. He was counted out.

But, to the consternation of the thousands packed inside the velodrome, the referee in the ring awarded the bout to Carpentier; his reason being that Siki had tripped him. It was a fix, and everyone in the Buffalo knew it. Confusion reigned for at least half an hour while the three ringside judges consulted the rule book and one another, and eventually overruled the decision. Battling Siki, almost unimaginably, had brought the legend of Georges Carpentier crashing down.

One of those ringside judges was Victor Breyer. Writing his report the next day in *L'Echo des Sports*, he conceded that Battling Siki had deserved to win, by every conceivable measure. But, as for his sympathies? They lay entirely with the beaten French fighter. This unexpected and chastening defeat effectively spelled the end of the mythical powers of a hero of French boxing in which the nation, Breyer included, had invested greatly.

The winner's life, Siki's, was short and unhappy thereafter. He was stripped of his title on some spurious technicality six months later, a decision which left the authorities wide open to the charge of racism. Though he fought again in Ireland and Paris throughout 1923, he failed to secure the lucrative bouts that might have changed his life permanently and set him up for retirement. He developed an addiction to the absinthe he used to feed to his lions. He moved to New York, where he fell in, and out, with the wrong crowd, made too many enemies, and ultimately met his premature, unexplained fate.

'RHEINLANDBASTARDE'

Both men's fortunes pointed towards two very disparate outcomes. Carpentier, as I had learned incidentally from my correspondent in Southwold, (remembering the testimony of her boxing journalist relation) went on to own a cocktail bar in the middle of Paris. He worked for radio stations, starred in films in Europe and America, and appeared in vaudeville shows. He commentated on boxing for radio stations. He wrote a novel. He died in his early eighties, in 1975, fully 50 years after Siki was shot dead.

It is worth recalling that, like Carpentier, Siki had served in the war. Both men had seemingly fought with distinction. Both were decorated veterans, having been awarded the exact same medals for bravery. It could well be, in fact, that Siki had sustained long-lasting lung damage from a German gas attack, injuries only discovered during the autopsy of his body in New York. That revelation made his athleticism all the more remarkable and would not have been known at the time. But by the time of his death in 1925, public opinion had hardened against Siki. When news reached France, for example, the editorial in *Le Matin* the following day read 'Battling Siki, by turns boxer, [lion] tamer, singer, emigrant, but always a negro ...'

Siki had served France with bravery and loyalty, just as his compatriots from Senegal continued to do in 1923, right in the line of fire, in the French occupation of the Ruhr. Senegalese soldiers were stationed across the territory. The presence of these African soldiers in Germany was being exploited by fascists in the most extreme racist terms, expressive of a prejudice that seemed to gain traction as anti-French resentment grew.

On 2 July 1923 the *Deutsche Allgemeine Zeitung* wrote of the border between Germany and the occupied zones being equipped with 'machine guns, tanks and loaded rifles' and manned by thousands of 'brown, black and white Frenchmen'. They, and the few hundred children who were born to the union of Senegalese soldiers and German women, were specifically mentioned, for example, by Adolf Hitler in *Mein Kampf*, in which they were referred to as 'Rheinlandbastarde'. The children of the Senegalese would be subjected to compulsory sterilisation and worse when eventually the Nazis came to power.

A TRIUMPH!

But what of Victor Breyer in all of this? By 1923, he'd at least partially settled whatever rivalries and disagreements he may have harboured vis-à-vis Henri Desgrange. Writing on the day of Henri Pélissier's triumphant ride into Paris, Breyer was fulsome in his praise for the race and its winner.

'*A success? It's more than that. It's a triumph!*' he declared gushingly from the front page of *L'Echo des Sports*. 'This gigantic race is, as everyone knows, the work of a man and a newspaper which we do not exactly hold dear to our hearts. But we should offer Henri Desgrange and *L'Auto* all the compliments that their success deserves. Moreover, we say this without the faintest trace of sarcasm, nor the least bitterness.'

In the end, I suppose, it was all a game, and Breyer and Desgrange were the game-masters.

BOTTECCHIA HEADS FOR HIS DESTINY IN THE ALPS

It is and it was an unstable world, full of extremes. Europe in flux, populations hoping, despairing, retreating and rioting. Governments looking over their shoulders, streets becoming battlegrounds. Now, as then.

The year 1923 was starting to get ragged. As the July heat built in France, a new weather system precipitated its collapse in distant Russia. Rostov-on-Don, close to the south-eastern border with Ukraine, though used to powerful summer thunderstorms, was struck by a cyclone of astonishing violence. Giant hailstones, some weighing a kilogramme, rained down on the town, slaughtering dozens of cattle and killing 23 people. This happened on the same day as stage 9 of the Tour, 10 July.

A week on from Beeckman's attack over the bridge, the race had reached and traversed the entire Pyrenees from west to east. It had dropped out of the mountains and arrived in Perpignan, before heading two days later for Nice via Toulon, where the Alps reared up ahead. If the stage had simply arrived in Nice via the most simple route, it might have been different. But, as so often with the Tour, it was not simple. The race route threw in a massive additional loop before the finish, taking in the coastal resort of Menton which sits directly on the Franco-Italian border, passing right by the house in which Augustine Tuillerie, that passionate, patriotic author of the *Tour de France par Deux Enfants*, had written her last book. She had lived a long life, but not long enough to know what happened next, dying as she did on 8 July.

At a mere 281 kilometres, stage 9 was far from being the longest one, but these extra, hilly kilometres were cruel and excessive. In 1924 Albert Londres would describe them in *Les Forçats de la Route*, when the race followed the same route once more:

> To get from Toulon to Nice, you have to go via Menton. Perhaps that surprises you. It's like this. They never seem to find long enough roads. Today they just added a hundred kilometres onto a straight line.
>   'It's no longer a Tour de France,' commented Alavoine. 'It's a Tour of Pigs.'

Ottavio Bottecchia was still leading the race and was looking increasingly confident in the yellow jersey. In Menton itself, on his way to Nice, Henri Pélissier punctured. Bottecchia did not wait for his teammate this time, but instead followed the Swiss rider Henri Collé and Jean Alavoine out of Menton and over the remaining climbs into Nice, where Alavoine took his fourth victory of the race. Bottecchia had extended his overall lead.

There was, understandably, tremendous support by the side of the road for Bottecchia. Italy was still rolling on a wave of populism that had prevailed in the fight against communism. Benito Mussolini had marched on Rome with his band of fascists and become prime minister scarcely eight months previously, in October 1922. Bottecchia's successes at the Tour to date had been widely celebrated in the Italian press, prompting thousands of *tifosi* (supporters) to cross the border and cheer on the first Italian rider ever to be in with a serious chance of winning the Tour. '*Bottecchia! Bottecchia! is all that one can hear shouted from the side of the road*,' according to a report in *L'Auto*.

After all, the race had now reached a corner of France which until 1860 had been in Italian hands, as part of the Piedmont-Sardinia Kingdom. It was as if they still laid claim to its blue waters and elegant towns clustered on the red cliffs. Augustine Tuillerie would surely have approved of the sense of Franco-Italian cross-border fraternity and of the healthy rivalry of Pélissier and Bottecchia. Italy, she wrote through the voice of her characters in *Le Tour de l'Europe*, was a noble friend: 'the Italian people, very intelligent, very hard working, are also very patriotic and very proud of their former glory'. In fact, such was the growing fanaticism that surrounded Bottecchia on the part of the Italian *tifosi* that the following year, in 1924, on a carbon copy of the stage and once again leading the race, Bottecchia would opt to wear his regular team kit rather than the yellow jersey, for fear that his supporters would pick him out and lift him in triumph off the race and out of contention.

At the finish line in Nice, Pélissier rolled in after a solo chase seven minutes and 44 seconds down, meaning that his deficit in the General Classification was now very nearly half an hour again. He was now under enormous pressure, and Bottecchia was being feted by none other than Henri Desgrange, who was becoming ever more unequivocal in his warm praise for the Italian, almost at the expense of the French star.

And Théo Beeckman? He finished an anonymous 47th on the stage. His story was fading to white, lost now in the dust kicked up by the race as it proceeded. Belgium was a long way off. But in 10 days' time the race would be rolling alongside the border with West Flanders, passing a couple of hours' ride from his home, and he would appear through the white cloud once more, this time coming very close to glory.

DEAD ENDS

All this while I had continued, very sporadically, to communicate with Beeckman's granddaughter Thérèse, and her husband Wim, in Belgium. I exchanged occasional emails with Wim, who eventually managed to download the film and watch it. He seemed to like it. At least that's what I gleaned from his concise response: 'It's great!'

I had already amassed a considerable and sometimes only partially relevant bundle of notes about Théo Beeckman's life. But I wanted to wait for the right moment to offload it all onto his only living descendants, and hope that they were interested. I intended to do this in person, but didn't yet feel as if I could ask to meet up for a variety of reasons, not all of them related to the difficulties of travelling during the Covid pandemic.

I didn't want to be humiliated by rejection, so I was hesitant to move the fragile connection with Beeckman's past any further and faster than I dared. Delicately, I tried to delve for a little more detail than the sparse reportage with which the newspapers of the age had managed to equip me. I wondered what else Wim could tell me about his wife's grandfather. A worryingly long period of time had already passed since Yolande, Théo's only daughter, had died, the last family member to have known Théo Beeckman in person. Wim was doing his best to help my research, but there was not much he could offer:

We will have to ask around about Théo, since Yolande died more than 10 years ago.

Théo died before Yolande got married, so her husband never met his father-in-law.

When he moved out of Ninove, most of what was left in the house (thus probably some souvenirs of Théo) were donated to a local thrift store. I do remember that there were some pictures, though. Whenever we find out something, we'll let you know.

My heart sank at that revelation. I could literally imagine nothing more rewarding than sifting through the contents of an imagined box full of junk with the name T. Beeckman written on the side, to hold in my hands anything which he had possessed, an ashtray, a pen, a cup, whatever.

Wim went on:

You probably do know that there is actually a 'Grand Prix Théo Beeckman' being organised every (normal) year in Ninove.

This was news to me, and briefly sent me into a spasm of excitement as I imagined booking a train ticket and getting over to stand by the side of the road and watch a race named after Beeckman himself. I searched for more on the race. It seemed the 'GP Beeckman–De Caluwé' was raced every summer in late July, with the finishing line in Ninove.

And yet, something was not quite right about what I could find. There were no positive references which identified this race as having been created in the memory of Théophile. In fact, I very soon discovered to my intense disappointment that the race was named after a rider called Camille (or Kamiel) Beeckman, who raced in the 1940s. The two men were not even related, as far as I could work out. How typical of a small Flandrian town like Ninove to have produced not one, but two outstanding Beeckmans.

Reluctantly, I reported this confusion back to Wim, and he asked around a bit among a few people in the area, including the race organiser who he used to know from the motor trade they were both in. Wim and

Thérèse had inherited the car dealership which Théophile Beeckman had set up in 1926. Indeed, when they finally sold the franchise in 2001, it still bore his name, Garage Beeckman. Ninove was a small town, and people knew each other. But in this case, they all drew the same conclusion, as Wim told me:

> *Just to let you know how much (or rather how little) we do know about him: it is indeed not after Théo that the race was named. It is not even certain that they are related.*

Then, a little while later, there was some more encouraging news from Belgium:

> *I have contacted Willy Verlé, who – also in his eighties – was involved in the organisation of the Ronde van Vlaanderen ('Tour of Flanders'), that as you know used to arrive in Ninove (Meerbeke). Willy actually remembers Théo, and claims to have once even got a bike from him. Anyway, he promised to look up whatever he could find and get back to me.*

This was the first promise I had of meeting an actual eyewitness, someone old enough to remember a man who died in 1955. And that he might have even obtained a bike from Théo was a tantalising detail. Eventually, Wim passed on Willy Verlé's details to me and I struck up a very brief correspondence with him. It ended far sooner than I had hoped. And it began with another disappointment:

> *Dear Ned,*
> *Thank you for your message. I am sorry to inform you that I haven't known Théo Beeckman personally, as I am not old enough for that. I will however try to obtain more information for you. I will contact you as soon as this is the case.*
> *Kind regards,*
> *Willy Verlé*

Many months later, just as I was about to follow up this lead and see if Willy could help, I noticed that his death had been reported in the local media in Ninove. Dr Willy Verlé had been a greatly respected local businessman, who had played such an important part in the life of Ninove, having brought the finish line of the Tour of Flanders to Meerbeke for almost 40 years. I watched a video online of his memorial service, attended by many of the great and the good in the professional Belgian cycling scene, who all paid tribute to him.

The memorial was held in Ninove's principal Catholic church, Our Lady of the Assumption, whose ornate baroque interior was impossible to divine from the austere Flandrian brickwork on the outside. I could not have known what role this church would play in the days to follow, and the place it would forever more occupy in my memory, though that connection was some way off still. All I knew now was that another delicate thread connecting me to the rider on the bridge had snapped.

ANOTHER DAWN BREAKS ACROSS FRANCE

The racing resumes after a rest day, on which the riders had enjoyed a swim, followed by a stroll along the Promenade des Anglais in Nice. Six more stages to Paris and the Alps still to come, starting today. France awaits another day of blistering heat.

At 2.15 on the same morning of 12 July 1923, a dark-green executioner's van pulls up outside the prison in the middle of Mont-de-Marsan, a modest little town in Les Landes. A large crowd has been gathering since midnight, gazing on in silence while the scaffold of a guillotine is unpacked from the back of the vehicle.

Inside the austere Napoleonic-era jail a young prisoner called Petit-Louis Bordes, convicted in the spring of 1923 of the callous robbery and shooting of two farmers, a husband and wife, is being read his last rites. Bordes is a rough, raging, damaged man; an ex-soldier who returned from service in Algeria to a lost life of crime. Standing in front of the priest in his cell, he listens to what is said and then replies, 'Your God does not exist, or he would not have allowed this.'

Bordes is then handed a cigarette, an eau de vie, a pen and some paper. He sits at a desk and writes four pages to his parents, underlining three times the phrase 'I AM INNOCENT'. Having done that, and despite his protestations of atheism, he attends a makeshift mass with a congregation of one. It is 3 a.m. now and he will die in an hour. The people waiting outside, many on rented balconies overlooking the prison, must wait a little longer. It is after all the first execution in the *département* for 19 years.

At the very same time in Nice, across the giant sweep of the Tarn and the Camargue to the south-east, the riders of the 1923 Tour de France, including Beeckman, Bottecchia and the Pélissiers, are pushing their way through similarly dense crowds of curious onlookers towards the tables which have been placed at the side of the road. It is also still dark in Nice. For the 10th time in 20 days, cyclists are signing on to race the Tour. Local rider Charles Cento is the first to appear, to the noisy delight of the crowd. Then Luigi Vertemati, whose presence makes clear how many Italians are in the crowd. Their support for the race leader Ottavio Bottecchia is noisier still. Of course, he doesn't know this yet but it will prove to be a fateful stage for Bottecchia's race lead, and a decisive one for Henri Pélissier. His brother Francis, who will play an important part in his brother's race-winning attack, is the last rider to sign on.

Meanwhile, in Mont-de-Marsan, the crowd are beginning to grow restless. Some are surging closer to the guillotine. It is only now becoming clear that those at the back will not be able to see the head fall into the basket. Those who fear they will miss out are trying to push to the front. A detail of Senegalese soldiers have been commandeered to support the local police and prison authorities in pushing the people back. It is possible that some of the Senegalese might also have been part of the guard of honour at the finish line of stage 5 into Bayonne some 10 days previously, standing smartly to attention to witness the victory of Robert Jacquinot. Their duties were varied, but this was all preferable to serving on the Rhine, and another world away from the horrors of the war.

With the crowd now under control and right on schedule, Bordes is marched out of the main entrance of the prison to take his place at the foot of the guillotine. His long hair is cut, and the cloth at the back of his collar is sliced away to allow the blade to fall cleanly onto his skin. It is noted by reporters that the prisoner does not flinch, 'as the condemned normally do'. Bordes has nothing more to say.

In Nice the riders line up; the 'aces' all at the front, wearily impatient for the race to start. It's a few minutes before 4 o'clock and dawn is beginning to glow light blue above. It will be perfect weather for the race. Henri Desgrange, checking his list, notes that only 54 riders remain of the original 138 from the start in Paris. After today there will be five stages still to race before the Tour comes to an end in the Parc des Princes. For the benefit of the spectacle, Desgrange could do with a French win.

The prisoner is pushed into a kneeling position. He too might have noted the slowly changing dawn blush beginning to illuminate the hundreds of faces watching, before his head was pushed downwards and all he would have seen was the basket. Without ceremony, the blade is released and Bordes has been put to death for the crime of murder. The crowd, most of whom would have been watching their first and only public execution, shuffle away. A general feeling of anticlimax is reported. It is over so quickly. The execution detail set about removing Bordes' mutilated remains and wash away the blood which has been spilt.

Minutes later in Nice, at exactly five minutes past the hour, Desgrange gives the signal for the race to start. Once more 'Le Grand Bob' Desmarets strides to the front of the peloton and, with a simple gesture towards the Alps, orders them to get going.

The race starts, and as the final vehicles disappear from view, another crowd slowly disperses, aware only that whatever fate has in store for the men they have come to watch is beyond their comprehension.

TIME TRAVEL

Back in my quiet online world, I find another silent film from 1923. This one is American.

It features an animated spaceman, dressed in not much more than leather flying togs and goggles, similar to those worn by the riders of the Tour. He is fired out of a monstrous cannon towards some distant objective. The film cuts to his point of view, as a city, maybe New York, recedes from view. Then a caption appears:

As we dash away, our Earth diminishes in size – and in importance.

We see the planet, rotating in the sunlight, and flecked with cloud, getting ever smaller as our spaceman ploughs on into space, leaving Earth to be swallowed into the inky blackness. It is an arresting image; one which, I subsequently discover, was one of the first attempts by filmmakers to consider this now familiar aspect of Earth, our collective self-image which the Apollo missions around a half-century later would make routine. At the time, it must have been a startlingly different perspective. I imagine rows of eyes under caps and hats, reflecting the light of the cinema's projection, widening slightly at the wonder of it, not just as a picture, but as an entire concept, as an exercise in imagination.

Hidden away in scientific cells across America and the continent of Europe, paradigm shifts in scientific thinking were piling up as the twentieth century was ramping up to its terminal speed. In just a few years' time, in 1927, the year of Beeckman's retirement from cycling, at a meeting in a restaurant in Breslau a curious group of rocket enthusiasts known as the *Verein für Raumschiffahrt* (the Spaceship Travel Club) would start fiddling around with liquid propulsion with pioneering success and occasionally comical failure. The club was made up of clever, sad, compromised, terrified men who would eventually be recruited by the Nazis to build their epoch-shaping dream of total destruction. Rocket technology, dimly understood at the time, had not specifically been banned under the terms of the Treaty of Versailles, a contract that had been drawn up as if the nineteenth century still held sway, under whose terms a boundlessly amoral and ambitious age of wonder was just beginning.

This silent animated short film from 1923, *The Einstein Theory of Relativity*, was the work of Max and David Fleischer, two brothers born respectively in 1883 and 1894 into a large, poor Jewish family from Brownsville, Brooklyn. Released for cinematic distribution on 8 February of that year, the film proved to be surprisingly popular, though ultimately it was little more than a footnote in the careers of the Fleischer brothers. They would go on to make the first *Superman* cartoons, as well as a 1923 cartoon film featuring Betty Boop.

There is a straightforward, honest awe about the way the Fleischer brothers attempt to explain Einstein's rewriting of the laws of the universe. The genre of the silent film, the use of captions, allows for complex ideas to settle before moving on; a speed of thought that permits the film to take the viewer through the most elementary conclusions of Einstein's devastatingly new thinking, which would stand physics on its head and change humanity's image of itself forever.

Towards the end of its 20-minute duration, the Fleischers' narrator hypothesises about the theoretical notion of time travel. The Earth turns on its axis, its rotation slightly jerky, and as it does so it trails out behind it captions of the numbered years: 1919, 1920, 1921 .... Then, just at the point at which 1922 fades off into oblivion and becomes 1923, another Rocket Man is shot into space, this time faster than the speed of light and therefore shooting backwards through the years: 1922, 1921, 1920, 1919 . . . ever faster in reverse.

The tiny time traveller comes to a halt in 1492, just in time to wish Columbus a safe voyage off the end of the world (the film was made for an American audience, after all). We observe his little flickering form, jumping around as the celluloid catches on the sprockets and leaps, set against all that starry sky and those scrolling dates.

Theoretical physics had never seemed so wonderful to me. I had been working for months now with a time machine of sorts. Every dark, rainy London morning that winter of 2020, I lit up the computer, the anglepoise light at my desk switched on to cast just enough of a yellow pool to allow me to scribble my notes, and fire myself back into 1923. Turbo-charged by the internet's endless murky depths of liquid fuel, I had gone travelling in time. I had been able somehow to punch a hole in space-time and escape.

EINSTEIN TRIES TO EXPLAIN

That wormhole enables me now to look closely at Théo Beeckman.

By the time the race arrives at the foot of the great Alpine stages, the Belgian is incubating a bacterial stomach infection that would affect him over the coming days. It has been brought on no doubt by the need to drink water from whichever mountain streams coursed down the hillsides of France, unclean from the cattle released onto their summer grazing pastures. France was at that time building back up its herds of grazing animals after the wide-scale requisitioning of all livestock to feed the French Army in the Great War. Millions of requisitioned cattle, sheep, goats, horses and pigs had been slaughtered in fields near the Western Front. Fifteen teams of butchers worked around the clock cutting 2,000 kilos of meat per day for just one infantry regiment. It had been the biggest charnel house the world has ever seen. Now the nation was re-stocking.

Ottavio Bottecchia, the *maillot jaune* once more, hauls his tired body and soul through the crowds of Italian fans and well-wishers at the start line of stage 10. It is time for his gruff, intimidating team leader Henri Pélissier to make his big move. There are only two more mountain stages left in which to haul the Italian back in. The querulous Frenchman does not yet know that in a matter of hours he will deliver the blow that will win the Tour de France. Nonetheless he is supernaturally confident that the fates will bend to his demands and that he will turn the race on its head.

In the Pyrenees, he had waited. There was no need yet to deliver the blow that would finally win him the Tour. Bottecchia could be allowed to carry on in the yellow jersey across the monster climbs of the Tourmalet, the Hautacam, the Peyresourde. Jean Alavoine could do what he always did and rack up some further stage wins. Henri Pélissier had his eyes on the ultimate prize. It will come in the Alps. And now they are in Nice, poised. Bottecchia's lead is indeed relative.

At the very same moment that the peloton of the 1923 Tour de France is gathering in the dark on the Promenade des Anglais in Nice for the start of stage 10, a 44-year-old physicist with frazzled greying hair and a thick, uncared-for moustache is sleeping fitfully in an elegant hotel suite in Gothenburg. The night is hot, even in Sweden. Later that afternoon, having fulfilled certain onerous public obligations, he will be called upon to speak.

As the riders on the Tour labour across the big Alpine climbs of stage 10, he is getting to his feet at the other end of Europe. The Nordic Assembly of Naturalists has gathered in the *Konsthall*, a masterpiece of modern classical design built to celebrate the 300th year of the city's foundation. In the front row, slumped in a chair with his head propped up by an extended hand, sits King Gustav V of Sweden. It is a sweltering day, but it is an auspicious one.

Albert Einstein, overlooked for a variety of odd political reasons, is to be retrospectively awarded the 1921 Nobel Prize in Physics for his work on photoelectric effect (a massively important evolution of Max Planck's original work, which is impenetrable to anyone without a serious understanding of the subject). But, by the time he turns up on 11 July 1923 to make the traditional speech which goes with the award (his $32,000 prize has already been paid to his ex-wife, as per the terms of their divorce), he has already become celebrated for something much more eye-catching than photoelectricity.

The Theory of Relativity is first expounded, in public lecture form, that stuffy afternoon in July 1923 in the echoing hall of Gothenburg's new landmark building. Einstein stands at the lectern, clad in a long coat and bow tie, trying to articulate the inexplicable to an audience which includes a European monarch in an itchy suit. As Einstein later confesses, when talking about his hypothesis that space-time was in fact bent; 'there are only about twelve people in the world who understand what I mean'.

$$ds^2 = \Sigma g_{\mu\nu}\, dx_\mu dx_\nu \quad (g_{\mu\nu} = g_{\nu\mu})$$

As the narrative caption of the American film from 1923 suggests: 'And, with the eyes of the world turned upon him, there sits in a quiet little study in Europe, a genius delving ever deeper into the mysteries of the Universe.'

Albert Einstein is incrementally picking apart the fabric of the universe to reveal a pattern of far greater complexity and beauty than anyone knew existed and that has been hidden all along. Science and its attendant impact on philosophy, theology and politics is moving at a pace that seems unsustainable. The world is being rocked on its axis. The boundaries of possibility quiver and dissolve. Matter and physics are not as they once were: reality is imprinted on celluloid, voices whisper along wires, and gravity is defied. There are conjuring tricks wherever one looks.

PÉLISSIER MAKES HIS MOVE

The helicopter was not yet fully airborne in 1923, though not for want of trying. On 1 April the French Aeronautic Federation announced the setting up of a 10,000-franc prize for any helicopter that could rise off the ground to at least one metre and fly for over a kilometre. This was finally achieved the following spring by the Frenchman Étienne Oehrnichen's Type 2 Quadrocopter.

The date of 1 April 1923 was also the day on which Théo Beeckman was one of 264 starters who set off from the Boulevard de Versailles in Suresnes in the west of Paris, heading for Roubaix. But it would be some 60 years before our understanding of bike races was revolutionised by the television coverage from cameras mounted on helicopters. These days, of course, such images are taken for granted; the bird's-eye view, or the camera's point of view gliding in parallel with the riders down some sinuous descent off a mountain, or following the peloton over the cobblestones of the Arenberg trench; all perspectives which didn't exist a century ago.

This God-like aspect of the viewing experience in the twenty-first century found a different expression back then, more likely resulting from the elaborate, hyperbolic, almost poetic race reports of the day;

sacred text to those who followed the race from newsprint only, each word imbued with meaning. You would have had to close your eyes to imagine the scene, as the race went largely unobserved save for fragmented impressions of eyewitnesses at the side of the road, and those shards of black-and-white light which lit up the faces of the viewers in the cinemas. The race was presented by Pathé and the press.

However, had the helicopter been able to follow the progress of the 1923 Tour into the Alps, then Bottecchia and Pélissier would have perhaps appeared as points of light, tiny particles, in a mysterious and ever-shifting landscape. Into the Alps they went and the race splintered. Their positions in the Tour de France, relative to one another, slid and resettled, changing the aspect of the race completely. In short, Bottecchia fell away, as Henri Pélissier capitalised on a moment of hesitation or weakness by the Italian debutant. And here, without the helicopter to record the moment, is where the limitations of the age come to bear.

Two different explanations exist in print for the reason why Bottecchia stopped at the foot of the penultimate climb of the day. Victor Breyer's *L'Echo des Sports* suggests that it was the pressing need to relieve himself which cost Bottecchia the race. But Henri Desgrange in *L'Auto*, along with the correspondent of the *Petit Parisien*, reported that the Italian had paused at the foot of the climb in order to change gear, which in 1923 still involved dismounting the rear wheel, turning it around, and then slotting it back in.

But even then, the selected smaller gear does not suit the climb and Bottecchia starts quickly to tire. Pélissier, by far the more experienced of the two riders, waits until the middle part of the climb before dismounting, changing around *his* rear wheel, and calmly regaining the lost ground to the group in which Bottecchia still finds himself.

Once back in the group, Pélissier attacks, supported by his brother Francis. At the top of the fearsome Col d'Allos, Bottecchia has lost two minutes to Pélissier. By the time they reach Barcelonnette, he is six minutes down. And on the final climb of the day, before the descent towards Briançon, Bottecchia's morale collapses entirely as he sees his chances of winning the Tour de France slip away over the endless horizon of jagged Alpine peaks.

At the top of the infamous Col d'Izoard he has shed an almighty 39 minutes, ceding the race lead to the Frenchman. On the long descent over the top, he loses still more ground. Théo Beeckman, who was a minute and half slower over the summit, even catches Bottecchia and overtakes him, finishing almost three minutes ahead of the *maillot jaune*.

By the end of the stage, Pélissier has taken 41 minutes back from the former race leader. Pélissier now leads by just over 13 minutes and will not relinquish his dominance for what remains of the race. The die is cast for his one and only Tour de France victory.

'His victory,' enthuses Desgrange, for so many years Pélissier's greatest critic, 'has the wonderful order and classicism of a work by Racine, the beautiful value of a perfect statue, a faultless canvas, a piece of music destined to stay with us in our remembrance.'

Within a year, Desgrange would be forced once again to suggest that Henri Pélissier, far from being the physical embodiment of Racine's orderly classicism, was actually just a commonplace scoundrel; a selfish bully and a cheat. How Desgrange railed against such dereliction of the soul, the corruption of his eternal race!

1924 – BEECKMAN, IN TRIUMPH

TWO MEN ON THE TOP – ONE TOO MANY!

This is a headline from the future. We must jump forward in time, by a year. Now it's stage 3 of the 1924 Tour de France; one of those days on which no one remembers the winner.

This long road from Cherbourg to Brest in 1924 has already staked a century-long claim as one of the most infamous in Tour history. The fact that Beeckman wins the stage is just a footnote; for when this stage is recalled to memory, the Belgian's victory is seldom deemed worthy of mention.

Beeckman's bad luck was to have picked the day of Henri Pélissier's mutiny, when he and his younger brother Francis paid the ultimate disrespect to the race. It was the day of historic sporting infamy, which called into question the basis of a sporting ordeal that had reduced them to the status of convicts, fed on a supply of cocaine and other substances simply to get through the day's race. It was also a national scandal. That evening outside the offices of *L'Auto* in Paris, crowds gathered hungry for confirmation of the news that had already started to circulate. There were demonstrations and counter-demonstrations, as public opinion was split asunder. So, it's easy to forget that the race had continued after the rebellion and without the mutineers.

Through Dol near the Breton coast they passed, at a moderate pace, under grey skies which were only slowly clearing. Towards lunchtime, the sky was clear, and the sun fierce once more. The rest of Brittany unfolded ahead of them and by the time they reached Dinan the front group comprised 47 riders. But no Pélissiers were present.

By Lamballe the front group had swollen again, and now counted 54.

1924 – THE WIDOW OF LAMBALLE

Lamballe, in Brittany. Once more the town fulfils its annual role as a checkpoint and a feed station, halfway between Cherbourg and Brest. A group of riders have just arrived, hastily signed their name against the time they reached the town, and now they are filling their lunch bags before remounting and continuing the race. These are not the big stars of the Tour. Those men have already passed through a while ago.

'Let me through, let me through!' A woman is trying to barge her way through a knot of people, including the journalist Henry Decoin. 'He's my brother-in-law,' she shouts and eventually reaches rider 225 in the midst of the melée. Briskly she takes his musette and stuffs it full of food, and after the briefest exchange, rider 225 pushes off into the distance, heading for Brest, still hours and hundreds of kilometres of dusty roads away.

She watches him go, and when she can see him no more, turns to leave. Decoin stops her, as she passes him.

'Who is rider 225?' he asks.

'It's Marie Aubry, my brother-in-law,' she says. Decoin notices that her eyelashes are wet with tears.

'Oh, you're the wife of his brother?' asks the reporter.

'Yes, except his brother, my husband, was killed in the war,' she tells him. 'Do you understand?'

Later on, during the rest day which followed, remembering the incident as he sat at a table in his hotel in Brest, Decoin wrote the following words in his newspaper:

But the crowd knows nothing. The crowd never knows anything. Now they're yelling enthusiastically because another group of riders has just arrived and has descended on the feed zone. 225 is her brother-in-law. She kissed him and he left. Off on the great road.

Decoin signs off his column for the day.

1924 – THE ELIMINATION GAME

Gradually the pace increased again after Lamballe, and a number of the lesser names started to drop away. Just before Landerneau, the last checkpoint before Brest and with only 24 remaining in the front group, the yellow jersey, Ottavio Bottecchia, punctured. It took him almost three and a half minutes to change his tyre, after which he was faced with an 18-kilometre chase to get back on. Amazingly, Bottecchia did just that, perhaps benefiting from a lack of commitment in the front group. They were riding at a steady 21 kph, *'numb with chill'*, according to *L'Auto*, with Bottecchia screaming along behind them at a constant 30 kph. The race leader (and eventual Tour winner in Paris) got back on just before Brest.

'All the sports fans of Brest were lined up along the roads leading to the velodrome,' reported the Belgian daily, La Dernière Heure. 'It's a picturesque spectacle as the peloton makes its way through the old roads of the Breton port, flanked by walls of curious onlookers, where women in white bonnets and old Breton men in their national dress cry out in their enthusiasm.'

When eventually the front group of 24 riders reached the Kerabecam Velodrome in Brest, the race was temporarily halted, while it was explained to the riders what would happen next.

In these pre-camera days, such a large group of riders contesting a bunch sprint finish would be impossible to rank. They might be able to pick the top three with the naked eye, but the judges would have had no chance listing them all the way down to 24 in the correct order. In accordance with the regulations, the race was therefore to be decided in the form of an elimination race on the track, whereby the last rider over the line on each of 23 laps must withdraw, until the final pair remained. This method was designed to provide a clear ranking.

They race. Riders are eliminated until eventually there are just two left, duelling for the win on the final lap. Victor Breyer, writing in his own newspaper *L'Echo des Sports*, described (not without some schadenfreude) some of the ensuing chaos: 'Unfortunately, the sheer number of contestants and, it must be said, the rather unhurried disposition of the officials were the cause of a total shambles. It would be better to have given the finish as indeterminate.'

The French-speaking Belgian national paper, *La Nation Belge*, saw things along similar lines: 'The number of competitors as well as the not exactly hasty dispositions of the "officials" were the cause of complete disarray.'

The Breton daily paper, *L'Ouest Éclair*, noted that the 'finish took place in some confusion, owing to the stubbornness of some riders who didn't climb off after they had been eliminated'.

One such rider, according to André Reuze, writing in *Excelsior*, was the great Belgian Philippe Thys, winner of three prior editions of the Tour: 'It was a pitiful muddle. The last rider from each lap was supposed to step off – but, not listening to the announcer, some simply continued. Thus, at the end, Thys comfortably outsprinted Beeckman, but had already been eliminated. So they declared Beeckman to be the winner of stage 3 and he laughed with joy on accepting his bouquet. Thys, Alavoine and others were still protesting, which I can understand.'

Eventually, and after such protracted deliberation which meant that almost every newspaper missed the final ruling, Thys and Beeckman were jointly awarded the stage win, although this fact has almost completely been airbrushed from the recorded results. According to *Het Laatste Nieuws*, this was a ruling that was justified, their lead reporter probably not wanting to rock the boat with either of the Belgian riders. Beeckman was ushered onto the podium and presented to the crowd as the winner of the race, while the wrangling continued. Henry Decoin was there to observe him, for *L'Auto*:

> *In the velodrome, the sun is baking. Beeckman has won stage three of the Tour de France. With his bouquet in his arms, he seems surprised, so surprised that the crowd are not sure that he's the winner. Beeckman is a timid man, modest, who never says anything except with his legs when they converse with the pedals.*

More confusion was to follow when the all-important General Classification was calculated. Beeckman's stage win also gave him a three-minute time bonus; an innovation in 1923 to the Tour de France regulations. Those three minutes catapulted him up the General Classification into joint first with Ottavio Bottecchia. By pure chance both riders were now on exactly 45 hours, 19 minutes and nine seconds after three stages. Once again, the regulations had to be examined to see which of the two riders would be wearing the famous yellow jersey the following day. Once again Decoin picks up the story:

> *The commissaires of the Tour de France met to discuss the issue, and, considering that Bottecchia had been wearing it since Le Havre, decided*

that he should keep it. This decision is a little contrary to the rules of the UVF [Union Vélocipédique de France]. According to the regulations, the first-placed rider at the end of the third stage should have assumed the prized jersey.

If that amounted to an admission that the rules had been broken for expediency, then the sentence that followed explained the rationale:

But are we really going to rise up against their decision, since Bottecchia is such a big star?

It was clear that Henri Desgrange, still no doubt seething from the Pélissiers' treachery, needed to keep his race firmly in the public eye, especially now that the great French hope for overall victory had abandoned the race. That meant Bottecchia should retain the race lead, rather than it be handed over to the rather more anonymous Théo Beeckman.

The decision came too late for the print deadlines of many of the daily papers. As a result, half of them had Beeckman in yellow for stage 4, and half of them went with Bottecchia, whose greater celebrity and race-winning potential had led to a transparently unfair decision.

One year on from the day of his attack on the bridge and over the exact same roads on the way to Les Sables d'Olonne, Beeckman *should* therefore have been wearing the yellow jersey. Never again would he come so close to the race lead.

A Belgian newspaper splashed the headline *BEECKMAN ZAL DE GELE SLUIER DRAGEN* (BEECKMAN SHOULD BE IN THE YELLOW JERSEY), but the political machinations of the race dictated otherwise. Desgrange, perhaps in conciliatory mode, wrote patronisingly of Beeckman's win, 'I'm sure his sister will be pleased – and his mother-in-law, if he has one.' It seems the director of the Tour neither knew nor cared to find out whether Beeckman was married, or whether he had siblings.

It's a curiously neglectful, throwaway comment, at which I found myself taking slight umbrage on Beeckman's behalf. For the sake of completeness, then, and because I was slowly becoming aware that perhaps only a handful of people in the world know what Desgrange had guessed at, I now feel duty bound to put the record straight.

Théo Beeckman did have four sisters who survived into adulthood, all quite a bit younger than him: Maria, Cesaria, Malvina and Susanna. But he would never have a mother-in-law. His bride to be, Irène, whom he would marry in 1925, lost her mother the previous summer. Emila van den Haute died at her home in 56 Brusselstraat, Ninove, just six days after the son-in-law she would never know attacked across the bridge into La Roche-Bernard.

Two years later, Théo and Irène would move into the house next door, number 58. Real lives lived in a real place.

HAVING WON

THÉO,

We'd known all day that the brothers had gone, and that other French guy. It hadn't taken long for word to spread, even before Desgrange pulled up alongside in his car and shouted the news at us. You could tell the old man was furious. Once he'd dropped back, we'd laughed hard for what seemed like most of the morning. No one felt anything but relief. We couldn't believe how pig-headed the brothers were. But, when eventually we fell silent as we started heading inland, I sometimes wondered whether we weren't the stupid ones.

No one said a word for the last half an hour, maybe longer. The racing hadn't been so hard, each one of us going to the front and slowing slightly, doing just enough to make it look like work, and then pulling over to the side and slotting back in down the line. I think already we were thinking about the finish, and holding something back. There were a couple of dozen of us left, including Ottavio. He was there again. We'd let him, and no one could say why, because no one was talking. We just let him come back, and it was a thing that you can't explain. But that's the way in races sometimes.

We all reached the velodrome in Brest together. They made us stop. We slid off the track and collapsed for a minute on the grass in the track centre, at least some of us did. I stood, my backside resting on the frame of the bicycle, as they tried to explain the rules. Ottavio looked shattered, a hollow look in his eyes I'd not seen before. Alavoine kept shouting out as they gave us our instructions, but no one could be bothered to laugh at his jokes. We slowly remounted, and I started to think about the race. A top ten would be good.

But then it was just me and Thys left on the track, who should have already been eliminated. I knew I couldn't ride away from him – he'd suck your wheel all the way to Paris given half a chance, just like he'd done to Pélissier in 1914. I pulled off the front with a lap to go, swung up the banking and settled on his wheel. We slowed right up, my heart almost coming to a stop. Then he hit me, and after that it was all too easy. The noise of all the French guys shouting – the hot evening air – hats thrown in the air. The whip-crack of the flag as he crossed the line. That's racing. You lose more than you win.

Except, it turns out I had won. I can't remember much of the podium, for all the arguing. The crowd were quiet, and I felt a bit ashamed, for some reason I didn't understand. It wasn't the feeling I was expecting it to be, there was no pleasure. I was tired. And when I stepped off, I knew something was wrong. I left the velodrome without the maillot jaune, and I knew that I would never again be so close.

I rode with a few of the lads into Brest, towards a sun dipping low over the sea. I didn't want to talk. Tomorrow I would sleep, then we'd ride again. I knew the story.

3. MOVING

'... from this moment history falls apart into countless individual asynchronous narratives.'

Daniel Schönpflug, *Die Kometenjahre*

A TRAIN TO BELGIUM IN A PANDEMIC

It was almost exactly a year to the day since I had first seen the still frame of Théo Beeckman against the light of my spare-room window. It was time to leave behind the desk whose smooth wooden edges had been the margins of the physical world I had inhabited while dropping back through time and, as if passing through a wardrobe hanging with furs, to enter a different realm altogether; a real one. I went off in search of him, or rather the traces he may have left behind.

After months of silence from Wim and Thérèse, our communication having ended with Willy Verlé's sudden death, I made hesitant contact once more. Worried that perhaps I had overstepped some sort of mark with my initial flurry of enquiries, I got back in touch with their daughter Charlotte, who had facilitated the connection in the first place. She assured me that her mum and dad were still keen to foster the connection, but that Wim sometimes took a while to respond. I picked things up with him again, and it wasn't long before I got a reply:

Evening Ned,

Sorry for this late reply. This doesn't mean that I am deliberately avoiding contact with you. It's just that I am quite busy professionally and at the same time rather sloppy when it comes to my personal mails. Mails I do not treat immediately rather easily tend to shift to the bottom of the list . . .

Heartened by his response I told him that I intended to come to Ninove, Covid travel restrictions permitting, and would be delighted to invite them both to a meal somewhere so that I could tell them all I had found out:

We would very much like to meet you in December. Even if Thérèse never actually knew her grandfather, whatever you discover about her family will certainly fascinate her.

Wim suggested a restaurant to meet in nearby Aalst, a handful of kilometres north of Ninove. Finally, I would be able to meet Beeckman's family and discuss this intangible figure with people who had a direct stake in his past, because it was their past too.

I picked quite the month to go to Belgium. A sudden freezing spell after a mild autumn in 2021 descended on the world from the Arctic in late November, rushing winter's rude privations into a world which had forgotten cold. And then, from South Africa, a new and worrying mutation of the Covid-19 virus had regimes across the world scrabbling to tighten once again their defences against this disease which, unlike the Spanish flu of 1919, was not allowed to blow in, devastate, and blow out. The vaccines were holding it just about at bay, but leaving societies in a state of permanent sparring with infection from which it seemed at the time there might be no exit.

The new lockdown measures, a deadening retrograde step for a world in denial that things were somehow normal, played out differently across the continent. Odd linguistic, cultural and international trends were there to be observed, as if the DNA of the old order which collapsed at the beginning of the twentieth century had not yet entirely been expunged. German-speaking countries numbered among their populations the most significant numbers of the vaccine-hesitant. Austria clamped down on its own, forcing a mandatory vaccination programme and effectively leaving those who refused to live their lives under house arrest. Germany battled itself; the Covid crisis had touched the still twitching nerve which connects the twin values of civic duty and individual freedom. The Netherlands, a linguistic cousin, erupted in outrage. The Hague saw pitched battles with the police, something mirrored in the streets of the neighbouring Belgium. Brussels hosted a sudden gathering of many thousands screaming their defiance until eventually they were dispersed by riot police.

A few days after the Brussels riots, and with new travel restrictions having just been announced, I boarded the Eurostar from London and dozed off with my face mask slipping, as the long, sleek train shot underneath the bedrock of the Channel across whose grey and churning waters ever larger numbers of refugees were seeking to escape. As I drifted between sleep and hearing, I was again gripped by the now familiar sensation of everything being in flux, coupled with a vague and no longer ignorable mourning for a past world which might never quite return in its familiar form.

I only awoke properly when we pulled out of Lille and headed across the border into West Flanders with its familiar, heavily churned brown fields, its sudden clusters of brick farmhouses, sullen steeples and piled heaps of sugar beet, scenes that appeared unchanged by the passing decades, centuries even. This was Beeckman's land. I glided by its wintry reality on an almost completely silent train at very nearly 300 kph. The drizzle streaked noiselessly in straight lines on the other side of glass so thick it denied the true hardships of the dark, wet world on the other side. The year 2021 was all about the illusion of security.

Arriving into Brussels Midi, I pulled my suitcase along the underground concourse, instinctively following the signs to a Covid test centre to satisfy Belgium's immigration regulations. In a once-grand side building, seemingly abandoned by whichever governmental institution might formerly have occupied it, and now repurposed to house a makeshift Red Cross operation, I queued with a few dozen others to fill in paperwork and get tested for infection, either to leave, or legally to enter the country. A tired-seeming doctor with an actorly presence, as if he'd been an incidental character in a major TV drama, flitted between French, Dutch, Italian and English, processing our various applications with softly expressed diligence and care, before directing us to the man with the apron and gloves who eventually stuck a swab up my nose and then ushered me out.

I passed the doctor on my way back to the station, who smiled at me and said, 'Courage, Monsieur!' as if he could read my mind. For many reasons, I was awash with trepidation: this country, after all, was where reality would potentially brush up against a year's worth of imaginings. I was worried that their fragile edifice might break.

'Merci, Docteur.'

On the regional train from Brussels to Ninove, which meandered through the East Flandrian countryside with a marked lack of intent, darkness drew in outside the windows. It was barely 3.30 pm, and already dusk. *Halle, Enghien, Herne* were announced by the driver. Schoolkids climbed on and got off, crackling with gossip behind their masks. *Geraardsbergen.* Here I sat up and paid attention as the train shuddered through the little town with the famous hill at its centre, whose cobbled climb and chapel occupied a central place in Flandrian cycling folklore. But the landmark was invisible from the railway lines, and I had to rely on my memory of watching races tear up its steep slopes to imagine it.

Instead, I noted on its outskirts an immense warehouse, open to the darkening skies. From a distance, I took the heaps to be coal but realised as the train lines switched ever closer to the compound, that Geraadsbergen boasted a wealth of manure, whose peaks and ridges were lightly steaming in the late afternoon dankness. A man opposite me cracked open a cold Jupiter beer, pulled down his mask and drained the can almost in one go. He settled back into his chair and immediately opened another, from which he started to sip.

Finally, the train slowed, pulled in, and I had arrived. Ninove's railway station was open to the elements; a post-war construction, charmlessly fashioned from drenched concrete and dripping steel. I dragged my case through the drizzle, along a semi-cobbled road on which gaggles of schoolchildren stood chatting animatedly through the faded light. Arriving almost at the centre of the town, far prettier and more appealing at first sight than I had thought it to be from afar, I quickly found the address at which I was to stay for a week. My host checked me into the recently refurbished attic room, with a brand-new kitchen and bathroom. An engineer by trade, he seemed particularly interested in making sure I knew that the timing switch he'd installed would shut off the heating every four hours, but that the WiFi was high quality. 'Here is the password,' he said, pointing at a laminated sheet pinned to the wall.

When he had gone, I carefully typed *imsosexy* into my laptop and sat down to type emails to several organisations and individuals in Ninove who I hoped might be able to help. These included two local news outlets. I thought that they might be interested in the case of a lone British journalist on a mission to discover more about one of the town's forgotten sons. I also thought that if they broadcast the message that I was looking for any information about Beeckman, I might be able to tease out a fresh source or two that way.

The evening ended with the sound of heavy Flandrian rain battering against the dormer windows. Caught in the yellow wash from streetlights, I could see the elegant tower of Our Lady of the Assumption. The red-brick baroque bulk of the church was a stone's throw from my attic room, right in the heart of old Ninove.

1926 – THE HARDEST STAGE IN HISTORY

The year 1926 was Théo Beeckman's last appearance at the Tour de France and, you might argue, his finest. One stage in particular, from Bayonne to Luchon, seemed to characterise his tenacity, as well as his particular habit of being overlooked by the history books.

It was raced under a freezing deluge from start to finish. Henri Desgrange, writing in *L'Auto*, noted that fans by the side of the road were lighting bonfires just to stave off the cold, and at one point he coyly describes having seen a gentleman trying to bring the sensation back to his frozen hands by '... *well, how should I say it? .... But I'm sure you have understood.*' For those wondering what he might have meant, he had seen someone pissing on their hands, quite a well-known cure for cold fingers among cyclists, borrowed from those among them who had been raised in the farming communities of the north, for defrosting fingers in extremis. This was not something you normally saw practised by spectators at the Tour de France.

It was another almost unimaginably hard day on some of the biggest climbs in the world, one after another. The Aubisque was the first of them, on which the defending champion Ottavio Bottecchia abandoned, having been spotted by a reporter who described seeing a haggard figure sitting by the side of the road. Bottecchia's last ever day at the Tour ended with him covered in mud and in floods of tears. Then came the Tourmalet, by which point the surrounding mountainside, high up, had simply been reduced to an ocean of freezing mud, the unsurfaced road almost washed away. By the time the few riders who were still able to mount their bikes had made it over the top of the Peyresourde, and started to descend to Luchon, this legendary stage had already become one of the hardest days that any riders would ever face, one of the most unreasonable in the long history of suffering with which the Tour de France is associated. 'The suffering of these men in the face of such untamed nature!' declaimed an editorial writer with thinly concealed delight, betraying a fetishisation for watching others in distress which endures in cycling reportage to this day.

Beeckman came over the finish line in fourth place. The first three that day were singled out for individual praise in almost all of the race reports: the Belgians Lucien Buysse and Léon Devos, along with the Italian Bartolomeo Aimo.

Few bothered to mention the slight rider with the sunken, staring eyes who rolled in 10 minutes and 11 seconds after Devos. But in doing so Théo Beeckman had had to show all the same qualities of resolve and determination as the others. His efforts that day have had to wait over 90 years to be recognised, you might argue. Until now, with this scant account.

BEECKMAN, BELGIUM AND THE WAR

If you search very carefully indeed, by which I mean combing through the regional press of the Denderstreek, a strip of Flanders that follows the meandering river Dender, a tributary of the more significant river Schelde, you might happen upon one single mention of Beeckman as early as 1914. It is, aside from the record of his birth in the Ninove town archives, the earliest trace I have seen of his existence. On 17 June, at the age of 17, Beeckman caught the eye of the cycling correspondent of *Sportwereld*, a publication with which he would have a continuous relationship for years to come.

This was less than two months prior to the outbreak of war, just 11 days before the assassination of Archduke Franz Ferdinand and his wife Sophie in Sarajevo. For most of the populations of Europe's nation states, life was still going along its humdrum way, and people were, as they always have been, preoccupied with the innocent pursuit of happiness. In this case, for racing cyclists like young Théo, this pursuit took the form of suffering on a bike.

Never really enamoured with racing on the track, which was every bit as important and lucrative in those pre-war years, Beeckman always favoured the road, and started to make his mark at a very early age. In teeming rain, he rode impressively at his debut in the 1914 Flanders Championships, remaining with the favourites, some of the best professionals in the world, in a front group that got smaller and smaller. Though he was eventually dropped, he rode on to claim ninth place, only five minutes down on the race winner. 'Beeckman deserves a special mention,' proclaimed *De Volkstem*. 'A double bravo for Filleken Beeckman of Ninove,' trumpeted *Sportwereld* ('Filleken' being a translated diminutive of Théophile and, like his surname, subject to multiple different spellings).

After that reference all trace of his life vanished from the record.

How had young Théo Beeckman spent the years of the Great War? Perhaps his youth saved him from the initial horrors faced by the massively outnumbered Belgian Army in the face of German military might. Théo's 18th birthday was on 1 November 1914, by which time Belgium had already been overrun. It was the same day that Parisians looked up into the cloudy skies above the Seine to see for the first time in their lives the horror of a Zeppelin emerging. The French capital was being struck once again by the Germans, just as it had been in 1871, but this time in an unimaginably futuristic way, from the air.

Germany had seized effective control of the entire apparatus of the Belgian state by November. They had taken the country's seat of government, its administration, press and judiciary. Half the Belgian Army had retreated into a tiny remainder of the country behind the front lines in Ypres, where they were being commanded by King Albert from his headquarters in de Panne some 37 kilometres away. The monarch, whose rejection of Germany's highly compromised 'peace' offering on 2 August had precipitated the invasion and signalled the start of war on the Western Front, stayed loyal to his troops throughout.

But thousands of his men had been taken prisoner, many thousands were dead already in the fiercest fighting to defend Antwerp and Namur, battles which at their peak of violence were claiming nearly 1,000 Belgian lives a day. Had Beeckman been a little older, he would have been among those fighting, after conscription had been introduced in 1913 to swell the ranks of the Belgian Army. At the start of the war it was bigger than its British counterpart.

East Flanders was the last of the Belgian regions to fall, with the towns of Termonde, Aalst, Saint-Gilles and Lebbeke seeing the worst of the fighting. The main thrust of Germany's three armies bypassed the territory to some extent, and so the incidents of reprisals against the civilian populations were often isolated, and yet extremely violent.

In late August 1914 scarcely 20 kilometres to the west of Ninove, a column of between 10,000 and 20,000 German troops were passing through Ronse on their way west. Three soldiers from the cycling brigade stormed the telephone exchange at the railway station, where its operator, George Desmets, was assaulted. They beat him at first, and then, when he tried to escape, they shot him in the gut as he dragged himself across the tracks. The infantrymen then carried him back into the exchange where one of them stabbed him with a bayonet through the right arm, as he sat strapped to a chair. For hours, they prevented any doctors from assisting him. Despite undergoing an operation the next day, Desmets died from his wounds. He became one of hundreds, perhaps thousands, of Belgian martyrs whose stories accumulated in the public consciousness and were picked up by the peddlers of propaganda on the Allied side of the settling front line.

Territory well known to and celebrated by successive generations of devotees to cycling's great Flandrian races became the backdrop to unimaginable horrors behind enemy lines. At Kwaremont, whose famous cobbled climb is a feature of the Tour of Flanders, the German army arrested a deserter who had been working for a local farmer. They tied his hands behind his back, put a noose around his neck and dragged him through the village behind a team of horses, while another soldier set about him with a leather whip. From there he was taken to their barracks, tied to a post, whipped again, and spat at by dozens of soldiers. Only then was he driven to a military tribunal in nearby Thielt, sentenced and shot.

Though some way from the front line, the local population of East Flanders witnessed much and endured more. One night, for example, a house in nearby Ellezelles, some 20 kilometres from Ninove, was struck by a crashing Zeppelin returning from a bombing raid on Paris. The occupants of the home, escaping unhurt, could hear the dying screams of the crew trapped inside, as the burning airship ripped off their roof.

With winter approaching and the front lines hardening, and as German control in occupied Belgium tightened, the population started to experience the full might of martial law. Death sentences for civilians accused of aiding the Belgian war effort were not uncommon, deportation to hard labour in Germany still more frequent. Hundreds of thousands of Belgian refugees fled the country while they still could, any which way they could; the Walloon population tended to flee westwards into France, while huge numbers of Dutch-speaking Flemish streamed over the Channel to England or across the border into the Netherlands to the east, which remained neutral. Almost a million chose that route, and many more tried to follow as newspapers carried small advertisements from individuals offering 'tourism' trips to the Netherlands. By the end of 1914, 20 per cent of all Belgians had left. The exodus across to Britain alone constituted the biggest single influx of refugee immigration the host country has ever witnessed.

By 1915, the Germans had erected a high-voltage electric fence along the entire length of the Dutch border from Aachen to Antwerp. It was known as the Death Wire, or *Dodendraad* in Dutch. In their desperation to flee the occupation, many Belgians still risked their lives to escape. Estimates vary as to how many were killed by electrocution trying to flee, but most historians believe the number to have been well in excess of 2,000.

One young Belgian who used to ride his bike across this lethal border, smuggling messages for the Belgian underground, would have been well known to young Théo Beeckman. His name was Paul Deman, the winner of the first ever Tour of Flanders in 1913. Eventually, Deman was caught, and only the signing of the Armistice in November 1918 prevented his death, as he was awaiting execution in a prison in Leuven. Having survived the war, he went on to win Paris-Roubaix, and three years later Paris-Tours. Beeckman finished in 17th place in the same race. That year was 1923.

Young Beeckman's war choices must have been stark: attempt the flight to France, Britain or the Netherlands; retreat behind Allied lines and await conscription; stay put in Ninove and risk becoming one of the estimated 6,000 French and Belgian civilians often randomly executed by German soldiers or face possible deportation to the Ruhr valley to be put to forced labour.

I could find no trace of his life in the war years. All I had managed to ascertain was this: By the time he married in 1925, he had indeed served in the army for a certain period of time, needing to prove that he had completed military service in order to be allowed to marry. But when he actually served and what that service might have been remained a mystery. The Belgian Army military archive showed no trace of his name whatsoever. Perhaps Wim and Thérèse could fill in the gaps for me.

IN NINOVE

In the morning, having slept badly, I woke, had a cup of tea, and then set out for a run. I passed the old town hall, and then the new one, which I believed housed the town's archive. I made a mental note to buy some chocolates and take them round to my original contact there, Sofie, whose diligent research almost exactly a year previously had unearthed so many of the starting points of further investigation. I wanted her to know that what she had started was still ongoing. And perhaps she might also be able to think of other avenues to explore.

Before long, I had crossed the river Dender. Here it was seemingly more of a canal than a free-flowing river, as it wound past Ninove's centre in curves which had been artificially hemmed in by concrete embankments.

Though I had a vague notion that I was heading in the right direction, I was still surprised to find myself on Brusselstraat before too long, stopping in the road, and looking at the three houses, side by side, that I had studied for so long on Google Street View. This was where Théo had lived when he married in 1925: No. 58, still with its garage doors, which must have once opened to reveal the premises of the Garage Beeckman, Nos. 60 and 62, little terraced houses which were once home to Théo and his wife Irène, as well as her Wachtelaer parents. All three of the buildings had seen such extensive adaptation and renovation that I found it hard, standing there, ridiculous in my running shorts, to feel any great connection to the past. I had thought so often about how this moment might feel. Inside the houses, dim lights shone. A curtain hung, half-drawn. The windows were dirty, sooted up from years of traffic passing along the street below. I felt suddenly self-conscious, staring at a stranger's house.

After that I ran on along the river, upstream and out of town, past sluice gates and herons, under grey skies from which lone gulls occasionally swooped. I passed two horses, biting slowly into the long grasses in a weed-strewn field next to a village. These were the roads that young Théo would have known in great detail as he headed away from Ninove, day-in, day-out, to criss-cross East and West Flanders; his endless training rides and the many races.

I crossed the river on a beautiful, gently arched iron footbridge (pictured), not completely dissimilar in construction to the bridge over the river Vilaine in my film, though tiny in comparison. Then I turned for home, surprised by an ornate Catholic shrine by the side of the road. I ran through a well-to-do suburb; big detached, modern houses. In their midst, a small, old dairy farm whose gates were open to reveal cows in old-fashioned yokes being milked by a farmer in blue overalls who was as surprised to see me as I was to see him. A lady with a big black dog had to yank it back on its lead as I passed. She apologised to me and I held up a hand as I ran on.

On I went, now through a stretch of scruffy woodland; stunted ash trees, and past a pigeon coop. I remembered, as I ran, one of the more collateral discoveries of my research: that pigeon racing was still big in Belgium, just as it had been in Britain in the 1920s, when the racing fraternity from the north-west of England often used to travel to Brittany to release their birds for the race back home.

I was almost back in town. Somewhere near the police station next to the town hall, I felt the need to wipe my nose and was surprised to discover that it was bleeding. I had never before had a nosebleed on a run. Back at the house I took my muddy shoes off, opened the door to my flat and walked slowly upstairs. When I got inside, I took a Covid test, then went to have a bath.

Twenty minutes later, and now clean and dry, I sat at my desk and planned my next move. It was only then that I glanced at the test result. A very faint second line was visible, and that changed everything again.

BEECKMAN STARTS TO RACE

Emerging the other side of the total black hole created by the Great War, not only in Beeckman's racing career but in his life, the results start to appear in print in the spring of 1919.

He wins the Junior Tour of Flanders in June, attacking so hard through the checkpoint in Aalst that the official's motorbike has real difficulties keeping up with him. A week later he wins a race of great local importance called the 'Denderwindeke'. Two days after that he takes the title at the Aalst Sports Club Championships. In August he places fourth in the hilly Circuit de Waterloo, even though his saddle works loose 100 kilometres before the end.

With a rapidly increased profile, the Beeckman family themselves seem by now to occupy a position of some status in the cycling world of this particular corner of East Flanders. 'Beeckman's mother Albertina,' reports *Sportwereld*, 'who used to be set against racing and would curse sportsmen, is now in seventh heaven. She warmly encourages her son, and bakes waffles for him if he wins.'

Albertina and her husband Camille's oldest child and only surviving son, Théo, is on his way to becoming a notable local favourite, despite his career having been put on hold for the duration of the hostilities. 'Filleken Beeckman is the darling of the Donderstreek!' declared *Sportwereld*, before reporting that 'his new bike was stolen at Esschen Railway Station. If the thief had ever been found, the people would surely have sorted him out.'

In October 1919 a new race is inaugurated; one which has survived in one form or another to this day.

The Groote Prijs of Hekelghem was the brainchild of the local cycling luminary Dr Alfred Tistaert, physiotherapist, masseur, race organiser, and purveyor of a miraculous-sounding embrocation, which sold for two Belgian francs for a small bottle, called La Musclophile. Like all good Flandrian races, the race looped crazily around the region, passing through the towns and villages of the Denderstreek several times. It included a circuit through Ninove, where there was a checkpoint set up after 28 kilometres and again after 78 kilometres, right outside the Beeckmans' front door. Beeckman attacked before the second checkpoint, first with a rider called Van den Bussche on his wheel, who punctured and fell away. This meant that Beeckman got to his own front door first with a two-minute lead over the peloton, collected a 10-franc bonus, and then carried on to win the race, where he earned a further 100 francs. At the finish he had five minutes on all the rest.

That race was renamed the following year and is now known as the GP Affligem, after the famous Trappist beer brewed in Hekelghem. Indeed, even in the 1919 race, the first 40 riders to finish entered a raffle in which they stood to win a selection of fine beers. The GP Affligem has been raced almost without interruption ever since.

In 2019, I noted, this race was won by Fred Wright. He is the son of a friend of mine with whom I used to ride on the track at Herne Hill Velodrome in London, and Fred would go on to race the Tour de France to great effect. I paused over this fact, curiously touched by it. I wanted to tell his dad, Phil, about my discovery but had no idea how to begin to explain to him my curious obsession with this forgotten Belgian rider whose accidental appearance in my life had assumed such bloated proportions, and how his career tangentially intersected with Fred's. I feared that if I tried to tell him about the wonderful symmetry of Fred winning the same race a hundred years after Théo, I would fail even remotely to articulate why this frail coincidence matters. Perhaps it didn't.

After Théo's victory, there were far too many people for the Beeckmans' humble home to accommodate, and so they adjourned to a nearby café where more speechmaking ensued. Théo himself felt duty-bound to make a speech, in which he simply thanked the mayor and the festival committee in 'a very few words'. That left the stage open for a lawyer called Cosyns to declare that Théo had 'fought for the name of Beeckman and for the honour of Meerbeke!' Then there were a couple of speeches by his sponsors, including a Mr De Clercq who suggested that Théo could go on to become one of the greats of the sport. Bertina (as Théo's mother was known) and his father, Camille, watching on, were seen wiping tears from their eyes. The party went on until late into the night.

But, despite this momentary flickering of self-awareness, the story simply called me back again. It shocked me to admit that I was no longer able resist the lure of turning over spade-full after spade-full of the past, in the hope that, every now and then, there might be a little something, a bright little coin of fact disturbed by my inquiry and brought suddenly from total oblivion back into the light.

And then there is the oddest kinship I felt with Beeckman, allied with the probably unwarranted sense of responsibility that came from my ownership of facts which he could not have known; that I know what had become of his only daughter, and was in contact with a grandchild he never met. That I had communicated with a great-grandchild he never knew. In part, this felt intrusive. But equally, I felt as though, by bringing these little stories back onto the page, Beeckman's story was becoming my obligation. I wanted to get as close to finding out as I could to his hidden nature; how his brushes with greatness should have secured him a place among the immortals of his cycling-besotted country. Should have but didn't.

In 1919, Beeckman's first full racing season came to an end. Over its course, he had lost seven kilograms in weight. '*Dat kleine Ding maar groot Kampion uit de Denderstreek!*' ('A tiny thing, but a great champion from the Denderstreek!') This depiction in the local Flemish press chimes entirely with how Henri Desgrange would go on to describe him as being '*mince comme un fil der fer*' ('as thin as a length of wire').

The following year, Beeckman was racing the Tour de France for the first time. Sponsored by the J.B. Louvet bicycle shop, and wearing their well-known red jersey with blue shoulders and sleeves, he bore the number 170, and was one of the 'second-class' riders, unsupported by a professional team and responsible for all his own mechanical repairs. One of his teammates, a certain rider known only by his surname Trabellesy, was forced to abandon the race before it even started, his bike having been stolen overnight in Paris before stage 1 got underway.

Beeckman was tiny, weighing in at an extremely lightweight 61.4 kg, compared to Henri Pélissier's 67.4 kg and his brother Francis's massive 79.9 kg. He struggled to make any significant impact, but learned a lot from the experience. His race came to an end on the relatively innocuous stage 8 to Aix-en-Provence, but the die had been cast the previous rest day in Perpignan. In the evening before the race, Beeckman, quite possibly seeing and experiencing the Mediterranean coast for the first time in his life, had eaten too many lobsters. With almost comical predictability, he'd spent an uncomfortable night with food poisoning, and had only been able to ingest a little Vichy mineral water before setting off on the following day's race. Through Montpellier, after 166 kilometres of racing, he was comfortably in the peloton. But, by Nîmes, he'd somehow lost almost two hours. After that, his name no longer features, except by its absence from the final results. And so his first participation in the race, in which he'd acquitted himself very respectably, came to a rather inglorious end. I find myself wondering how on earth he made it home to Ninove, with his bike and all his luggage, clambering aboard a series of trains, no doubt.

He missed the 1921 Tour for reasons I have not been able to ascertain. But he was back again in 1922, carrying with him high hopes from the Belgian cycling press. *De Standaard* suggested that on his debut at the Tour in 1920 he'd 'showed us some beautiful, if a little untidy, moments. But now he has come back wonderfully and we are convinced that we will see him win many races.'

In the spring of 1922, he won a prestigious one-day race in Wallonia whose past and future had a shadow cast across it. Heure-le-Romain – Malmédy – Heure-le-Romain. The start town, near to Liège, had seen the most atrocious massacre of civilians and the destruction of 83 houses by the German army in August 1914, and Malmédy, close to the German border, would be the scene of a mass execution of civilians and American POW's in the next war in December 1944. The race was held only once. Beeckman also finished 2nd in Paris-St Étienne, an important two-day stage race organised by *La Tribune Republicaine* in which he was noted by *L'Auto* for 'another fine performance'. 'The man is one to watch,' they concluded.

Beeckman went to the 1922 Tour de France in good form. Though he didn't win a stage, he did finish in 24th place overall, and was the best placed of the second-class riders. This represented a noticeable and undeniable upward trajectory in his performances. And the longer the race went on, the better he got. Three times in the second half of the race, Beeckman broke into the top ten. Along with his great friend and fellow resident of Ninove, Alfons ('Fons') Standaert, who finished fifth in the second class, his progress around France was followed with pride by their fellow Flandrians.

When the two young riders arrived home on 27 July, there was a civic reception in Ninove to welcome the returning local heroes. Hundreds of people and a marching band accompanied them first from the railway station to the town hall, where speeches were made by pretty much everyone who mattered. And from there, the crowd split into two: half went to the Standaerts' house in central Ninove, while the rest trudged off to the Beeckmans' tiny family home over the river Dender in Meerbeke, fully intending to carry on the party. Arriving home, Théo found that his mother had attached a bow to the front door, bearing the legend 'A Tribute To Our Brave Champion!'

DARTS

With hindsight, I had almost certainly caught Covid at the darts. The previous weekend, I'd been presenting darts coverage for television at Butlins holiday camp in Minehead. All that weekend we'd made jokes about the tournament, with its 4,000 residential guests, being a Covid 'super-spreader' event, little knowing that a few of us would indeed go on to catch the disease.

John McDonald had of course been at the darts at Butlins, introducing every player onto the stage in his inimitable way. From time to time, I'd tried to open a conversation with him about the film he'd linked me to a year previously. But with no great success; John didn't seem greatly interested beyond to say, 'great, glad to hear it'.

In my mind the film and its welter of associations and meanings had already expanded like loft-insulating foam, to fill every nook and cranny of my free mental space.

In short, I was still all alone with my obsession. I had been figuratively stuck, and now I was literally stuck.

A RETURN

I had also been awaiting further news from Paris, where the Pathé archive had promised to get back to me *'rapidement'*, an adverb that turned out to mean a delay of several months in which they maintained a consistent and stoical silence.

At one point during that prolonged delay, we drove out to have dinner at the house of a distant relative of my partner, a lovely old stone house in the Wiltshire countryside. He was a lawyer who specialised in copyright and intellectual property law in the creative industries. For many years he had represented one of the biggest rock bands in the world.

The following morning, over coffee, and gazing out over the rolling English hills behind him, we discussed the case of my film. He was kind enough to feign genuine interest, not just in the story of the film, but in the legal niceties of who it belonged to. After all, it was unusual to be in possession of the physical object without the right to use it, and for Pathé the situation was the mirror opposite: their ownership of the rights to the film meant nothing if they didn't actually own the copy. Either way, he was of a view that the rights to the film almost certainly did reside with Pathé, and that I would need to clear with them if I wanted to duplicate or distribute the images in any way at all.

'But', he warned, 'it's complex. The danger you run is that Pathé might not know how to deal with your case, and though it's very important to you, it's perhaps not very high on their list. And the most efficient way of dealing with complicated, annoying things,' he warned, 'is simply to say "No" to them.

'Sometimes the most risky thing you can do is to raise the issue at all. But, not raising it is also a risk.' I had been backed into a curious corner by my ownership of the little reel.

But eventually word came back from Paris, from the administration of Pathé's *Base des Données* in their archives; the head of donations. She confirmed that, after extensive research in their catalogue, nothing like the film existed in their collection, and that they would be very keen to acquire it for the archives. What, she asked, would be my terms for handing the material over? I replied, telling them I'd be happy to donate it to the collection, if I could be allowed to make limited use of it in print and on TV.

I was also relieved to hear that they'd looked for it and failed to find it. I'd invested a lot in the film's uniqueness. To have discovered that Pathé already had an identical copy knocking around collecting dust in the archive would have been a very significant disappointment. To have it confirmed that the film was, as far as anyone could tell, a one-off survivor, this validated the whole year's work, conferring on it the seal of approval of the iconic French company, an institution which, like the Tour de France, has been at the heart of French public life for well over a hundred years. And, here they were, asking me what my terms were, expressing interest in and gratitude for my offer to return to them a piece of their past, their *patrimoine*.

Eventually, a legal document was drawn up, detailing their waiving of rights in my favour, and, with the cooperation of the facility in London which had stored it for a year or more, the reel of film was carefully and safely transported to Paris. They even sent me a photograph of it on its arrival, and now satisfyingly installed in its new, permanent home in Saint Ouen, in between Saint-Denis and Clichy.

The film would be listed on their online database under the reference number 1923PDOC00563, searchable under the keywords:

France; Brittany; Lorient; Brest; Vannes; La Roche Bernard; Théo Beeckman; Cycle race.

THE ROOF OF A CHURCH

Locked inside my apartment in Ninove, I would now have to stay isolated for the 10 days that were the legal requirement in Belgium. Once I had established that I could get some food delivered by Carrefour, I relaxed to the extent that I could now begin to rearrange my plans for the week, all of which had just been washed away by the positive test results from my antigen test and the PCR test which I had done on arrival in Brussels. That too came back positive, and there could now be no doubt why I had a pounding headache, an itchy feeling and persistent nosebleeds.

My plan for the first day had been to walk up to the cemetery in Ninove, about a 15-minute stroll out of the town centre, I estimated, from my attic apartment. I knew that Théo Beeckman had been born, married, lived and died in Ninove, and I saw nothing to suggest that he hadn't been a steady Catholic, as most professed to be in East Flanders, certainly then and probably still to this day. I had been looking forward to the task of patrolling the rows of neatly kept gravestones, looking for the one name that mattered to me. I had imagined finding his grave and wondered how I might feel if I did.

Instead, I was reduced once again to scouring the area right outside my four walls from the false altitude of Google Maps, occasionally dropping down into Street View. The flat I had rented had three small dormer windows, set into the sloping roof space at an angle. They opened only partially, and not wide enough for me to stick out my head without bending my neck at an unlikely angle. Every now and again over the 10 days to come, I'd walk to one of the windows, throw it open and thrust my face into the chilly drizzle being whipped across Ninove's rooftops, trying to catch the metallic tang of rain in the air amid the drifting diesel fumes and extractor fans from the town's many *frituur* chip shops. And when I wasn't doing that, or helping myself to another ladle of an enormous pot of bean stew I cooked as soon as the bag of groceries had been delivered, I was once again sinking into the quicksand of 1923, returning to the race, re-entering the world I had assembled from the loose skeleton of information I had about those four weeks in that hot summer. The sun was always bright and the days always long on my computer, but outside darkness had fallen by half past three every day.

On those rare occasions when the winter sun shone, it set with a honeyed glow and cast long rays of light, first on the brick buttresses, then the tiled roof and sharp spires of Our Lady of the Assumption, which dominated the view from my apartment. It presented its south-facing flank to me, graceful, tall and somehow consoling. Because it was the only building of note that I could see, filling my view, because it was a church, and because the play of light from morning, through the wintry days and into night, meant that its aspect never remained the same, I gazed at it for hours on end, knowing that Théo Beeckman would also have known its outline.

When I had arrived from Brussels, still unaware of my positive status, I had stretched the elastic of the regulations for new arrivals to the extent that I had very briefly popped my head into the church, and, finding it quite empty, had briskly walked around it. It was a mellow, mahogany and gilt church with a tall drop from ceiling to stone floor, slightly over-literal stained glass, a colossal pulpit and an almost inaudible, gentle hum from an idling loudspeaker system. How often had Beeckman visited this cold and quiet space, with its faint scent of candle smoke?

All day, from my vantage point, I could watch its elderly visitors come and go, sometimes alone, sometimes in pairs and always masked. Some walked in with the help of sticks, others briskly, almost at a canter if a rainy squall happened to catch the moment they had chosen to drop into church that day to say a prayer and light a votive candle. Perhaps even to confess. Over the coming days, I started to recognise certain individuals, and my imagination, attuned already to filling in the gaps, began to extemporise and invent identities for them.

BEECKMAN'S LEGACY, THE LEAST NOISE

I sent an email to Wim and Thérèse explaining that I would not be able to meet them for lunch on Sunday:

Hi Wim
The good news: I am in Ninove.

The bad news: I just tested positive for Covid. So, I am now in isolation for the next 10 days.

I am SO sorry – I was really looking forward to meeting you both. We'll have to do it another time.

N

Wim replied within the hour:

Bad news indeed!!
Let us know if we can plan it again in the future.
In the meantime: take care!!

The central-heating thermostat clicked and the boiler ignited, rumbling hot water through the pipes. I glanced out of the window, in time to see a pigeon swoop suddenly down and settle on the parapet outside my window. It paused there for a count of five, then was gone again, dropping steeply towards street level.

What I had glimpsed of Ninove before needing to isolate had conformed to all the standards of a small Flemish town: a strange mixture of austerity and a welcoming cosiness. Architecture and shops on a human, relatable scale, an environment built with an understanding of place. Ninove is not a tourist destination. When I had messaged my friend and colleague from Belgian TV to tell him of my predicament, he was highly amused that I had landed myself in isolation in such a backwater, as he saw it.

Yet I have always admired small-town Flanders, ever since my first brushes with the country in my early twenties. Ninove had an old town hall, as well as new purpose-built premises, a grand-enough church, one main shopping street with twinkling Christmas decorations, a Chinese restaurant, lots and lots of shops selling pizzas, kebabs and chips, and a complex of terraced roads leading towards the centre; tiny two-storey houses with windows flush to the front walls, each one slightly different from its neighbour, in good Belgian tradition. These roads had seen many hundreds of bike races throughout the decades: kermesse races, criteriums, one-day tests, classics, amateur, junior, monuments. Théo Beeckman would have known them all, had raced them all, and won his fair share of them, too.

Five years into his post-racing retirement, Beeckman was the proprietor of a business called Garage Beeckman. His business premises

were at Brusselstraat, right next to the house where his father-in-law
Ernest Wachtelaer lived. Beeckman and his wife Irène had moved
into number 58 shortly after their wedding in 1925. My suspicion was
that his new father-in-law, whose profession is listed on the marriage
certificate as 'businessman', might have set Théo up in the car trade,
so as to provide for his daughter. For the last couple of years of racing,
Beeckman managed to juggle his business commitments with his
racing. After finishing the 1927 season, in which he switched teams
to the less prestigious Peugeot outfit in the middle of February, he
dedicated himself to building the business which for the first four years
exclusively sold Fabrique Nationale cars. These were built in Herstal by
the same monolithic Belgian engineering company which had started
off manufacturing firearms, including, coincidentally, the pistol with
which Archduke Franz Ferdinand had been assassinated in late June
1914. After that, Beeckman switched the business to become a Renault
franchise, which it remained for many years, right up until Wim and
Thérèse sold it in 2001.

Beeckman still kept an interest in cycling though. And, as many
retired riders did, he started coaching. A report in the *Sportwereld*
newspaper from June 1928 mentions a young rider who is being coached
by Beeckman. The youngster went by the excellent name of Leopold van
Snik. 'The former professional,' writes the reporter, 'can be very proud to
have such a talented rider under his command, and Leopold would be
well advised to listen to his warm words and to draw on his knowledge
of how to turn you into a good rider.'

One of the very final traces of Théophile Beeckman, as reported in the
press, is less complimentary. The scene was the Junior Tour of Ninove
in 1932, which was routed, like most Belgian races are, over a series of
convoluted laps and circuits, threading the peloton repeatedly through
the centre of the town to be greeted no doubt by loud, knowledgeable
crowds of neighbours, relatives and general supporters. On the third lap
of the circuit, there was a lone attacker, a young rider called Sandeur.
Suddenly, it seems, 'Fiel' Beeckman appeared on the course. He had
driven onto it in his Renault:

*Fiel Beeckman, who gets in the way in his car at every race, got involved
here, too, interfering in matters that do not concern him, giving Sandeur a
signal for which way to go, and sending him the wrong way.*

These were the first openly critical words I had ever read in the press about Beeckman's behaviour. He was usually portrayed as a man of quiet humility, inscrutable. When the 1923 Tour came to its close in the Parc des Princes, the track-specialist writer François Mercier wrote in *L'Auto* that Beeckman, who finished 14th overall, five hours and four seconds outside the time of Henri Pélissier, had 'ridden a courageous race, as was his custom'. Such a sparing summation was typical of the way in which he is normally portrayed; simple, dignified, brave. Yet, here, the impression was quite different. And the suggestion that he was a repeat offender was even more surprising to note.

The article went on to single him out for particular blame, and even went so far as to raise an eyebrow about his possible motivation for sending the rider the wrong way. 'I don't want to suggest that this was done with any bad intentions,' the writer reports, thereby suggesting that it might have been done with bad intentions, 'but as an ex-rider he should know better than anyone that he is not needed here. It is hoped that this lesson will teach him to stay at home in the future, for which we thank him in advance.'

If the impression given by this article was reflective of a widespread view of Théophile Beeckman, then it ran counter to the impression of the man I had built up thus far.

I stared out of the window at the cobalt-blue sky just starting to lose its light. The ridge of tiles along the top of the roof of the church was starting to fade to black, to become silhouettes. That Beeckman became a pariah, unwanted at bike races, shunned by the Ninove cycling fraternity: it was as if they're talking about a different man altogether.

Perhaps he was not as well-liked as I had thought all along. I think about the Dutch website that bemoaned the fact that Meerbeke had never erected any kind of memorial to Beeckman. I remember discovering that the GP Beeckman bike race was not in fact named after him, but after Kamiel Beeckman, whose surname was nothing more than a coincidence, whose list of achievements was far more modest than Théo's, and who was described in one account as being 'not a great rider, but full of fight'. And I recall then having to tell Wim and Thérèse that the race they believed to be named after Thérèse's grandfather actually had nothing to do with him, and the disappointment I thought I'd detected when Wim realised I was correct.

One newspaper, more than any other, had consistently documented the ebb and flow of Beeckman's professional career: *Sportwereld*. This was the paper which promoted Beeckman's prospects throughout his active years, praising him for his physical attributes – '*His muscles may be made of steel, but he also has a stomach of iron*' – as well as for his growing mental fortitude. In 1921, for example, their sportswriter praises the hitherto timid-seeming Beeckman for raising an objection with the judges after he had been impeded in a sprint in some one-day race or other. This was considered to be evidence that he was '*showing signs of becoming a man*'. It seems that Beeckman latched onto the tacit understanding that he had with the influential paper, the pact that so many athletes (and politicians, come to that) have always entered into with the media. In March 1923, on the day after he'd travelled to Sanremo in north-western Italy, he took the time to send the newspaper a postcard from the seaside, which he got half a dozen riders to sign, including Jean Alavoine.

And it's in the pages of *Sportwereld* that eventually I reach the end of the road. The very last searchable mention of his name comes about in 1936, in an article that explores the legacy of the Flemish pioneers of road racing. Beeckman is put in the same category as Albert Dejonghe, who won Paris-Roubaix in 1922 as well as stage 4 of the 1923 Tour, and after whom there are streets named in two Belgian cities. Beeckman is also compared favourably to Félix Sellier, like Dejonghe a winner of Paris-Roubaix and a three-time stage winner at the Tour. Sellier is famous for being the subject of an iconic photograph in which he is seen furiously trying to attack the driver of a car that has just run into him on stage 13 of the 1925 Tour de France.

But what of Beeckman's legacy? Nothing. No photo. Not one single memory.

The local news organisations in Ninove which I had contacted proved to lead to two dead ends. Neither channel replied to me, a judgement of my irrelevance which I took to heart, as one of the stories they ran that week was about the repainting of a bench. I emailed the late Willy Verlé's colleagues on the local organising committee which hosted the finish line of the Tour of Flanders (when it used to finish in Meerbeke/ Ninove) and the Omloop Het Nieuwsblad race. They didn't respond. I contacted the encyclopaedic resource at the Ronde van Vlaanderen but their historians collectively drew a complete blank, though they did reply to me after a bit of digging:

> *Hi Ned!*
>
> *We did contact our connection Nico, but he doesn't find anything more about 'Théophile Beeckman'.*
>
> *If he does find something, he will contact us and we will keep you up to date!*

I read the very last instance of his name in print, and it came 13 years after the film on the bridge ensured that he might be gone, but not entirely forgotten. The *Sportwereld* article, having made the comparison with Dejonghe and Sellier, concludes by stating, 'But of the three, Beeckman made the least noise.'

PÉLISSIER TAKES TOTAL CONTROL

The 1923 race was nearing its end.

It was 14 July, Bastille Day, and while the Champs-Elysées bore witness to a parade of the massed ranks of the French Army, flanked by representations from their Allies in the Great War, a tradition since 1918, the 1923 Tour de France continued to wind its way onwards.

Henri Pélissier was already firmly in control of the race after his massive Alpine raid on stage 10 to Briançon. Now, two days later, he doubled up on the road out of the Alps to Geneva, finishing ahead of his brother Francis. This was also the day that Jean Alavoine was forced to abandon the race, feeling the effects of his crash on the previous stage; mixed fortunes and high, contrasting emotions for the two duelling French challengers.

Alavoine climbed into Henri Desgrange's Peugeot, where he sat and wept, his arms wrapped in numerous bandages. This image of 'Gars Jean', weeping in the race director's car, knowing that his chance of winning the Tour de France was probably gone forever, is just one of any number of vivid moments on another day of great drama on the Tour. In the race, and at the sides of the roads, you never could tell what lay around the corner.

Sometimes the casual way in which matters of life and death are reported in the papers is so perfunctory and incidental that I find myself re-reading the column several times until I can be confident that I have not mistranslated it. Under the heading '*Un incident tragique*', a bizarre detail emerges: As the race passed through the checkpoint at Barcelonette, a large, unruly crowd was there to greet the riders. One of the *touriste-routiers* riders dropped a tin of 'Second Patches' tyre-repair kits, and there was an almighty scrum to get hold of it. Somehow, in the middle of the chaos, a local amateur rider, called simply Sansavoine, was bundled to the ground and killed in the mêlée. It goes without saying that a tragedy like this might well halt the race nowadays and would have made headlines across the world, overshadowing the sporting context completely. But in 1923, in a world inured to senseless death, it barely warranted a mention.

The Tour de France was in the unshakeable grip of Henri Pélissier after stage 11. 'Only a serious accident,' wrote Desgrange, 'can prevent him from winning the race now.' Even though Ottavio Bottecchia had now shuffled back up into second place, moving ahead of the unfortunate Alavoine, the Italian lost a further 16 minutes on the stage and now trailed Pélissier by very nearly half an hour.

After Pélissier's victory, a striking scene was recorded by eyewitnesses: the two Pélissier brothers falling into one another's arms on the finish line, as the moustachioed Henri planted a kiss on Francis's dust-covered cheek. Henri Desgrange, writing in *L'Auto*, speculated poetically as to what this simple gesture might have meant, what message it could have imparted, inventing on Henri's behalf an imagined speech to his younger brother, giving Henri a voice he probably didn't merit: 'You see, kid, when I have retired,' extemporised Desgrange in his column, 'and it is your turn to win the great race, you can now see how it is done. Don't let the inevitable setbacks get to you. Don't push too hard at the beginning when you feel a moment of weakness. And if you don't win the game in the Pyrenees, dream of how the Alps are the supreme, fearful, magnificent second chance, where those who know how to fight the best will get their recompense.'

Meanwhile Théo Beeckman had moved up from 19th place in General Classification to 17th. He had suffered a horrible bout of stomach cramps on the rest day in between the two Alpine stages, probably because he'd drunk from that mountain stream the previous day on the road to Briançon. He was grateful that on stage 11 he was starting to feel better, telling the reporter from *Sportwereld* that if he'd had cramps like that during the race, he'd never have been able to finish. His trajectory was upwards again, and in a few days he'd come close to victory.

THE LOST SPOILS

I stop what I am writing and just listen. There is the sound of rain on the red rooftiles above me. Somewhere in the distance I can just about make out the passage of an ambulance, or a police car, whose siren drifts on the edge of audibility, kept airborne by those squally gusts that rush through the damp surrounding streets.

Days pass softly here. You could find a year has slipped by without you knowing. It's conceivable. Time is almost stopped and yet is moving so fast that nothing survives in its wake. All the characters, once flesh and blood, are now just ghosts in a story which is anchored in nothing much more than this never-ending Flemish wind.

Often, in my frustration, I think of the plastic bag of Théo Beeckman's stuff that they took to the charity shop and dumped. Out with the old.

STRASBOURG IN A STORM

On the day of stage 12, the heatwave finally broke in France and the mercury in the thermometers plummeted. A westerly wind brought huge banks of clouds in from the Atlantic. There was no part of France which escaped the storms. Lightning strikes and heavy rain rolled through every town and village, every wood, valley and hillside in the land.

Across France and beyond, histories, some distinct, others obscure and most entirely forgotten, were being lived. Guillaume Seznec, arrested a week earlier on suspicion of the murder of Pierre Quémeneur, was transported to Morlaix from Paris. Accompanied by two prison guards, in a separate third-class compartment, he made the long train journey to his home town with an attitude of calm detachment. In Morlaix he was treated well by the authorities, given the best room in the prison, and allowed to meet his wife and embrace his children. The following day, he would face examination by the investigating magistrate, and the mystery would deepen. It would be almost 18 months before his case would come to trial and the guilty verdict handed down.

On the same day it was also reported that the big rematch between Georges Carpentier and Battling Siki, scheduled for 16 September, had been suddenly thrown into doubt, when the French boxer asked the Federation for a delay to the date for the fight. It was a rematch that was destined never to happen; a failure to make the fight which almost certainly accelerated the decline and fall of the Senegalese fighter.

And tragedy struck at the Nancy-Verdun-Nancy bicycle race, when a M. Garçon was hit by a rider called Clément Maurice as the race passed through Montauville. The victim was thrown to the ground and suffered a fractured skull. He was carried to his home in the town, where he died. Maurice himself was driven to hospital in Pont-à-Moussin where he was treated for concussion and severe bruising.

The Tour de France, beginning its long arc towards Paris, now headed through the rain for Strasbourg. With the Pélissier brothers in complete control and both the Alps and the Pyrenees behind them, there was an opportunity to be seized if a lowlier rider wished to launch a long-range raid. Fittingly, since the route was passing through Alsace-Lorraine, it was a rider from the region who won the stage alone. It was to be Joseph Muller's finest hour.

Muller had been born in the half-timbered Germanic world of Orschwiller, just to the south of Strasbourg, a little town overlooked by the fairy-tale, turreted bulk of the Château du Haut-Kœnigsbourg. The castle, built into the side of a Vosges mountain, overlooks the Upper Rhine Plain, affording strategic views into Germany which stretch as far as the Black Forest. Though it had fallen into ruin by the late nineteenth century when the Prussians took the Alsace, Kaiser Wilhelm II claimed ownership of the castle and personally saw to it that it was restored.

It should, he announced, stand as a grand symbol of German civilisation, and tighten the bond with the *Vaterland* felt by the citizens of Alsace-Lorraine. In 1919 the terms of the Treaty of Versailles returned the region to the French state. These days, the local tourism industry is the beneficiary of the Kaiser's expensive renovations.

Muller had been showing some glimmers of good form in the Alps, having climbed the mighty Galibier on the wheel of the *maillot jaune* Henri Pélissier just two days previously. Lining up at the start in Geneva,

Muller, along with the remaining 48 riders, would have felt the chill from the first rainfall of the race. Across both mountain ranges, the sun had shone unrelentingly, and the heat had been unbearable in the far south. But now, as they headed off on their long pilgrimage north, the high pressure cracked spectacularly as it so often does during July in France.

The deluge dampened spirits in a weary peloton. It turned the roads into a muddy quagmire on the Col de la Faucille in the Jura mountains. By the time they got to the checkpoint at Pontarlier, and started out along the Doubs river valley, the front group totalled 30 riders, each one indistinguishable from the next, due to the mud which covered them from head to toe. On the industrial outskirts of Belfort, Muller chose his moment to attack. At first he stole 100 metres, then 200. Then the Pélissiers started to react. The peloton began wearily to claw their way across to the lone leader. Over the course of 12 kilometres they chased and had almost reeled him in when Henri Pélissier punctured.

That was the key moment, knocking the stuffing out of the chase group. Francis Pélissier stopped riding, and even Ottavio Bottecchia decided to relent, not wishing to take advantage of the misfortune that had struck his teammate and race leader. The stage was effectively won in that instant.

The front cover of *Le Petit Journal* depicting Muller's victory

The victory of Joseph Muller was lovingly rendered on the front page of *Le Petit Journal* on 29 July 1923. The local rider is pushing his way up a hill towards the finish line in the velodrome, past typical half-timbered Strasbourg houses, to the acclaim of the local population who line the street on either side. Muller has turned to smile at some children who are cheering him home. The location of some victories carried more significance than others and Strasbourg was always loaded with meaning for the French.

ALONG THE FRONT LINE

I have arranged on the desk printed photos of Théo Beeckman, as well as the front page of *Le Petit Journal*. I read again through the pages of scribbled notes I made back in London, picking through the newspaper reports from the front line of the bike race. In mid-December the sun rises late and sets early. Outside my window, Ninove's red-brick houses are, more often than not, dark. But inside, lights illuminate people quietly going about their lives. I count the days down. I am creeping towards the end of my isolation, falling into a step march with the last days of the 1923 Tour.

Stage 13 was from Strasbourg to Metz. Under fresh blue skies, in much milder conditions, the race through the 1870–71 battlefields was a tight affair. Henri Pélissier, sensing how close he now was to victory in Paris, was not minded to take any risks. In the knowledge that only mechanical misfortune or a crash could realistically prevent him from winning, he told the press at the start line in Strasbourg that 'his bike was more important to him than his eyes'.

The race tracked alongside ripening orchards, heavy with fruit. It passed through the lush green landscape, whose sheer abundance was lapped up by the French press in a spirit of celebration for a paradise refound. Yet this part of the land, still so recently reclaimed by France, was heavily populated by military bases. The correspondent for the *Petit Parisien* noted that he had 'never before seen so many soldiers at a bicycle race. Cheers and fanfares all the way through Bitche, Sarregemuines, Forbach and Wissembourg; names which resonate so painfully in the ears of our ancestors!' They were the sites of the series of defeats which the Prussians had inflicted on the Republic in 1870–71.

No one wanted to let an attacker like Muller go, as they had done on stage 12. At one point Francis Pélissier attacked, taking with him a couple of others. But they too were kept on a tight leash. As a result, the race ended in a bunch sprint, with Romain Bellenger taking a first stage win of the Tour to go with the temporary yellow jersey he'd been presented with as the race had entered the Pyrenees. Bellenger outsprinted Félix Goethals and Beeckman's old friend from Ninove, Alfons Standaert. That was Alfons's best-ever finish at the Tour.

Théophile Beeckman was having a quiet race at this point. Indeed, writing on the day of the race for *L'Auto*, the great Henri Desgrange was already starting to sum up the 17th edition of the race, and to draw his emphatically expressed conclusions. I have no idea whether or not Beeckman read the newspaper, though I suspect he would have found it hard to avoid. But, if he had, he would have perhaps scanned the editorial for mentions of his name, and discovered that Desgrange simply dismissed him with the damning '*I do not believe very much in Beeckman.*'

Beeckman had, in truth, been racing hard, but without making much of an impact on the Tour. His 18th place into Metz was indicative of a rider who, it might have appeared, had found his level. But he would have one more day left in which to shine. His fate on the penultimate stage 14 of the 1923 Tour serves as metaphor for his almost-but-not-quite-great career.

A SPLINTER OF IRON

The penultimate stage of the 1923 Tour de France traced a wandering course northwards, from Metz to Dunkirk. Beeckman had spent the previous rest day cruising around Metz with Alfons Standaert and the veteran Walloon, Benjamin Mortier. Outside the Café Français at the start line of stage 14, Beeckman was brimming with confidence. By the middle of the morning, and just after the checkpoint at La Capelle, he could wait no longer and attacked, '*the first to get bored of the walking pace and stride out,*' according to the Flemish daily *Het Laatste Nieuws*. This brief breakaway was not dissimilar to his filmed attack on stage 4. He gained 200 metres on the bunch, and then sat up.

Beeckman reached the checkpoint at Mauberge in first place, driving the peloton on, a group which had been reduced to just 30 riders. After Mauberge, the riders hit cobbled roads, and the average speed plummeted, many of them opting for extreme caution and even deciding to walk from time to time. Then the race started skirting the Flemish border with Belgium, passing through the heavily scarred farmland landscapes still unrecognisable from their pre-war peaceful appearance. Beeckman was first again into Valenciennes, 307 kilometres into the stage.

It is possible that some of his family may have made the short trip across into France to see him race; his father Camille perhaps, with Bertina, who agonised for her son when he raced. He was, after all, their eldest child and only surviving son. Perhaps friends and supporters from Meerbeke made the trip to France, just as Bottecchia had enjoyed Italian support across the border. Maybe that was the case, since Beeckman is recorded as having been the first rider at the checkpoint in Valenciennes to sign in; the closest the race would come to Belgium. Perhaps he was inspired by the sight, reported in *Vélo-Sport*, of a sea of black, gold and red flags held aloft as the race route hugged the Belgian border. It was, according to *Sportwereld*, a *'beautiful race from Fieleken Beeckman'*.

Whatever his motivation, Beeckman had good legs that day. He made the final selection; a group of five riders including the yellow jersey Henri Pélissier went clear with 10 kilometres to run. The Belgian was 'the big unknown' in the group; unproven at this very high level, and without a stage win yet to his name. He and his fellow Belgian, Hector Tiberghien, were riding 'with their nose to the window', looking for a moment to attack that never came.

But there was a reason why Beeckman was never going to be able to attack, nor sprint effectively, if it came to it. A little iron splinter which had presumably jumped up off the road (this being five years after the end of the war, there must have been any amount of exploded ordnance and shrapnel fragments still littering the ground), had embedded itself in his brake callipers and was rubbing against the rim. Such was the pace that there was no way Beeckman could have stepped off and plucked it clear – if he'd done that, the race would have got away from him. He simply had to ride on and take his chances. Henri Desgrange is the only writer on the race with a sufficient attention to detail to notice Beeckman's handicap.

Somehow, Beeckman manages to sprint to third place on stage 14, his highest-placed finish in the 1923 race. Though it's Félix Goethals, born and bred in Calais, who takes the stage into Dunkirk, Beeckman's podium place is a notable achievement, especially given the clear disadvantage he has suffered. This does not escape the notice of the writer from *Le Petit Parisien*, who comments that he is *'riding ever more strongly'*.

Beeckman would, of course, win a stage of the race in 1924. But that would be overshadowed entirely by Henri Pélissier's mutiny and would end in the chaos of the badly managed elimination race in Brest, then the denial of his right to wear the yellow jersey the following day. That was hardly a satisfactory apotheosis of all that he had worked for, but this was typical of Beeckman's overlooked career.

His second stage win at the 1925 Tour came the following year and would also come and go with a singular lack of fanfare.

IN LOVE

THÉO

I married on St Valentine's Day in 1925. It was a happy day, and I think we looked all right together, like a man and a wife should look. Irène was watching out for her father all day, and from time to time I felt a bit envious. I think she missed her mother, and it was sad for her that I had both my parents with me.

Then we got on a train, and everyone was there on the platform to wave us off. There was a lot of confusion with the bags, and for a long time on the train to Brussels I worried that I'd forgotten something important. Irène thought it was funny that I kept jumping up to look through my kit bag for another thing I feared I had left at home. I almost got cross with her, but when I was happy that I hadn't left anything behind, I sat down and could smile at myself.

We didn't have long in Paris, really. Just time to dash across the city in a cab to the service course of Alcyon. I needed to pick up all my kit for my new team this year, which felt exciting, but strange. In the train to Lyon, I held up my new jersey and showed Irène. She liked the sky blue, and so did I.

And now here we are in Nice. The sun is so warm here, that even though it is February, Irène can drink good coffee on the balcony, while I build the bike, paying attention to each little part. I look up at her from time to time and I can see how still she is, just gazing out to sea. I remember how I felt the first time I saw it, and I imagine she must feel the same. Sometimes, my left thumb reaches out for my wedding ring, and I turn it around. It is a bit loose, and still feels strange.

Tomorrow Marcel Huot arrives from Paris, too. He has agreed to leave Griffon-Dunlop to join Alcyon this year too, and we are going to ride up over the Col d'Eze and into the mountains, while Irène explores Nice. It's not long now till the Tour of Flanders.

PARIS AND *PATRIE*

On 22 July the 1923 Tour de France reached the Parc des Princes and Henri Pélissier's crowning achievement was complete. Stage 15 was won by Félix Goethals again, who, on reaching the velodrome, attacked a group of 30 riders without hesitation and rode clear. The huge crowds in the stands rose to their feet, thinking that his orange racing jersey was in fact Pélissier's yellow jersey, then sat back down again when they realised it wasn't the race leader. Despite Francis Pélissier leading out his brother in a counter-attack, Goethals had judged his sprint to perfection, and held on to take a second victory in three days.

In third place, Pélissier rolled over the line and was engulfed by supporters, lifted off his bike and hoisted onto their shoulders. The spell had been broken, the Belgian stranglehold on the race had been loosened, and France once again had a champion. The race, one of the slowest ever given the severity of the climbing and the heat through which the riders had been forced to race, had lived up to its billing. It was compared favourably to some of the great pre-war editions, such as 1910 when France followed the great duels of François Faber and Octave Lapize. Even the Belgian press acknowledged its significance. Jean le Walloon, writing in the Belgian paper *Vélo-Sport* willingly conceded 'The French victory is a good thing for everyone. It's good for the French in whom it has provoked a wave of enthusiasm for which the sport as a whole can benefit. That, in itself, is already a good thing.'

Henri Pélissier's triumph in Paris was recorded of course by the cameras of Pathé. But the newsreel of the day's events includes scenes from the end of the bicycle race which are underwhelming in a certain sense. They simply depict groups of smiling men standing around in a field, some in suits, some on bikes, clutching unrecognisable trophies and wearing laurels. But they are also deserving of great attention, these rare fragments that are laced with meaning, if something is known of each individual's journey to that point in space and time.

This, then, is the scene projected onto Parisian cinema screens: Henri Pélissier is the first French champion of the Tour since 1911. He looks relieved, more than anything else, happy that it is over. After a relatively few and somewhat perfunctory seconds of Pélissier trying to smile naturally for the cameras, the film cuts.

The scene which follows is of a very different but similarly ceremonial nature.

CUT

French Prime Minister Raymond Poincaré stands with Marshal Foch at the base of a new war memorial in Villers-Cotterêts in north-eastern France. The two old men are unveiling its austere statuary and names engraved in stone to a crowd of local dignitaries, press men and important townsfolk, many of whom will have been reflecting on great personal losses.

This modest little town has always carried a specific and enduring significance in the history of the notion of French nationhood. The Ordinance of Villers-Cotterêts of 1539 was signed by François I, the de facto first King of France. The document changed the national language of the country from Latin to French and laid down the requirement for baptisms and deaths to be registered. It was here, some historians argued, that the first foundations of the French state were laid down.

Poincaré makes a speech in which he reminds the French public of the destruction wreaked upon the Département de l'Aisne while at the same time stresses the fact that the Ruhr valley across the border in occupied Germany had remained unscathed throughout the war. 'Those who wish to make the comparison,' he declares to the listening masses, 'should visit the devastated Aisne and then the Ruhr, intact.' The French Prime Minister is in no mood for conciliatory words. His not unreasonable calculation was that this political steadfastness might have found favour in Villers-Cotterêts, a town that had been partially razed to the ground by a late German counter-offensive in the final months of the Great War.

In July 1918, after a lengthy siege, and at great cost, the Allies had won a victory here against the enemy, in which much of the fighting and loss of life was born by the Senegalese *tirailleurs* and the British Indian Army. Perhaps General Ferdinand Foch, by now in his early seventies, standing to the side as his prime minister continues to address the crowd, might have allowed his thoughts to wonder. The memory of the victory his troops had secured exactly five years previously in Villers-Cotterêts might still have been fresh, and its significance not to be ignored.

Or perhaps Foch's thoughts, unreadable in the fleeting shots of that Pathé newsreel, might have been with the current ongoing occupation of the Ruhr and the French soldiers deployed on German soil. His sentiments would doubtless have chimed with those of Poincaré, for Foch was also of the opinion that the Treaty of Versailles was too soft on Germany. 'This is no peace,' Foch had previously declared. 'This is a 20-year armistice.'

Foch had been the man to whom, as Supreme Commander of the Allies, Germany had surrendered on Armistice Day, 11 November 1918, in a lonely railway carriage in the woods outside nearby Compiègne. He had, according to some accounts, kept the German delegation waiting for an hour, before walking into the carriage and asking the gentleman, 'What do you think you are here to discuss?'. Foch's power play was forcing them to concede defeat, to acknowledge that this was not a meeting of equals.

The Marshal's feelings of insecurity in the face of Germany were commonplace among French leaders of the age. André Maginot, a wounded hero from the Battle of Verdun and now the Minister of War in Poincaré's cabinet, felt much the same. 'Having won the victory, we now have to win the peace,' Maginot wrote in 1923. 'The occupation of the Ruhr is the guarantee for the debt that we are owed. If we'd agreed to the four-year moratorium proposed by Germany, we would have found at the end of the moratorium that Germany had reorganised.'

Maginot went on to give his name to the series of massive fortifications in Alsace-Lorraine which cost many billions of francs to build and were designed to keep the Germans forever at bay in that disputed territory.

It didn't, of course. History had something else in mind.

TIME: ISOLATION

Sometimes half a day can pass without me noticing it go. I lie on the couch in the flat, looking out at the church, watching the changing light, waiting for the next line of rain-bearing clouds to blow in from the west and push pulses of freezing drops at the glass. All the while, heating ticks a ponderous rhythm throughout the long course of my confinement. Outside, Ninove shifts through the hours of its day, its comings and goings, without sentiment, and with an eye only on the present, not lingering as mine was on the past.

Other times, I sit at my keyboard and vanish entirely into the story. When this happens, I see things with a dubious clarity that I feel I cannot trust. The pictures are sometimes so vivid that their colours blur and seep across, the one to the other. I no longer know where one thing ends and another begins. The characters dance.

FOCH, BERNHARDT, DUMAS – SERVICE, SENTIMENT AND SACRIFICE

Marshal Ferdinand Foch, whose Germanic family name derived from an ancestry that led back to that same disputed Alsace, lived his entire life defined by the German question. As a teenager he had enlisted in the war of 1870 declared by Emperor Napoleon III against Bismarck's Prussian alliance. Though Foch did not see combat, he fell victim to the retreat towards Paris as the French capital was besieged. In Paris he reportedly entered a makeshift military field hospital established in the famous Odéon theatre. Here he may well have encountered another key figure in French history whose biography crosses lines curiously not just with Foch, but with the town of Villers-Cotterêts. The temporary Odéon hospital, created to take in the wounded from the encircled French army as they fell back from the Prussian advance, had been created at the behest of the rising star of French theatre, the charismatic Sarah Bernhardt.

Sarah Bernhardt, the darling of French theatre

Bernhardt persuaded the theatre management to support her efforts, which resulted in beds being set up in every conceivable nook and cranny of the establishment: in the lobbies, the dressing rooms, the corridors, even on the stage itself. She called in favours from her long list of well-connected admirers to supply the makeshift hospital with food, as well as wine and brandy. And she spent every waking hour doing what she could to nurse the soldiers back to health. For the brief duration of the war and the subsequent uprising, the actress devoted herself to the care of wounded soldiers, something she considered to be her patriotic duty.

Already hugely popular in French society for her work on the stage, this period of Bernhardt's life cemented her reputation with the wider public. The unanimity of admiration for Bernhardt was itself something of a surprise given her unconventional lifestyle (she often dressed androgynously, slept in a coffin, collected rare animals, and took many lovers). But it was even more trend-bucking given her partially Jewish origins. The Dreyfus Affair was about to tear French society asunder and embolden the already deeply embedded anti-Semitic tendencies in France, and the fact that Bernhardt side-stepped this particular and ancient prejudice is a curious anomaly. She continued to be adored across all strata of French culture, through into old age. Having suffered an amputation of her right leg at the age of 71, she nevertheless toured the front lines during the Great War in support of the troops.

Bernhardt died on 26 March 1923. A month or two later, during the Tour de France, the vast amount of her personal effects were being auctioned off, day by day, as the race progressed.

And here, in multiple unexpected ways, the story of Bernhardt and Foch, of Pélissier and Poincaré, of the two ceremonies of victory and remembrance recorded by Pathé on that day in 1923, all intertwine. They circle back around one another to meet in the plump and extravagant figure of Alexandre Dumas, author of *The Three Musketeers* and a son of Villers-Cotterêts. There is a florid statue in the town that depicts him flourishing a quill and manuscript.

Several accounts of Sarah Bernhardt's extraordinary life credit Dumas for having introduced her as a girl to the theatre and with encouraging her to enlist in the Conservatoire. Though the liaison between the writer and the young Bernhardt is shrouded in obfuscation and gossip, it seems clear that, regardless of the exact nature of the relationship, there was a long collaboration between the two that saw her perform plays by Dumas, as well as those written by his son, Dumas *fils*.

It is also likely that by the outbreak of the Franco-Prussian War, whatever contact there had been between the two had broken down completely. Besides, in December 1870, as Germany tightened its grip on Paris, Alexandre Dumas fell ill and died. He was buried in Villers-Cotterêts, where now, 53 years later, the old man Foch stood to attention and listened to the familiar words of warning about Germany, words he had heard repeated throughout his long life.

Alexandre Dumas was of mixed-race heritage. Foch might indeed have passed by the statue to Dumas and noted his appearance, accurately rendered in bronze. His father would have been perhaps even better known to Foch than the great novelist was.

General Thomas-Alexandre Dumas had been born into slavery in the French Caribbean colony of Saint-Domingue, his mother being a slave of African descent. Taken to France by his white father, he entered the army before rising to the very top, becoming the first person of colour to reach the rank of brigadier general. He led an astonishing life, which involved campaigns of epic proportions, a spiky relationship with Napoleon, and any number of other adventures. But his extraordinary journey ended in poverty and disease. He died of stomach cancer in 1806, also in Villers-Cotterêts.

This anonymous town, in a region of France to which it is hard to ascribe a definitive character, flickers through the timeline of this story of nationhood, paranoia and pride. It is a curiosity to find it brought back to prominence by the camera lens of Pathé on the same day that the 1923 Tour de France, complete with its French champion, comes to an end in the capital city. The tangled themes seem curiously aligned.

Now, a hundred years later, Villers-Cotterêts is in the hands of nationalists once more. Franck Briffaut, an ex-soldier from the parachute regiment, is the mayor of the town. He is a member of the Rassemblement National (formerly, the National Front). Briffaut was first elected in 2014, and then subsequently re-elected in the middle of the Covid pandemic in 2020.

During his time in charge of the town, Briffaut has confiscated works of art from public exhibition that he deemed to be too critical of the right. He has insisted that musicians who perform at the town's festivals sign a 'political neutrality' clause, and he has refused point blank to organise any commemoration to the abolition of slavery.

Change is often slow, but sometimes it crashes in where memory fails.

LEAVING NINOVE

I turn the handle, step out into the dank air, and let the door close behind me. It's early, still half-light really. Overnight, a cold rain has fallen, leaving the roads and pavements wet, catching the sodium lights from overhead in the half-hour before they will switch off and the low winter sun appears in the sky. No one is about, other than me.

Wheeling my suitcase as quietly as I can, conscious that Ninove is still asleep, I walk along the cobbled street I have only gazed down upon since my arrival in Belgium. After 10 days alone, with only the ghosts of Foch, Bottecchia, Bernhardt and Beeckman for company, returning to this world is a rich sensation, in which everything feels like a gift. The light movement of cold air, the distant sound of a motorbike in a side street, and the flight of a single bird across the brightening sky. At the railway station, I stand alone on the platform, waiting for half an hour for the train. I watch as a lemon-yellow sun rises suddenly behind the line of electric pylons that follow the track to the east, towards Brussels where I am heading.

A man appears, walking agitatedly. When he approaches me, he asks me something in Flemish that I can't grasp. I shake my head and apologise, so he switches to urgent English.

'Have you seen a guy carrying a small black dog?'

'No, I'm sorry.'

'He stole my fucking dog.' He rushes away, retracing his steps back along the platform. This is the first human interaction I have had in 10 days.

I watch the man retreat, as the Brussels train pulls in. Then I get on board, leaving Beeckman's home town behind me, without so much as a backwards glance.

1925 – A GLITCH AND SOME GLORY

In 1925, after two years racing for Griffon-Dunlop, Théo Beeckman had seemingly agreed to move to the Alcyon-Dunlop team; a switch to higher status and more money, no doubt brought about after his high-profile success at the 1924 Tour de France. Shortly after his wedding in February 1925, *Sportwereld* reported on Beeckman's honeymoon trip to

Nice with his new bride (Irène), and how it had been inextricably bound up with work. The couple had stopped off in Paris to pick up his new Alcyon bike, and they'd met with Marcel Huot in Nice. The Frenchman, a former teammate from Beeckman's old team, was moving to Alcyon, too. The account is surprisingly detailed, and the reporter was clearly very well briefed, presumably directly by Beeckman.

But, and this throws me off-kilter, Théophile Beeckman never made the move to Alcyon. Somewhere along the line, shortly before the racing season began, the transfer must have collapsed. For he is a Thomann-Dunlop rider the next time the Tour de France comes around in 1925. The reason for the move breaking down is lost to time, unreported and now unknowable. But it is further evidence that Beeckman may not have been the most straightforward man to manage, after all. Still more confusingly, there is that striking picture of him with a bouquet in a velodrome. It looks like he is wearing a wedding band, so it must have been taken after February 1925. But he is wearing a Griffon jersey, a team he reportedly left at the end of 1924.

Regardless of this confusion, it is true that the following summer Beeckman turns up at the Tour as a Thomann rider, and Huot, as the original article accurately reported, has indeed switched to Alcyon.

Either way: 1925 was a decidedly different Tour de France. Henri Desgrange had overseen one of his periodical revolutions in how it was run, with a departure from the repetition of identical race routes that been used for the previous five editions. Three more stages were added, and three of the longer stages were halved in length, including the Brest–Les Sables stage. Stage 8 was the last of the much-derided shorter stages, which attracted almost universal disdain in the sporting press. They were deemed to be footling little affairs, at just over 200 kilometres, which demeaned the grandeur of the race. It was one of these that Beeckman had the misfortune to win. There is scant detail in the press as to how it unfolded because most of the writing from the day's racing simply dwelt on the inadequacy of the spectacle.

'No fatigue. No event. No worry. A "little girl" of a stage' was the blunt angle with which the special correspondent for *Le Matin* chose to describe the race. Instead of bothering to report on the action, he filled most of his column with the complaint that he couldn't get a hotel room in Nîmes because everything had been booked up for a bullfighting festival, that he'd been forced to sleep in the open air, and was therefore filing his copy from a bar, surrounded by people with strange Provençale accents. The *Miroir du Sport*, normally assiduous in its detailed reporting, omitted stage 8 entirely. It had been too late for the 8 July edition and deemed too dated to merit inclusion in its edition of 11 July. And the *Echo des Sports* ran the headline: '*A Stage Without a Story!*' The article then went on to describe Beeckman's solo attack from the bunch a few kilometres from the finish line, and how he'd held on to win by 100 metres:

> It is appropriate to congratulate the valiant *Théo* who, ever since the beginning of the Tour, has always behaved in a most honourable fashion, who has had to defend his fortunes energetically in the mountains, and what's more, has been a very valuable man for his team. This victory is just reward for his meritorious efforts.

But Beeckman's win is once again overshadowed. Henri Desgrange is in a foul mood, it seems, stalking around the start line in Perpignan snapping at people. He is complaining vociferously about the attitude of the riders, casting aspersions and making dark insinuations about malfeasance in the peloton in coded, mysterious-sounding practices such 'good bottles' and 'interposed people', which imply all sorts of cheating. The socialist newspaper *L'Humanité* is less concerned with Beeckman's win than taking the side of the worker in its ongoing antipathy towards the establishment, in this case Henri Desgrange:

> *We think that all workers who follow the Tour would like to know these improper stories, and not hear them being divulged elsewhere, because that would be detrimental to the marvellous affair which is the Tour for some. M. Desgrange has said too much and not enough. Will he have the courage to back up his assertions?*

As for the stage itself, *L'Humanité* sums it up in one simple word: '*Monotonous.*'

Those at the finish line in Nîmes were in a state of feverish excitement, nonetheless. But sadly, not really because of Théo Beeckman's imminent arrival. Instead, large crowds had gathered not just for the arrival of stage 10 of the Tour, but also because a film was being shot using them as a backdrop.

Le Roi de la Pédale was in production that summer, a silent movie made by Pathé's erstwhile rivals Gaumont about an unlikely cycling hero, starring an extremely well-known comic actor by the name of Georges Biscot; a kind of French Norman Wisdom of the era. With a pleasing symmetry, given that Gaumont and Pathé would go on to merge, this film now sits online in exactly the same archive as my found footage of the 1923 Tour.

Le Roi de la Pédale was produced in association with *L'Auto*, and had been co-written by their regular cycling journalist Henri Decoin. It tells the story of a cycling-obsessed hotel bellboy called Fortuné, played with impressive lack of restraint by Biscot, who finds himself, through a series of unlikely and comedic events, finishing third in the 1925 Tour de France, behind Ottavio Bottecchia and Nicolas Frantz, both of whom actually featured in the real race; Bottecchia winning it, and Frantz picking up four stages in bunch sprints. The General Classification on the day that Beeckman won in Nîmes had Bottecchia and Frantz in the top two, and there is a shot in the film of Biscot posing with them. The storyline of Fortuné finishing third overall might have been improvised to retro-fit the story to the images, since that shot of Biscot with Bottecchia and Frantz was perhaps just what they happened to get.

They'd also needed to film Biscot's character finishing a stage of the Tour, so they made use of the actual crowd that was in Nîmes that day. This allowed Biscot's fictional cyclist to appear in front of a tumultuous knot of real spectators a short while before Beeckman did it for real. Some reports suggest that the reception accorded Biscot eclipsed that given to the Belgian, which would seem entirely plausible. Something always stood in the way for Beeckman.

Georges Biscot, in typical cheeky-chappy mode

THE BEGINNING OF THE END

On my way back from Ninove in December, I had bought a huge antique, leather-bound Belgian book. It contained a detailed account of Germany's war of conquest in 1914 and had been published not long after the war. Its tone was monumental, and spoke of atrocity and grievance at the hands of the enemy. One assertion struck me: namely that Germany had expected the Belgians meekly to submit to their invasion, given the cultural and linguistic closeness of Flemish and German. According to this (highly partial) publication, the Kaiser had expected Belgians to lay down their arms and accept occupation. I had translated the words in the Eurostar on the way home, and had written the phrase down. Belgium provided:

> ... the fertile ground for Kaiser Wilhelm tragically to misunderstand the changing complexities of the European map. Germany thought that their Flemish cousins might simply acquiesce in the face of aggression in 1914. They were mistaken.

For Germany in 1914, read Russia in 2022. For Belgium, Ukraine.

I was working in the United Arab Emirates when a war actually broke out in Europe again in February 2022. Vladimir Putin ordered tens of thousands of Russian soldiers to pour across the border into Ukraine and there it suddenly was again: bombs, tanks, soldiers, murder. In Jeddah and in Abu Dhabi, they opted not to take phone calls from the president of the United States. NATO and the EU were being sorely tested. Old alliances were falling apart. Countries were scrambling to understand a new world order, as if it were 1914 all over again.

By Monday morning that week I was back in London as the financial markets in Moscow re-opened. The rouble immediately sank to a historic low. The Russian Central Bank, technically unable to deploy its $600-billion fund to prop up its plummeting currency because of hastily assembled sanctions, had been forced to raise interest rates to 20 per cent. Rapid hyperinflation was predicted, as Russians stood in line to withdraw their money from a banking system facing ruin. Vladimir Putin raised the level of nuclear readiness in his military machine.

The words from Pope Pius XI from 1923 return to me, speaking across the ages, warning in urgent terms of 'resentments which would remain a continuous threat of new and more ruinous conflagrations'.

By telling this story, I had intended only to trace distant, centennial echoes, to *imagine* the waves of history lapping in succession on our continent. I did not for a minute think that these shocks would be real and would land with such ferocity on houses, homes, bodies and hearts. This turn of history was too much. It ceased to be a story when real shells were falling, real bones were breaking, and great populations were quivering, or fleeing for their lives.

AT WORK

THÉO

They never asked me about the race, back then. But even if they had, I doubt I would have been able to tell them. Even if I'd chosen to. It wasn't how I was. I was never the first to talk, always the first to leave it and move on.

But sometimes now, when I am with a customer in the Brusselstraat garage, or trying to scrub the grease from under my fingernails in time for the dinner that Irène has put on the table next door, where Yolande has already gone to her cot . . . Sometimes then, it comes back.

Or when I return to the desk in the office after dinner, look at its ringed surface, scored with marks from hot drinks, or pocked with dropped cigarette ash. I sit down, and it comes back, especially when another car has just left the garage. That's when it arrives in a rush, a gust you can't locate. It blows the candle flat for a moment.

There's the ridge of the Tourmalet, a summer mountain mist whipped over its shoulder of road by the rising winds, in your back on the way up. The sun is out again, and the boys crest the top. The Pélissier brothers, Léon, Alfons, Albert, Robert, Philippe, Romain, Gars Jean and Ottavio. Below us is where the rest of life has vanished. Beneath us lies all of that.

MUNICH

I arrived early one spring morning in 2022, stepping off the sleeper train which had taken me on its rumbling course through the night, and across the Alps from Milan. I was on my way home from working on the Milan-Sanremo one-day race, and was visiting friends in Munich I had not seen for a long time.

I passed through the concourse of the Hauptbahnhof, heading for the exit. At the main entrance there was a makeshift reception centre for processing Ukrainian refugees, with words of welcome in Ukrainian printed on a large hanging display. The displaced people were arriving in a steady stream, met by volunteers in red tabards bearing the word 'CARITAS' on them. A family of three Ukrainians, met by a couple of volunteers and what I took to be a host family, stood by the taxi rank. Their two children, dressed in bright winter clothing and carrying heavy rucksacks and trolley bags, looked happy, though that is undoubtedly the wrong word. Maybe it was only that they were relieved their journey was over, at least for now. And down the escalator, moving into the subterranean U-Bahn complex, a teenage girl and a volunteer walked briskly towards the platforms heading for some unknown destination in the city. The girl, also pulling heavy luggage, was trying to message on her phone as she went.

That afternoon, I walked along the Viscardigasse. It's a narrow, cobbled street just behind the monumental Feldherrnhalle façade, in front of which it eventually became mandatory for Germans to salute the Führer. Those who refused to do this often chose to pick a route through the alleyway behind and slip past the guards unnoticed. Nowadays, there is a ribbon of polished bronze cobbles implanted among the stones which recognises this unofficial protest against Nazi rule.

I was the only visitor that afternoon to a special exhibition in the City Museum about Munich under National Socialism. On my way in, an elderly museum attendant with a newspaper, reluctant to get up from his chair, asked from a distance if I had a ticket. I took it from my top pocket and showed it to him. He waved me through, almost irritably, and resumed his reading of the paper.

It was an ordinary, dutiful sort of gallery, with posters, photos, but not much else. There was a copy of *Mein Kampf*, the first one I had ever seen, and an original at that. I was sure that, when I had lived in Germany, possession of the book had been illegal. Perhaps it still was. I stood for a while in front of the first widely published photographic portrait of Hitler; the work of his personal photographer, Heinrich Hoffmann, in 1923. This was the year that the Hitler myth came of age.

The exhibition loosely charted the rise of Nazism in Munich, but attributed much importance to the events of 1923, starting with huge simultaneous rallies around the city in January, all of which were attended in person by Hitler, who sped from one to another, railing against the occupation of the Ruhr and threatening to overthrow the Bavarian government.

The Circus Krone hosted perhaps the most explosive of all the meetings. The photos of the event show Hitler goaded on by a seething crowd, as if at a prize fight. It looks like something from the boxing rings of Paris.

Leaving behind the darkness of the museum, I headed back out into the bright sunlight. While I unlocked my hire bike, I took in the people around me, the final state of post-war European people: on phones, scooping ice-creams, whipping by on electric scooters. And among them and already invisible, the displaced from Ukraine, in ever greater numbers.

EASTER

A date in my diary neared. On Easter Sunday, I was going to head off again to Ninove; a second and final attempt to meet Wim and Théo Beeckman's granddaughter, Thérèse. So, two days before our scheduled meeting, I got on the Eurostar again and set off. I had booked the trip to coincide with Paris-Roubaix, a race in which Théo, in a characteristic near-miss, would finish in 4th place in 1923, just off the podium.

Some 99 years later, the famous one-day race was held not in its usual place in the calendar, but a week later, in order to avoid a clash with the first round of elections for the French presidency. Easter Sunday, falling in between the two rounds of voting, would see ferocious campaigning between the incumbent Emmanuel Macron, and his far-right rival Marine Le Pen. As I travelled into France once more, the outcome was far from certain. All eyes were on France.

The day after Paris-Roubaix, with most of Europe still basking in the kind of surprisingly warm mid-April weather that seems too delicate to last, I took the train again to Brussels. And from the Belgian capital, once more, I travelled on the long, slow looping train through a dozen sleepy Flandrian villages, until I reached Ninove for a second time. Now a deep winter had turned into an unsettling spring.

BACK IN NINOVE

Four months had passed since my ill-fated attempt to connect with the fine surviving threads of the Beeckman dynasty, such as it was. Free from illness now, buoyed by the sudden sunshine, and admiring the acid green of the slender leaves unfurling from the branches of oaks, poplars and beeches, I watched Ninove's church of Our Lady of the Assumption slide past the train window, and I disembarked again.

Dropping off my suitcase this time at Ninove's only hotel, I walked off in search of traces of Théo. I stopped again outside the row of modest terraces which constituted the known addresses of the family in Brusselsstraat. The last time I was there, I had been on a morning run, unaware of the Covid infection I had brought into Belgium. This time, I walked there, at a less encumbered pace. Standing in front of what had been the original premises of Garage Beeckman, I took a photo.

A lad appeared, striding suddenly across the road. He was about my height, perhaps 16 or 17, and pretty muscular. He marched up the pavement towards me, as I meandered away from the spot I had paused at to take the picture. He stopped in front of me, almost imperceptibly squaring up. I was aware of at least two other people watching us: a lady who might be his mother and a middle-aged man who'd pulled up in a car to use a cashpoint. The lad asked me something in Dutch, which I only partially got the gist of. He seemed agitated.

'I'm sorry. I only speak English.' I smiled in a manner I hoped might disarm him, but I felt instead the dull weight of my lack of Dutch.

His brow was furrowed. 'Why are you taking pictures of our house?'

'Ah, OK. Let me explain ...' and I started again on another attempt to explain away the oddness of my mission, standing on another European pavement. At the word 'famous cyclist', however, I noticed his features soften from aggressive concern to mild curiosity.

'He lived in this house?' he asked, pointing at the butcher's shop next door to number 50. 'That is where we live.'

'No, sorry,' I said. 'It was next door.'

Satisfied that I was simply an eccentric fool who liked bicycles, he sauntered off to join his mother, who was by now in deep conversation with the man at the cashpoint and was still shooting suspicious glances my way. The young man seemed to be telling them about the famous cyclist, and they looked at me one last time, but more forgivingly now.

I walked on, crossing the main road to Brussels, heading towards the old village around which the town of Meerbeke had grown. It was now Easter Monday, and apart from my brief encounter with Beeckman's future neighbours-to-be, not a soul was to be seen out on the streets. It was quiet in a way that I was unfamiliar with from my London life; a shuttered, complete silence seemed to penetrate behind the windows and doors of each esoteric Belgian house. As I walked, a stork flew quite low overhead, its legs tucked improbably into its belly as it arrowed through the air. It too made no noise in flight, a deep sky rising endlessly above its slender form, soft, blue and welcomingly warm.

I arrived at Meerbeke cemetery, intent on searching for Théophile Beeckman's last resting place. The gravestones were set in a neat rectangle of Flandrian earth, surrounded by ploughed fields, enclosed by a low parapet. I noted that the nearest rows to the entrance were very new graves, some as recent as the Covid pandemic, and that the further back they went, the older they were. Knowing that Théo had died in 1955, I made my way right to the back, only to establish that no gravestones seemed any older than the early 1970s. I was in the wrong place.

As I made my way back through the cemetery, I passed an elderly couple who were just remounting their step-through bikes, having tended to someone's grave. I asked them if they knew whether Meerbeke had an older graveyard. There was a lot of shaking the head and sucking the teeth as our conversation veered between Dutch, shaky French and English, eventually drawing in a passing family whose daughter was carefully carrying a bunch of flowers to lay. A consensus was reached. The old church up the road had a few overgrown graves around it, but no one visits them any longer. It might be worth trying there.

'What was the name of the cyclist?'

'Théophile Beeckman.'

Further shaking of heads.

A 10-minute walk and I reached the church of Sint-Pieter and Sinte-Berlindi, the centre of what used to be the village of Meerbeke, before it sprawled down to the Dender to merge with the town of Ninove. It was another surprisingly grand and imposing baroque church, surrounded on three sides by a walled graveyard. This was a tumbledown affair, through which I carefully picked my way. By now the sun was beating down with unusual strength for the time of year. From a surrounding house, through an open window, I could hear the sound of a TV show being streamed through a phone, and elsewhere the light crackle of something frying. A dog barked six or seven times in the distance.

Here the graves were arranged with none of the regimented order of the municipal cemetery. Some were from the late nineteenth century, but most reflected the calligraphic and design fads of the passing decades of the twentieth century, and were jumbled up. Many were cracked, subsided or covered in weeds. Few were tended. A peaceful sense of decay pervaded the still air which drifted through the stones, set at collapsing angles.

My eyes worked fast, as I walked in slow motion through the vestiges of rows, looking for the unique name that had become stamped into my imagination, like a watermark in the surface of my thoughts. There were Timmermans, Appelmans, Evenepoels, De Pluses. There were Breckmans, and Beeckmans. There was even the odd Beeckman, but there was no Théophile Beeckman. After almost an hour, I had scoured every stone. Defeated, I headed for the exit, passing by a beautiful memorial to the fallen of 1914–18, which featured a grieving family surrounding a dead soldier.

Then, emerging from the shadow of a newly greened tree, I saw a statue to the Tour of Flanders, reminding the town of how the great annual race used to pass by this church en route to its finish in nearby Ninove.

There was a poem engraved onto a fashionably rusting plate, written in Dutch by a man called Willie Verhegghe. What little I was able to translate sounded intriguing; something about a world of wheels, glinting in the sun and pushing through a madly screaming throng to triumph and eternal fame. I stood in front of the statue, with its twin riders, one exultant, the other defeated, and googled the poem's author. Willie Verhegghe was Ninove's poet in residence, and had documented the life and history of his home town for more than a decade, it seemed. Within a few minutes I had an email address for him and had sent him a message. Not long after that he rang me up.

'Why don't we meet up?' he said, with an excitement that mirrored mine.

'I'd love that. When?'

'Well, tomorrow I have to go to the dentist.'

'Oh, bad luck,' I commiserated. 'I could come to your house now, it's a nice evening, and I would very happily walk there. If you're at home, that is?'

About an hour later, I arrived at his house having walked in glorious sunshine along the same stretch of the river Dender to the little iron footbridge that I already knew from my December visit.

WILLIE

The Tour of Flanders, when it finished in Ninove, used to come almost directly past Willie's pristine white-washed and blue-windowed cottage in the village of Pollare. The last little climb of the race was just up the road, the testing little hillock leading away into the gentle sloping woods which marked the rolling periphery of the Dender river valley. Willie was deeply ensconced in Flandrian cycling, personally connected to numerous riders going back many years. Going back, indeed, to Eddy Merckx himself.

Introduced to one another only because of a chance encounter with a statue, he and I now sat in the garden, a Trappist beer in hand, and the warm late afternoon sun drenching his lawn with golden light. I noticed that Willie wore a yellow 'Livestrong' bracelet, something I had not seen for well over a decade.

'I still respect Lance,' he explained. 'He was a fantastic man to me.'

Willie then explained how he had met Armstrong in the French Alps in 2010. The Texan had invited him into his hotel room during the Dauphiné Libéré (a race sponsored by a newspaper named after the expulsion of the Germans in 1945). The two had talked privately, for a long time. Willie explained to Armstrong that he had lost his

10-year-old son to cancer in 1981. That is what, among other things, the two men had discussed.

Willie's son had been called Miguel, and his son had been uppermost in his thoughts over that Easter weekend in 2022. 'He was born in 1971 on the day of Paris-Roubaix, and he died 10 years later, also on the same day as Paris-Roubaix.' It was a startling coincidence, especially given the fact that I had been in Roubaix only the day before to see the 2022 edition of the race. 'It is the anniversary of Miguel's death.' Willie went on with the faintest watering of his eyes, and an almost imperceptible hesitancy in his words. 'He would have been 51 today.'

For a long time, as the sun started to sink lower, we spoke about racers, racing, and the feelings it invoked in both of us. I was struck by the manner in which road racing knits together so much of the invisible fabric of our lives: villages, biographies, the past and the present, stories and memories of people and places. I showed him the film, which he watched with acute concentration, and he then showed me his collections of poetry. There were dozens, if not hundreds, written on the theme of cycling, including a whole book about Tom Simpson's life and the cyclist's premature death. Willie's sentimental heart had been gripped by the sport of cycling and had never been released.

But, for all that he was at the heart of Ninove's cycling world, and the wider Flanders scene, Willie confessed that he knew almost nothing of Théophile Beeckman. He knew a fair bit about the other Beeckman, the one with the race named after him: Camille Beeckman, who had finished 3rd in the Tour of Flanders in 1943. 'They called him *De Boereke*, the little farmer.' He asked me if the two Beeckmans were related to one another. I told him they weren't and he shook his head again in self-reproach.

'Do you remember the Garage Beeckman?' I suddenly asked. He did, after all, drive a Renault, which was their brand. Perhaps he had bought cars from there, or at least got them serviced.

'Of course!' he said.

'Well, that was his company. That was Beeckman's garage.'

'Mea culpa,' he said, in surprise. 'Mea maxima culpa.' Then he admitted to me that before I'd arrived at his house, he'd looked Beeckman up on the internet to remind himself. Just before I said goodbye to Willie, he announced that he was going to write a poem about Théophile Beeckman. 'The Forgotten Rider, something like that.'

'That would be amazing. We could include it in the book.'
'He was *really good*, wasn't he?'
'He was, Willie.'
'And completely forgotten.'
'It seems so.'

SOFIE

Nerves meant that I had some difficulty passing the morning before I was supposed to meet Wim and Thérèse for lunch. But it was another in the string of perfect spring days that year and the market was in town. Ninove was bustling with contented life. I slipped out of the hotel entrance and joined the flow, stopping first at a chocolatier to buy an assortment of Belgian truffles in a box tied up with a ribbon. Then I strolled across the street to Ninove's modern town hall.

Following the signs to the 'Archief', I bypassed the reception desk and headed down a set of stairs and into the basement. Following a council official, I opened the door to the town's archive room, unsure whether or not I had any right to be there. Inside, there was a large room, flanked by shelves supporting rows of box files and vintage ledgers. Oil paintings of nineteenth-century notables hung on the walls, and there was a general light clattering of keyboards. A woman got up from her office swivel chair and came to greet me, looking slightly concerned at my unannounced presence.

'Hello, I'm looking for Sofie.'

'That's me,' she answered with an uncertain smile. By now, unbidden, I had the attention of everyone in the subterranean office.

I told Sofie how greatly she'd helped me launch my mission to track down the descendants of Théophile Beeckman, and explained how I was in Ninove to meet with his granddaughter and her husband. Then, with a superfluous further word of thanks, I handed her the chocolates. She looked reassured that I wasn't completely insane, but also slightly embarrassed by all the attention. Around the office, her co-workers grinned at the scene. Then, with perhaps an overly cheerful goodbye, I left this mine of local history, having at least fulfilled one of my obligations to the people of Ninove. I made my way back upstairs and out into the bright sunlight.

WIM AND THÉRÈSE

Finally, it was time to head for the restaurant that Wim had recommended. It was a modern bistro on a busy crossroads on the outskirts of the town, the kind of place you'd normally drive to. I arrived on foot, and at exactly midday. Wim was already there. Though we had no idea what the other looked like, there was something about the slim, smartly dressed man sitting alone in the corner of the restaurant that chimed with the tone of his emails: considered, well-constructed.

'Wim?' I offered, as I approached his table. He broke into a smile, we shook hands, and I took a seat opposite him. 'Thérèse is on her way,' he explained. 'She's coming from home.' Some years ago, Wim and Thérèse had moved out of Ninove to Dendermonde, the little town at the confluence of the Dender and the Schelde. While we waited for her to arrive, he explained to me how he'd taken a few hours off work to come and meet me. He was a busy property developer, working across Belgium in retail parks, very successfully I suspected. But for a long time prior to that, he and his wife had run the Garage Beeckman in Ninove.

The first thing I noticed when Thérèse arrived, neatly dressed, and with a cautious smile, was her eyes. Quiet, soulful, serious, she had exactly the same gaze as her grandfather's. They were Théo's eyes. 'I can't believe how much you look like him,' I said to her. Of all the things I had imagined or expected, a striking resemblance had not been one of them.

She nodded in amused agreement. 'I know,' she conceded. 'My brother looked even more like him, I think.'

This was the first thing she said that was news to me. I had no idea that Thérèse had had a brother. I had always thought that she was the only child of Yolande, who was in turn Théo's only child. Thérèse, with the help of Wim when she faltered in her account, as we switched between English and French, told me more about her younger brother Peter.

Peter had been destined to take over the running of the Garage from Yolande, who had been in sole charge of the thriving business after Théo's death. But, one day in 1986, Peter was killed in a car accident on the road to Brussels. He had been only 25 when he died. This meant that Thérèse, who was running a clothes shop in the town at the time of Peter's death, had to change her plans and would eventually take over the running of the garage; something she did in obedience to the wishes of her mother ('I always do what I am told') and with considerable success until with her husband Wim she sold the business in 2001.

Remembering was hard. At first Thérèse was apologetic and felt that she had nothing to add to the story, as plates of steak, white fish and asparagus were served at our table in the corner. She shook her head repeatedly and claimed that there was little or nothing she could tell me about her grandfather. After all, she had been born four years after his death. How could she know much?

So, as we ate, I began instead to talk. Slowly, and feeling my way so that I didn't rush any of the details which I believed made Beeckman's story so poignant, I began to recount his rise through the ranks, the civic reception which greeted his return from the 1922 Tour de France, his best results of the 1923 race, and how both his 1924 and 1925 stage wins had been overshadowed in different ways by bigger stories. How his racing career had been curiously condemned to a sense of anonymity. Wim and Thérèse listened intently to what I had to say, occasionally expressing wonder at how little they had known, and how richly mysterious the hidden reality of his career had been. The story of how Théo Beeckman had been denied his right to wear the *maillot jaune* seemed to resonate particularly.

To be the gatekeeper to so much information was both a responsibility and an honour. From time to time, I checked my words and asked if they wanted to hear more, which they did. I told Thérèse about my meeting with Willie Verhegghe, and about his intention to write a poem to remember Théophile and finally to mark his largely airbrushed name into Ninove's collective memory. Thérèse, a shy, undemonstrative woman, appeared to be moved by this idea, and there suddenly hung around the table a strange kinship of purpose, as if we were gathered around a little fire which was almost going out.

We talked some more, switching now back to their place in the lineage of Beeckman descendants. When the plates were being cleared, Wim shook his head in disbelief. 'I think,' he said after listening to all that I had to say, 'that all the time I have known this family, I have never once heard them talk about him. Not once. Now I wonder why.' Thérèse's expression was impossible to judge. But then she too conceded that Théo's only presence in the house was in the form of a framed picture which hung in the hallway; standing with his bike, tyres coiled around his shoulder. There were no trophies, no cuttings, no other memorabilia, and very little discussion about the absent patriarch in a home of strong, independent women.

Wim had known the family for a long time. He had known Théo's indomitable widow, Irène. She had died at the age of 94, but 'would have certainly lived to be a 100' if she hadn't taken a fall down some stairs in the house that she shared with her daughter, Yolande. And Yolande, who took over the garage after Théo's death from cancer in 1955, ran her business entirely (her husband Frans played a silent role in the background). Yolande had been known by everyone in Ninove as

'Madame Beeckman', despite having married and taken her husband's name. She carried on in charge until 1992, when she passed the business on in turn to her daughter Thérèse and to Wim, perpetuating a line of female garage owners of the original business established by Théophile Beeckman in 1926. Wim had a picture of four generations of the family, with Théo's widow Irène at the centre, holding Charlotte, her youngest great-grandchild. Thérèse sat behind them.

Wim and Thérèse sold up and moved away in 2001, clearing out the house of all the remaining physical links to Théo and Irène, including the sole framed picture of the bike rider from the Tour de France whose mysterious presence had brought us to this table.

'Where was Théo buried?' I asked Thérèse.

'In the churchyard, in Meerbeke,' she explained. It was indeed the one I had unsuccessfully searched through the previous day. 'But the grave is no longer there.' Though Thérèse could remember visiting with her mother and grandmother to tend her grandfather's grave as a child, at some point they stopped going. In Belgium, unless you extend the lease after 30 years, gravestones are removed and the burial site recycled. This is what happened to Théo's memorial. His name, however, was recorded on Irène's gravestone in Ninove cemetery when she was finally interred some 40 years after her husband's death.

'My biggest frustration,' I explained to Thérèse, 'is not knowing what happened to your grandfather in the First World War.' It was a complete blank, and now, as we all conceded, it was unknowable.

'There's no one left alive who would know,' conceded Wim.

'I think I know what happened in the *Second* World War,' Thérèse announced suddenly.

THÉO AND FRANCE

Thérèse remembered hearing her mother talk about her childhood. From a very early age, Yolande, who had been born in 1928, visited France. Every summer, as she was growing up, her parents would close the garage for the month of July and take a holiday. Loading up their big, swanky Renault, they would cross the border and head for the start of the Tour de France. A month later they would return, having followed the route of the race all the way round.

Théo, having finished with his own racing career, would still have known some of the riders in the peloton, and was clearly a besotted fan of the sport. According to Thérèse, the family had a profound and enduring affection for France, and there was not a corner of it they hadn't visited by following the consecutive and changing routes of the Tour. I learned to my surprise that the whole family were excellent French speakers, something which, though common, was not an automatic assumption in Flanders at the time, and still is not today. Yolande had the fondest memories of these trips, and would later proudly boast to her daughter that she had been one of the few Belgian six-year-olds to have developed a taste for foie gras.

'I think that my grandfather was someone who enjoyed the good things in life. He was a *bon viveur*,' Thérèse suggests. It is an impression of Théo which I find surprising. It runs counter to the one gleaned from all the reports of his racing career which stress his quiet, unassuming, humble nature. She also said that her mother and her grandparents were all extremely religious and were regular churchgoers.

But she has further evidence, pieced together from fragments of overheard, perhaps half-remembered, family anecdotes, that Théo enjoyed the finer things in life. There were memories of extravagant holiday excursions to the seaside resort of Knokke, again driving to the coast in their unusually grand Renault, to stay in the best hotels and wine and dine in style. Irène had also seemingly enjoyed these shows of affluence, having come from a family that had done well for itself; her sisters often claiming that none of them would have to work for a living. Both Irène and Théo had come from big families. But they were the parents of an only child, something which puzzles Thérèse. As we discuss this, Wim, who has spent much of the time listening, suggests that the reason they stopped having children after Yolande was born was simply to ensure that she would want for nothing, and that she might grow up financially secure.

Thérèse is even able to augment the story of Théo and Irène's honeymoon in France with a telling detail. 'They went for a whole month to Nice, travelling by car instead of train, and they stayed in the Negresco Hotel, right on the Promenade des Anglais.' It amuses Thérèse to hear that my understanding is that they stopped in Paris to collect some cycling equipment and that Théo spent most of the honeymoon out on long training rides. But it was news to me that they'd gone there in a private car. That's not how I'd imagined it.

When a German army swept into Ninove for the second time in Théophile Beeckman's life, he was 43 years old. This time around it was indeed possible to know what happened. His business was confiscated by the invaders, who set about converting the premises into a depot for the maintenance and repair of their tanks. Even before the arrival of the enemy, the Beeckman Garage was in the thick of it. By early September 1939, the business had essentially been requisitioned by the Belgian Army. A stream of orders for the supply of fuel and the repair of vehicles were filed by the military in preparation for the war to come. (Months after my meeting with Thérèse and Wim, Sofie from the Ninove archives unearthed a screed of orders in both French and Dutch, and invoices for

the services supplied to the Belgian Army, signed by Théo himself, with
a hurried-looking script.)

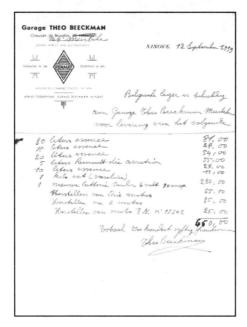

With the arrival of the Germans, the Beeckman family – Théo, Irène and Yolande – packed up their things and fled across the border into France. And there they stayed for the duration of the Second World War. A French family gave them shelter for the war years, which they spent on a farm, though Thérèse has no idea whereabouts it was. But she recalls her mother telling her how she had made a close friend of her age during those years in which they lived on the farm as refugees. Yolande would have been in her early teens.

It is very probable, therefore, that Théo Beeckman was still in France on the very day that a wave of ink-black clouds swept in from the Bay of Biscay on 15 August 1944. He would have heard the claps of thunder and perhaps marvelled at the violence of the storm.

It struck most fiercely in the west of France, in La Roche-Bernard.

Lighting a candle in Sint-Pieterskerk, Meerbeke

LA ROCHE-BERNARD

Two days later.

It was true that I had long daydreamed about visiting La Roche-Bernard. But now that I was here, the richness of the experience took me by surprise. I had not been prepared for the feeling of disjointed well-being that swelled within me as I sat gazing up at the high windows above me. Behind me, to the right, I sensed the presence of the big Gothic church from the film. All I needed to affirm that I had landed in the middle of the century-old scene was to glance over my shoulder, and glimpse its tall windows and grey stone, set back from the road, at a slight angle, and casting their judgement on all that lay below, on the bar, on the parked cars, the shiny, lightweight aluminium tables and me, my back warming in the early evening sun, and my thoughts settling like the white seedheads drifting in the spring air.

I really *was* in La Roche-Bernard. This was a different dimension altogether to the maddeningly finite world of the film; whose parameters were forever constrained, whose timeline was petrified, whose lifespan was finished and immutable. This was water-in-a-sieve reality, trickling on in uncatchable ways.

Outside the Église Saint-Michel, La Roche Bernard

Twenty minutes earlier, I had walked into the bar, ordered a beer, and asked a question I had been saving up for over a year. '*C'est à vous le bar, monsieur?*'

The tall, slightly unshaven barman of Le Saint Bernard looked up from the glass which he was tapping my beer into. It wasn't his bar, he explained with a smile and a polish of a glass with a tea towel, as if he were in a film. He just worked there. '*Pourquoi vous demandez?*'

I explained. Balancing my laptop on a pile of betting slips on a shelf by the counter, I quickly found myself surrounded by a clutch of late-afternoon drinkers in boilersuits and wellingtons. I was showing my film for the first time to people who not only knew the street through which Théo Beeckman is accelerating; we were watching it play, actually standing in one of the houses it had incidentally illuminated.

There was a lot of nodding, some occasional pointing, and general smiling. Once the little film had finished, I flipped down the laptop, shook a few hands, and they all sauntered back to their end of the bar, with the odd word of encouragement in my direction. There was, after all, not much to say, other than to agree that we were where Théo Beeckman had been, and that a hundred years had passed. After that, I drank my beer slowly, enjoying the slow churn of their conversation about who had bought a new car, when they were going to book a holiday, and whether or not FC Nantes stood a chance against Bordeaux at the weekend.

This was the first of a series of encounters as I drifted somnambulantly through La Roche-Bernard, absorbing impressions of the town's quiet industry, passing landmarks from the film and noting what remained, and what had changed. The stone wall, for example, along which Beeckman races as he leaves town on the Rue de Nantes now housed a building site. Where mature trees had once stood, overhanging the wall (it had then been the garden of the town's notary, a Monsieur Théophile Rancher, I would discover), now a row of three-storey residential homes were being finished off. The garden was gone, the wall stood, though it had been covered in part with election posters that bore testament to the febrile state of French politics during the spring. In fact, around every corner of this prosperous, perfect Breton town, there was a reminder of the forces at play across the land.

MICHEL

I had in mind a particular end to my journey. But before that moment of arrival, I wanted at least to seed the strange kernel of this story across the town which had unwittingly given rise to it. Urged on by a no longer quite containable desire to share what I had discovered with those people for whom the town was not a silent black-and-white fiction, but a bustling daily reality, I pushed open the door of the town's second-hand bookshop, a blue-fronted shop with the golden-lettered *LIBRAIRIE* above its windows.

Picking up a second-hand copy of Pierre Assouline's biography of Albert Londres (whose chapter on *Les Forçats de la Route* I later read over a coffee by the market), I approached the till where a man I later found out was called Sacha sat filling in some paperwork. He looked up, his white hair tied back in a ponytail, and took the book from me. It was priced at €10, but he asked me for €8. I told him I was happy to pay the full price, and he brusquely dismissed my offer.

'I decide here what price is paid,' he snapped, not without a certain aggression. I put my hands up in mock surrender, at which he then laughed. I asked him if he had any old maps from the early part of the twentieth century, and after a lot of rifling around through the disorder of the shop, he drew a blank. 'But I have a friend who might be able to help. Leave your number here, and I'll ask Michel,' he suggested. 'Also, two doors down the road there is a lady who sells vintage maps. Try her.'

Mélody, who I visited next, was fascinated by the film I showed her. Together in her neat little shop called Phileas Fogg, we pored over a map from the 1950s that pre-dated the construction of the new motorway connecting Vannes with Nantes. We were trying to figure out which of the two or three different roads the Tour might have taken as it wound its way south. The only street scene in the film I had not been able to place was the final one, the small collection of houses through which Beeckman passes before the film abruptly reaches its end. That this location was somewhere along the 20 kilometres of countryside between La Roche-Bernard and Pontchâteau was all that it was possible to know; but that left a huge number of different possible locations, many of which might no longer exist. Mélody thought she half recognised the street, and that it might be near where a friend of hers lived. But she wasn't sure at all.

'There is a man in the town who knows all about the history of La Roche-Bernard. I can't remember exactly where he lives, but I can find out for you. His name is Michel Chatal.' I looked up from the map at Mélody, as she scrolled through her phone looking in vain for his contact details. 'You simply must talk to him. He *has* to see your film.'

I bought an old postcard of the iron-arched bridge for €3, thanked her very much, and left to go for a walk down on the riverfront, where dozens of yachts were moored, their masts minutely swaying with the almost imperceptible swell of the Vilaine's dark waters running peacefully out towards the sea. It didn't take long before my phone rang.

'*Monsieur Boulting. Içi Michel Chatal . . .*'

ARRÊTE-LÀ!

'*Arrête-là!*' I stopped the film on the clipped command of Michel Chatal. He sat forward on his leather armchair and looked intently at the blurred image on my laptop; the crowd in La Roche-Bernard parting to reveal Théophile Beeckman.

'That's the old Citroën garage,' he said, pointing at the building in front of which the checkpoint has been set up. The sign which reads 'CONTRÔLE' has been strung across the road. Beeckman is unfussily remounting his bike, urgently continuing his attack, pressing on. 'That was their old showroom,' he continued, jabbing a finger at the shadowy shape across the road, 'and there on the other side of the street was their workshop. That building is still there. Next to the garage is the Hotel La Boule d'Or, and there's Bouet's café and wine shop which burnt to the ground in 1944.' I scribbled down the information and tried to keep up as best I could. He never once consulted any notes.

Tall, elegant, white-haired and trim, Michel Chatal exuded warmth and welcome. Inside his deceptively spacious house right in the historical heart of La Roche-Bernard, whose modest exterior looked across to the town hall, he told me about his lifelong obsession. Looking up from his coffee table strewn with clippings from newspapers detailing La Roche-Bernard's intertwined history with the Tour de France, he explained his life's work.

'You see that bookcase?' He pointed at floor-to-ceiling shelves, groaning with books and box files. 'I have many more upstairs. All the books, everything, relates to the history of La Roche-Bernard.'

I turned back to look at him, now with his arms, in pastel knitwear, benignly outstretched in supplication. He grinned at me. 'I am 64 now. I have been obsessed with the history of my home town since I was 10 years old! Half a century!' He laughed as if he had been caught doing something mildly disreputable.

We continued to look at the film. Michel straight away noticed the gendarme, or at least the uniformed figure which I had taken to be a gendarme. 'He was not actually a gendarme, but the *garde champêtre* of La Roche-Bernard. Each town had just one rural policeman. This man's name was Monsieur Boëffard. And those cars by the side of the road? Slow down the film! Can we see the numberplate?' They blurred and remained maddeningly indistinct. 'Even if we can't decipher the numberplate, I can try to cross-reference them against photographs. Cars were still pretty rare in 1923. On the opposite side of the street there were two hotels, one of which is still there.'

For a few hours we spoke about his home town, about the Tour de France, about his cherished ambition to pull all the threads of research together into one huge volume. And then we talked some more about the coincidence of our encounter, the shared interests, the fact that we had been brought together by the accidental unearthing of this rare film, which meant so much to him and to the people of this beautiful river harbour with its rocky outcrops and wooded hillsides. He used the word *patrimoine* on more than one occasion, and always as he did so, stressing it.

'And have you returned the film to Pathé? Is it back with them?' he asked, and sat forward in his chair. I told him it was, and he nodded his approval. 'Then you have done the right thing.'

We were working towards a conclusion. 'You and I will stay in touch,' Michel promised me. 'And next year, when you have finished your work at the Tour de France, when the race has reached Paris, you should come back to La Roche-Bernard, with the film, with your book. I will put something on for you here.' He smiled broadly at me. 'I don't know yet what it will be, but people will love to hear your story. Will you please be our guest?'

I told him that I could think of no greater honour. And for the first time in this whole unpredictable endeavour, I very nearly cried. And I couldn't really explain why, save for the connection we had forged within such a short, but also very long, period of time.

SUMMER STORM

Through the summer of 1944, the Americans had been drawing ever closer to La Roche-Bernard, advancing their positions across the fielded plains of Morbihan, rolling their forces through hamlets and farmyards, past churches and villages, weary already from two months of fighting their way south from Normandy. Ahead of them lay the Vilaine river, a formidable natural barrier to their advance on St Nazaire, the fortified submarine base which the German army would defend until the end.

La Roche-Bernard was in the hands of the enemy, though the moment of violent change was growing closer. Conversations in the town grew less and less frequent, lips more pursed, brows more furrowed. From time to time the sound of shelling could be heard from the other side of the river, some distant, some very close. The Americans had moved to within 500 metres of the iron bridge.

Two more of the townsfolk were dead. François Mitaille, a 35-year-old father of two, and his much younger sister Thérèse had been taken by the Germans to the north bank of the river, and there in the woods, with La Roche-Bernard at their backs, they had been shot dead for their part in smuggling messages to the Americans. It was 7 August when they died, and their father would not discover their bodies for another nine days, by which time everything had changed.

Aware of the inevitability of the Allied advance, German troops had placed a dump of explosives on the bridge. Detonating wires ran back along the road and into the fortified positions on the south bank of the river, from which the Germans intended to defend La Roche-Bernard.

The heat was intense, the very height of summer. On the afternoon of 15 August, just as the day was reaching its hottest hour, a wind picked up. It swept up along the width of the Vilaine, bringing warm, wet Atlantic air inland. The treetops on the hillsides started to sway, as did the tops of the masts in the harbour below. The skies started to boil with ever darker clouds, separated clumps of dark grey and pure white interspersed with swatches of bright blue at first, before drawing a long hanging thick veil across the horizon, at which point the first drops of rain started to fall in isolation on dusty roads, on rooftops, car bonnets, and on the giant iron arch high above the river.

At 3 p.m. the thunder started. A few distant claps at first, but then right overhead, a violent crashing. Rain began to batter La Roche-Bernard, filling the streets with noise, and forming instant rivers that cascaded down into the Vilaine's seething waters. And again, more thunder, until successive claps started to merge. The town was now at the very centre of the storm.

That was when the lightning struck. No one saw the moment the old arch was hit by a fork of lightning, but they heard what followed: a second later, the mightiest explosion. A fireball tore away from the bridge in every direction – massive iron girders were wrenched apart, simply blown into fragments. The road instantly lost its shape and fell into the river in defeated, huge clumps. The arch twisted and groaned, gyrated, turned almost on its side, and then ripped itself apart, the highest point of its curve falling gracelessly asunder.

Watching on from his window, 'Docteur Cornudet', the mayor of La Roche-Bernard, could not believe his eyes: 'Suddenly I saw our beautiful arch collapsing heavily into the Vilaine. The storm was rampaging with such violence that I couldn't distinguish the noise of the explosion from the rolls of thunder.'

Théo's bridge had fallen.

RETURNING

THÉO

When the war was over, Irène, Yolande and I went back to Ninove in the old Renault we had fled in. There was a lot of paperwork to fill out, a lot to do to reclaim our business, so at first we stayed at my sister Malwine's place. She and her husband Prosper saw us right, until we could move back to our old house.

Yolande was very quiet for a few weeks. I noticed for the first time that she was a young woman now, though she'd been a child when we left. Her years in France had been good to her. She would be fine, would Mlle. Beeckman. Perhaps, one day soon, she might even be a mother.

It was hard to remember what it had been like before the war. The garage needed sweeping, scrubbing. There were windows to replace, tiles missing. There was engine oil in every corner. The Germans had taken many of our tools, and left others. I wondered if they'd had to leave in a hurry. Irène and I found the old order books, lying in a heap under the desk in the office. We dusted them off. I have to admit, I felt very tired knowing that I had no choice but to start again.

It wasn't long before I met some of the guys. I asked what I had missed.
You know they raced the Ronde van Vlaanderen every year while we were
gone? As if nothing was happening, as if it were all completely normal?
Camille, the 'Boereke', did well though. He was 3rd in '43. Best result of
any Beeckman, better than me.

I'd had my moments, though. I could race.

LA SURETÉ

'*Arrête!*'

I had paused the film again. Michel had narrowed his eyes at the
final scene, the low-rise houses to the left, the large restaurant with the
three high windows on the right, the wide sun-bleached road at the
crossroads where Beeckman's story is about to fade to white. Then he'd
grabbed my pen and notebook and scribbled:

fin du film MISSILLAC – lieu dit LA SURETÉ.

And later that day, driving 12 kilometres south, I would discover that he
was completely right. Without hesitation, Michel had located the precise
point of the minor road between La Roche-Bernard and Pontchâteau
where the film ends. I parked at the side of the road, opened the door,
and got out.

There was the big house, with its three windows facing the camera. On
the lintel above the ground-floor window, white paint now obscured
the lettering which a century ago had born the word *DÉBITANT*. The

road was quiet and wide, and remarkably unchanged in a hundred years. Only there were no people to be seen, and no rider from the Tour de France alone on the road and a long way from home.

I stood at the exact spot where the film halted as it caught on the bulb of the projector and smouldered, fading all sense of resolution to little more than white light and burnt dots. The point in both the past and the present beyond which it was impossible to go.

VITALY

I read the news that in Ukraine a young marine named Vitaly Shakun has been killed in combat defending Kherson province just north of Crimea. Charged with laying mines on the Henichesky bridge, he noticed an advancing Russian tank. Realising that he wouldn't be able to install the remote detonation device in time, he opted instead to blow the bridge, taking himself with it.

A picture of the blasted iron structure reveals two torn roads, contorted and unnaturally halted in mid-air with nothing between them but the clear waters of the Dnipro river running fast to the Black Sea, as an army advances.

VERTIGO

To get onto the ruins of the bridge at La Roche-Bernard, I had to climb over a small parapet. Then, there was a narrow strip, no wider than a foot, on which I would have to walk the 100 yards or so until I had reached its furthest extremity; the highest point above the water, where iron had once met stone, and where now the stone arch gazes blindly out across the water at its counterpart on the Vilaine's other side.

I had never before known the sensation of vertigo. But, inching my way further along the narrow path, unprotected in any sense from a sheer drop which grew ever bigger on the other side, I found I could scarcely put one foot in front of another. At one point, I was seized by the need to sit down, but knew that if I did so I would not be able to find the courage to stand up again, and would have to send for help. And so I continued my teetering progress, my upper body instinctively flinching away from the void, the fragile stability in my legs and ankles the only things keeping me from the drop.

Somehow, I made it to the end. Where once the road had spanned the great river, and the giant iron bridge had risen elegantly around it to lift its perfect form above the water, now there was nothing, just air. Across on the other side of the river, the arches faced their equal and opposite twin; vast, defiant, stone legs, striding out across the water.

There was no noise. Absence hung in the light. The woods behind me, the trees beyond, the slow drift west of the Vilaine; they were indifferent witnesses to the tiny human story that had played out here, a pinhole point in time that had been extinguished and then glimpsed again by chance.

Closing my eyes to the sun, I let the film run once more, watching its century-old ritual re-enacted. I saw again that tiny figure shoot across the bridge for one last time: Théophile Beeckman, his liminal existence caught between nations, between wars, between ages, between success and failure, fame and anonymity, an unknowable life erased by time and lost to space.

And then I felt the whole invisible edifice slump, the tumorous growth that had coalesced around the magic reel of film; all the interconnected lives and deaths, passions and beliefs, pictures, words, fears, threats, laments, delights, futures and pasts. I thought of Beeckman, the Pélissiers, Alavoine and Bottecchia, the men who had raced across this now invisible space, and all the writers, thinkers, fighters, schemers and dreamers whose stories had sliced through or run alongside the race with its headlong charge across the mined fields of 1923, its portent of cataclysm and its grand utopian hopes. All this second-hand stuff I had piled high and haphazardly, a notional, transparent stack of thought: I felt it all collapse under its own weight, leaving only nothing.

On the other side of the river, the torn-off arm of the bridge reached bluntly into the void; the woodland behind slowly encroaching on its stone, saplings taking root in the gaps, weeds becoming shrubs, creeping taller.

I waited a moment or two longer. I wanted to see the river and never forget it. Then reluctantly I turned away, closing the story behind me as I walked very slowly back to the shore. Though I had come far, I understood that there was no further step to take.

And by evening time on the same day, I was home.

*   *   *

THÉOPHILE BEECKMAN,
DE VERGETEN KAMPIOEN

voor Ned Boulting

Het dorp Meerbeke, waar ooit de grootste, Merckx,
voor een tweede keer de Ronde van Vlaanderen won,
is zijn beste renner ooit vergeten, van hem en zijn roem
is niets meer overgebleven, alleen een metalen letternaam
op het graf van zijn jong weduwe geworden Irène.

Of hoe deze kampioen achter de duistere gordijnen
van de ongenadige tijd is verdwenen, hij die driemaal
net buiten het magische Tour de France-podium viel en
in diezelfde Tour twee ritten won, zich ook bijna kroonde
met de eeuwige kasseien van hellestad Roubaix.

Zijn atletische Parnassus bereikte hij op 6 juli 1926,
in een Pyreneeënrit die de renners meedogenloos
met modder, ijzige kou en stortregens verlamde,
een zwarte katafalk waarop pijn en labeur heersten:
Lucien Buysse won in Luchon, Beeckman werd vierde
op deze dag die als het topinferno van het wielrennen
wordt beschouwd, meer dan 17 uren onmenselijk zwoegen,
de grote Ottavio Bottecchia weende toen als een kind.

Théophile rust nu door mijn schuldige pen in eer hersteld,
ik zie zijn gestileerde en bruin gebrande benen glanzen,
zijn karakterkop getooid met een aureool van bloemen.

Willie Verhegghe, 2022

THÉOPHILE BEECKMAN,
THE FORGOTTEN CHAMPION

For Ned Boulting

The little town of Meerbeke, where once the greatest, Merckx,
won the Tour of Flanders for the second time, has forgotten
its greatest rider. Of him and his fame nothing
more remains, save for his name in metal letters
on the grave of his young widow Irène.

Has forgotten how this champion behind the dark curtains
of merciless time is gone; he who thrice fell just short
of the magical Tour de France podium but won
two stages of the very same race, and nearly
crowned himself with the eternal cobblestones
of the City of Hell, Roubaix.

His Mount Parnassus came on 6 July 1926
on a race through the Pyrenees which ceaselessly
froze riders with mud, icy cold and torrential rain,
a black catafalque on which pain and labour reigned:
Lucien Buysse won in Luchon, Beeckman was fourth.
on this day they say it was the ultimate cycling hell.
the seventeen hours of inhuman toil left
the great Ottavio Bottecchia weeping like a child.

Théophile now rests in peace, honoured by my guilty pen.
I can see his sculpted, burnt brown legs glint,
His head, his character, adorned with a halo of flowers.

Willie Verhegge, 2022

1906 – competition announced for new bridge
design won by Eiffel (?) + built on the foundation
of the suspension bridge it was finished in 1911.
The Germanruie was struck by lightning in a storm
on Aug 15th 1944 – at 3 pm.
Docteur Cornudet, the mayor of La Roche –
"I was at my window, watching the terrible storm that
was battering the whole region, when I suddenly saw
our beautiful arch collapse heavily into the
Vilaine. The storm was rampaging with such violence
that I couldn't distinguish the noise of the explosion
from the rolls of thunder."

POSTSCRIPT

Months after finishing this book in the early summer of 2022, its convoluted narrative continued to uncoil, and in so doing, from time to time sprang back into my life in unexpected ways.

In the autumn, I set off on a national theatre tour of the UK, performing a one-man show about the Tour de France to live audiences up and down the country. One morning, travelling by train from London to Manchester, I passed through Wolverhampton. Here the train tracks briefly follow the line of locks which mark the passage of the canal as it drops away from the city centre. It was along this tow path, at which I gazed from the window of the slow-moving train, that I had run in the company of John McDonald over a decade before he had innocently provided me with the online link to the film. A week or so later, John suddenly messaged me again, this time with a photo he'd taken on a run that morning; the same locks. He was back in Wolverhampton, reliving our shared memory.

Another time, I found myself backstage in the fabulous Tyne Theatre, waiting for the curtain to go up on my show. As was often the case, the walls of the dressing rooms acted as a gallery for posters of previous performers. They were always fascinating to look at. But on this occasion, one name stood out. In July 1897, Sarah Bernhardt had come to Newcastle to perform *Tosca*.

Bernhardt's story had been a constant low-key presence alongside the months of writing *1923*. It had been the year of her death, and the race had passed so close to her beloved former home on the island of Belle Ile. The coincidence of our crossed paths along the dark corridors to and from the raked wooden stage of the Tyne Theatre, separated by 125 years, was further evidence that the tentacles of 1923 were never really going to loosen their grip on me entirely.

At around about the same time, I learned of the death of Brian Robinson, at the age of 91. Brian was not only a fabulous man, generous and humble to a fault, but also a genuine trailblazer for British cycling. He was the first man from these shores to win a stage of the Tour de France, something he achieved for the first time in 1958.

At Brian's memorial service in November, I learned from the eulogy delivered by the Yorkshire cycling writer Chris Sidwells about the first of those two victories. It was a story I had never heard before. Beaten in a sprint by the Italian Arigo Padovan, Brian had had to settle for second place, only to find that the race commissaires would later reverse their decision on the basis of Padovan's illegal sprint. That evening, long after he had given up on any sense of justice, he was told he'd won after all.

Then came the detail which resonated: the finish line had been in Brest. Like Théo Beeckman, Robinson took his first stage in the Breton port, and like the Belgian, he lost the sprint, only for the result to be overturned. It was a remarkable coincidence. Like Beeckman, Robinson would win just one further stage, with a solo attack, in a not dissimilar fashion. Both men spent the majority of their post-racing lives in relative obscurity, the scale of their achievements overlooked for the most part.

I returned one more time to Beeckman's home town of Ninove, at the beginning of December 2022, one year on from my ill-fated first visit during which my plans had been struck down by Covid. The occasion of my visit was the launch of a collection of cycling poetry by Willie Verhegghe entitled *Tot aan de meet* ('All the way to the finish line'). In front of an audience of hundreds, including several former Tour de France stars, Willie read aloud his poem about Théo Beeckman, explaining how the story of this forgotten local rider had come to his attention when I had visited him in the spring.

Later that evening, I met Wim and Thérèse. They had not yet had the occasion to read the poem which Willie had included in his collection. I was able to hand them a copy. Watching Thérèse's obvious delight in reading these heartfelt words about her grandfather felt like the appropriate moment, finally, to draw some sort of a line under the whole adventure.

I doubt, however, that there will ever really be an end to it. And I don't want there to be.

FURTHER READING

Assouline, Pierre, *Albert Londres, Vie et Mort d'un Grand Reporter 1884–1932*,
  Éditions Balland, 1989
Bastide, Roger, and Leducq, André, *La Légende des Pélissiers*, Presses de la Cite, 1981
Benson, Peter, *Battling Siki*, The University of Arkansas Press, 2006
Bernstein, Jeremy, *Einstein*, Fontana/Collins, 1973
Blondin, Antoine, *Sur le Tour de France*, Éditions de la Table Ronde, 1996
Bouëdec, Gérard Le, *Lorient et le Morbihan*, Presse Universitaire de Rennes, 2019
Bracher, Karl Dietrich, *The German Dictatorship: The origins, structure and
  consequences of National Socialism*, Penguin Books, 1970
Breyer, Victor, *La Belle Époque à 30 à L'heure*, Éditions France Empire, 1984
Brocheux, Pierre, *Ho Chi Minh: A Biography*, Cambridge University Press, 2007
Bruno, G., *Le Tour de France par Deux Enfants*, Librairie Classique Eugène Belin, 1907
Bruno, G., *Le Tour de l'Europe Pendant La Guerre*, Librairie Classique Eugène
  Belin, 1916
Cobban, Alfred, *A History of Modern France*, Penguin Books, 1965
Cuvelier, Joseph, *La Belgique et La Guerre, II: L'Invasion Allemande*, Henri Bertels,
  1921
Dumas, Alexandre, *The Regent's Daughter*, 1845
Fenby, Jonathan, *The History of Modern France*, Simon &Schuster, 2015
Gachet, Stéphane, *Naissance des sports dans le Morbihan*, Éditions Les Oiseaux de
  Papier, 2014
Gottlieb, Robert, *Sarah: The Life of Sarah Bernhardt*, Yale University Press, 2010
Hazareesingh, Sudhir, *How the French Think*, Allen Lane, 2015
Hemingway, Ernest, *A Moveable Feast*, Jonathan Cape, 1936
Hemingway, Ernest, *Fiesta: The Sun Also Rises*, Jonathan Cape, 1926
Hemingway, Ernest, *A Farewell to Arms*, Jonathan Cape, 1929
Huxley, Aldous, *Antic Hay*, Chatto & Windus, 1923
Huxley, Aldous, *Music at Night*, Chatto & Windus, 1931
Jarry, Alfred, *Ubu Cycliste*, Éditions Le Pas d'Oiseau, 2007
Krumeich, Gerd, *Die unbewältigte Neiderlage*, Verlag Herder GmbH, 2018
Lierneux, Pierre and Peeters, Natasja, *Beyond The Great War: Belgium 1918–1928*,
  Lannoo, 2018
Londres, Albert, *Les Forçats de la Route*, Éditions Arléa, 1992
Mohr, Joachim, Patalong, Frank, Schnurr, Eva-Maria, *Deutschland in den Goldenen
  Zwanzigern*, Penguin Verlag, 2021
Richards, Denis, *Modern Europe, 1789–1945*, Longmans, Green and Co., 1950
Ritchie, Andrew, *Major Taylor: The Extraordinary Career of a Champion Bicycle
  Racer*, The John Hopkins University Press, 1996
Rouz, Bernard, *L'Affaire Quéméneur-Seznec*, Éditions Apogée, 2006
Schönpflug, Daniel, *Kometenjahre, 1918: Die Welt im Aufbruch*, S, Fischer Verlag
  GmbH, 2017
Verhegge, Willy, *Tot aan de meet*, Les Iles, 2022

INDEX